FINANCIAL ACCOUNTING
A Casebook

GLENN M. PFEIFFER

ROBERT M. BOWEN

University of Washington

PRENTICE-HALL, INC., Englewood Cliffs, New Jersey 07632

Library of Congress Cataloging in Publication Data

Pfeiffer, Glenn M. (date)
   Financial accounting.

   1. Accounting–Case studies. I. Bowen, Robert M. (date)
   II. Title.
HF5635.P54 1985   657   84-9902
ISBN 0-13-316639-2

Editorial/production supervision and interior design: Barbara Grasso
Cover design: Wanda Lubelska
Manufacturing buyer: Ray Keating

Printed in the United States of America

10 9 8 7 6 5 4 3 2

ISBN 0-13-316639-2 01

Prentice-Hall International, Inc., *London*
Prentice-Hall of Australia Pty. Limited, *Sydney*
Editora Prentice-Hall do Brasil, Ltda., *Rio de Janeiro*
Prentice-Hall Canada Inc., *Toronto*
Prentice-Hall of India Private Limited, *New Delhi*
Prentice-Hall of Japan, Inc., *Tokyo*
Prentice-Hall of Southeast Asia Pte. Ltd., *Singapore*
Whitehall Books Limited, *Wellington, New Zealand*

FROM _____

_____
_____
DELIVERY POST OFFICE
COMPUTE POSTAGE DUE
(See 919.7 Domestic Mail Manual)

SPECIAL FOURTH CLASS RATE

MERCHANDISE RETURN FEE _____

TOTAL POSTAGE DUE $ _____

POSTAGE _____

MERCHANDISE RETURN LABEL

PERMIT NO. 29   WEST NYACK, NY 10994

PRENTICE HALL   RTE 59 @ BROOK HILL DR

POSTAGE DUE UNIT

U.S. POSTAL SERVICE
WEST NYACK, NY 10994

You can help stop the rising cost of textbooks!

The enclosed copy is being sent to you for adoption consideration.

However, if you don't wish to consider it, please use this postage paid label to return the book to us. The book will then be available to send to a colleague for review.

Your cooperation can have considerable impact on the price of textbooks.

Thank you.

(4/87)

A parcel mailed using this label may be mailed at a Post Office or in any mail deposit receptacle.

This label is coated with a dry-gum adhesive. To use, moisten this side and affix label to parcel.

CONTENTS

ALPHABETICAL INDEX OF CASES

PREFACE

The purpose of this book is to provide problem materials that help students and instructors bridge the gap between the traditional accounting textbook and the "real world" of financial reporting. While almost all financial accounting textbooks are oriented toward the preparation of financial statements, most students in introductory financial accounting classes will ultimately be *users* of accounting information. We believe that the ability to read and interpret published financial statements is an essential, yet often overlooked, objective of accounting education.

When students who have had some training in accounting attempt to apply their training outside the classroom, they are often overwhelmed by the very things that textbooks take pains to eliminate—nonstandard terminology and format, detail, complexity, and incomplete information. We have found the case method to be an effective way to overcome this difficulty, as it forces students to extend their inquiry beyond the textbook to realistic situations and applications. As a result, the student's ability to understand and use published financial data is substantially improved. Additionally, we have found that the case studies stimulate greater interest and student participation in the required financial accounting course.

The cases in this book were originally written to be used in our introductory financial accounting course at the University of Washington. The approach has proven to be very successful. The course has been rated by graduating students as the most useful course in the MBA curriculum. Several of the cases have since been adopted in undergraduate classes (especially at the intermediate level) and many have been used effectively in executive programs.

The vast majority of these cases are based on published corporate financial reports. While most of the cases require numerical solutions such as computations, journal entries, or statement preparation, these numerical solutions should be viewed as only a first step in the process of preparing and discussing the cases. Pushing the numbers is an effective way to become familiar with the case while at the same time reinforcing textbook concepts. We encourage students to go beyond the listed requirements to attempt to develop an understanding of the issues and concepts behind the numbers.

The cases have been grouped into chapters by subject area so as to be compatible with any introductory financial accounting text. Each case is constructed to be independent of the others and can be used under any reasonable ordering of topics. Also, several cases have been divided into parts "A" and "B," etc., allowing the instructor the flexibility of assigning part of a case.

An instructor's manual is available to accompany the casebook. The teaching notes to each case include a discussion of the objectives and pedagogical aspects of the case as well as a numerical solution. In addition, the introduction to the instructor includes course outlines and case descriptions to assist in course organization.

Acknowledgments

The approach embodied in this book has evolved over several years. We apologize in advance to those who have contributed but whose names we have omitted below. The majority of these are our MBA students, who from 1980 to the present were required to tackle many first drafts of cases that appear (as well as many that do not appear) in this volume.

We first became exposed to cases of this type at Cornell University and Stanford University, respectively. Cases written by former teachers and colleagues, especially Tom Dyckman and Bob Swieringa at Cornell and Robert Sprouse at Stanford, have influenced our thinking. We are also indebted to Pete Dukes and Eric Noreen at the University of Washington, and Bob May at the University of Texas for providing case materials that are included. While we are pleased to acknowledge these individuals, we accept full responsibility for the final product. We welcome comments and we would appreciate suggestions for interesting case situations.

Invaluable editorial and typing services have been cheerfully provided by Joanne Carlsson, Judy Gilmore, Debbie Malestky and Nancy Pearson. We are also thankful for the financial support of the Accounting Development Fund at the University of Washington.

Financial Accounting: A Casebook is dedicated to our families, broadly defined, with appreciation for their support before, during, and after this project.

BASIC FRAMEWORK OF FINANCIAL ACCOUNTING

Case 1–1

Personal Statement of Financial Position

Presented on the following page is a standard supplement required as part of a residential loan application. The form is similar to a balance sheet prepared for a business.

Required

1. Complete the statement of assets and liabilities for your own situation. Estimate those items that are difficult to value or locate. (You will not be asked to divulge any information on your statement.)
2. List the important items that appear to be omitted from your personal balance sheet.
3. How does this balance sheet differ from a corporate balance sheet prepared on the basis of historical cost?

EXHIBIT 1
STATEMENT OF ASSETS AND LIABILITIES
(Supplement to Residential Loan Application)

Name _____

The following information is provided to complete and become a part of the application for a mortgage in the amount of $ _____ with interest at _____ % for a term of _____ months and to be secured by property known as

Street Address _____

Legal Description _____

ASSETS		LIABILITIES AND PLEDGED ASSETS			

Indicate by (*) those liabilities or pledged assets which will be satisfied upon sale of real estate owned or upon refinancing of subject property.

Description	Cash or Market Value	Creditor's Name, Address and Account Number	Acct Name If Not Borrower's	Mo Pmt and Mos left to pay	Unpaid Balance
Cash Deposit Toward Purchase Held By	$	Installment Debts (include revolving, charge accts)		$ Pmt Mos	$
Checking and Savings Accounts Show Names of Institutions Acct Nos					
Stocks and Bonds No Description					
Life Insurance Net Cash Value Face Amount $		Other Debts Including Stock Pledges			
SUBTOTAL LIQUID ASSETS	$				
Real Estate Owned (Enter Market Value from Schedule of Real Estate Owned)		Real Estate Loans			
Vested Interest in Retirement Fund					
Net Worth of Business Owned (ATTACH FINANCIAL STATEMENT)					
Automobiles (Make and Year)		Automobile Loans			
Furniture and Personal Property		Alimony, Child Support and Separate Maintenance Payments Owed To			
Other Assets Itemize					
		TOTAL MONTHLY PAYMENTS		$	
TOTAL ASSETS	A $	NET WORTH (A minus B) $		TOTAL LIABILITIES	B $

SCHEDULE OF REAL ESTATE OWNED (If Additional Properties Owned Attach Separate Schedule)

Address of Property (Indicate S if Sold, PS if Pending Sale or R if Rental being held for income)	Type of Property	Present Market Value	Amount of Mortgages & Liens	Gross Rental Income	Mortgage Payments	Taxes Ins Maintenance and Misc	Net Rental Income
		$	$	$	$	$	$
TOTALS →		$	$	$	$	$	$

LIST PREVIOUS CREDIT REFERENCES

B – Borrower C – Co-Borrower	Creditor's Name and Address	Account Number	Purpose	Highest Balance	Date Paid

List any additional names under which credit has previously been received._____

I/we fully understand that it is a federal crime punishable by fine or imprisonment, or both, to knowingly make any false statements concerning any of the above facts as applicable under the provision of Title 18, United States Code, Section 1014.

NOTE: The signatory of this form must also sign the aforedescribed application

Signature _____ Date _____

FOR LENDER'S USE ONLY

(FNMA REQUIREMENT ONLY) This application was taken by ☐ face to face interview ☐ by mail ☐ by telephone

_____ (Interviewer)　　　　_____ Name of Employer of Interviewer

Case 1–2

Haystack Bookstore

For several years, Arthur King dreamed of owning his own business. One afternoon, he noticed a newspaper ad for the sale of a bookstore in Cannon Beach, Oregon:

Business for Sale—$125,000

Small bookstore in popular summer vacation resort. Possible owner financing. Contact M. Becker, Cannon Beach, Oregon.

The ad provided a telephone number, so King called Mary Becker and arranged a meeting for the following week.

When he arrived in Cannon Beach, King discovered a small store on a busy street in the heart of town. The building that housed the shop was an attractive older structure that had been remodeled and was in good repair. Inside, the fixtures were clean and well maintained, and the shelves were stocked with best-sellers, travel guides, cookbooks, "how-to" books, and the usual bookstore merchandise.

Mary Becker had owned and operated the Haystack Bookstore for over 20 years. She showed King her accounting records disclosing the cost of inventories and the earnings of the bookstore for the past 5 years. She also indicated that Cannon Beach was growing more popular as a summer resort and as a year-round residence.

King wanted to purchase the business but explained that he could only afford to pay $45,000 in cash. Becker was eager to sell, so she proposed to settle for $45,000 cash and a 10-year loan for the remaining $80,000. The loan would be secured by the land and building, bear a 10% interest rate, and require annual payments of $8,000 plus accrued interest. After some discussion, King agreed to these terms and signed a purchase agreement.

King immediately began organizing his business. He was able to contribute $60,000 in cash to the firm after depleting his personal savings and cashing in an insurance policy he owned. On March 31, the title was transferred from Becker to King. As part of the closing process, King paid $5,000 in legal fees and other costs related to the purchase of the land and building, in addition to the $45,000 down payment.

King decided to allocate the $125,000 purchase price as follows: $20,000 for the land, $80,000 for the building, $8,500 for fixtures and equipment, and $16,500 for inventory. He based this allocation on the appraised value of the land and building and the historical cost of the merchandise in inventory. The next day, King was busy preparing his store for opening.

a. He purchased a fire insurance policy covering the building and its contents and paid the $600 annual premium in advance.

b. Additional fixtures were purchased for $1,300 cash.

c. A shipment of books arrived accompanied by an invoice for $2,800.

3

On April 3, King opened his store and greeted his first customers.

   d. Sales for the 9-month period ending December 31 totaled $66,300. All sales were collected in cash.
   e. Between April 3 and December 31, Haystack Bookstore took delivery of inventory costing $43,900. This merchandise was purchased on account.
   f. King paid $42,100 in cash to suppliers for the merchandise purchased in c and e.
   g. Inventory on hand at December 31 was valued at $19,600.
   h. The cost of telephone service, electricity, and other utilities came to $1,900 during the April–December period. These costs were paid in cash.
   i. King paid $2,800 to part-time employees during the busy summer season.
   j. King determined that the building had a useful life of 20 years and that the fixtures and equipment should be depreciated over 5 years.
   k. King paid himself a salary of $9,000.

   Required

   1. Prepare a statement of financial position as of April 3 for the Haystack Bookstore.
   2. Prepare a balance sheet and an income statement for the 9 months ended December 31. Did the Haystack Bookstore earn a profit?

Case 1–3

Lookout Inn

In February 1982, John and Sandra Darby purchased the Lookout Inn near Waterville, New Hampshire. Located on the eastern slope of Lookout Mountain, the inn had been in operation since 1924 when it was converted from a nineteenth-century farmhouse. Waterville had always been a popular summer and autumn vacation area. However, the growing popularity of Nordic skiing has made the area a busy winter resort as well.

The inn offered nine guest rooms on the second and third floors, including the bridal suite, which featured a fireplace and a private bath. The main floor had two sitting rooms, one with a large fireplace, a dining room, kitchen, and a parlor that was used as an office. The price of a room included breakfast, which was served "family style" each morning in the dining room. The inn did not serve lunch or dinner, and breakfast was available only to overnight guests. The "bed and breakfast" format was popular among visitors from eastern metropolitan areas such as Boston and New York, and the Darbys soon discovered that many guests returned regularly.

The Darbys had no formal business training or experience. However, Mr. Darby was an experienced carpenter and was able to handle most of the repairs and maintenance himself. The Darbys worked full time operating the inn. In addition, they hired a part-time employee to handle cleaning and miscellaneous chores around the inn. Overall, they were pleased with the success of their business in 1982 and felt that they had learned a great deal about running the inn during their first year.

One morning, Mr. Darby read an article in the business section of the local newspaper that stated that, due to the recession and cool summer weather, 1982 had been a bad year for tourism throughout most of New England. The article noted that several businesses had declared bankruptcy and that many others had been forced to renegotiate loans and take other measures hoping that 1983 would be a better year. John was concerned about this news and decided to visit his accountant.

Bill Martin, a local C.P.A., had been retained by the Darbys to prepare their tax return for 1982. Nevertheless, he was surprised to see John Darby enter his office. Darby immediately explained: "This article has me a bit unsettled. You see, Sandra and I plan to close the inn for two weeks in April, when business is slow, and take a trip to Florida. Now I'm not so sure that we can afford the vacation."

"It sounds as if you could use a set of financial statements," Martin said. "You know, a profit and loss statement and a balance sheet. They will tell you how well your business did last year and where you stand at year end."

Darby interjected: "But isn't a profit and loss statement just the same as our tax statement?"

"Not exactly," replied Martin. "The objectives of the tax return and profit and loss statement are somewhat different. I think it will be easier to explain after I prepare your statements. I'll stop by the inn tomorrow to get the information I need."

The only records that the Darbys kept for their business were a checkbook register, which included detailed explanations of all checks drawn, and a file of all invoices received. Mrs. Darby explained to Bill Martin that she was sure that the inn earned a profit in 1982 because the cash balance in the checking account had increased by $20,000. Martin gathered the information he needed and returned to his office to prepare the financial statements.

Upon returning to his office, the first thing Martin did was prepare a balance sheet as of February 28, 1982, when the Darbys took over the Lookout Inn (see Exhibit 1). He noted that they had invested $36,400 of their own capital and had borrowed the remaining amount to finance the business. Next, he prepared a summary of cash deposits and withdrawals based on the Darbys' checkbook (see Exhibit 2). Once he had completed these statements, Martin began to piece together the information he needed to prepare an income statement for 1982.

a. The Darbys did not accept credit cards or other forms of credit. Also, when they began operating the inn, they instituted a policy of requiring a $50 deposit for advance reservations. By December 31, 1982, they had collected deposits totaling $3,900 for reservations in January and February of the following year. These advance payments had been deposited in the Darbys' checking account and were included in the $59,400 total collected from customers.

b. Martin determined that, out of the $10,080 paid toward the Darbys' mortgage, $9,780 was interest and the remaining $300 was principal.

c. The $600 paid for insurance provided fire and casualty coverage for the period from March 1, 1982 through February 28, 1983.

d. The Darbys purchased food and supplies on account. At year end, they owed a total of $1,750 to various suppliers. In addition, they estimated that year-end inventories of food and supplies totaled $550.

e. Employee wages, utilities, and advertising expenses had been paid in full by year end.

f. Mr. Darby estimated that the firewood remaining in the woodpile at December 31, 1982 had cost $490.

g. Martin determined that depreciation of the building, furnishings, and equipment totaled $7,680 during the 10-month period ending December 31.

Martin had just about completed the financial statements for the Lookout Inn when he received a phone call from Mrs. Darby. She explained that she had just received a tax statement from the Town of Waterville. According to the statement, the Darbys owed property taxes totaling $1,140 for the 12-month period ending February 28, 1983.

Required

1. Based on the information provided, prepare a statement of financial position as of December 31, 1982 and an income statement for the 10-month period from March 1, 1982 through December 31, 1982.
2. Did the Lookout Inn have a "good" year or a "bad" year? Explain.
3. Explain why the Darbys' income tax return differs from the income statement you prepared. Would your answer be different if the Lookout Inn were a corporation?

EXHIBIT 1
Lookout Inn
Statement of Financial Position,
February 28, 1982

Assets	
Current assets	
Cash	$ 1,600
Food and supplies	800
Total current assets	2,400
Land	22,000
Building	86,000
Furnishings and equipment	24,600
Total assets	$135,000

Liabilities and Owners' Equity	
Current liabilities	
Accounts payable	$ 600
Total current liabilities	600
Mortgage payable	98,000
Total liabilities	98,600
Owners' equity	36,400
Total liabilities and owners' equity	$135,000

EXHIBIT 2
Lookout Inn
Summary of Cash Deposits and Withdrawals,
March 1, 1982–December 31, 1982

Deposits	
Receipts collected from customers	$59,400
Total	$59,400
Checks drawn	
Mortgage payments	$10,080
Insurance	600
Food and supplies	8,100
Wages	8,400
Utilities	1,650
Advertising	1,200
Firewood	780
Withdrawals by owners	8,590
Total	$39,400

Case 1–4

Lake Michigan Gasket Company

Lake Michigan Gasket Company is one of many small manufacturing companies in the Grand Rapids, Michigan, area that serve the automobile industry and other large manufacturing concerns. The firm is operated by Ed Kent who founded the company in 1969 and is currently the majority stockholder. The company's largest customers are General Motors Corporation in Detroit and the Whirlpool Corporation in Benton Harbor, Michigan.

The company manufactures all types of gaskets from materials including cork, rubber, and paper. However, the firm specializes in self-adhesive neoprene rubber gaskets. The characteristics of neoprene rubber, which include heat and shock insulation qualities, make the material especially useful in certain applications.

Manufacturing Process

Gaskets are produced on a job order basis only. That is, the gaskets are manufactured only when an order is received from the customer. The manufacturing process consists of five steps:

1. Set-up. First, the engineer designs the gasket to the customer's specifications. This includes specifying dimensions, tolerances, and materials to be used. A full-scale drawing is prepared for use by the die-maker. The die-maker constructs a cutting die for use in the stamping process described in step 4. The die is made of a wooden block with protruding metal blades that "cut" the gasket out in the stamping step.

2. Shearing. Next, the neoprene rubber, which comes in sheets that are approximately 50 inches square, is sheared into strips. The width of the sheared strips depends on the size of the finished gasket as the strips of material must be ¼ to ½ inch wider than the gasket. This step is also necessary for cork and paper gaskets, as cork comes in 30-inch by 48-inch sheets, whereas the various grades of paper used by the company come in 500-foot rolls that are 30 or 36 inches wide.

3. Gluing. For self-adhesive gaskets, the next step involves gluing a sheet of plastic-coated paper to the strips of rubber. The glue is applied directly to the rubber and then the paper is attached. Once the glue dries, the thin plastic coating on the paper is bonded to the rubber. When the paper is peeled away, the adhesive that gives the gasket its self-adhesive property is revealed. (The paper remains a part of the gasket until it is removed by the customer.)

4. Stamping. In the next step, the cutting die is mounted into a punch press. The strips of adhesive-backed neoprene rubber (or cork or paper) are fed through the punch press, which stamps out the gaskets one by one.

5. Picking and Packing. In the final step, the gaskets are "picked." That is, the gasket is removed from the surrounding material. The holes and centers of the gasket are then removed. While much of the material is wasted, not all of the holes and centers are disposed of. Larger pieces are saved as these can be used in the future for making smaller gaskets. Finally, the gaskets are packed for shipment to the customer.

Financial Data

A balance sheet prepared on December 31, 1983 is presented in Exhibit 1. The following additional information relates to events that occurred during fiscal 1984:

a. **Sales.** Sales totaled $195,000 in 1984. All sales were on account, with payment due 30 days after the gaskets were shipped. The company collected $197,000 in cash from customers during 1984.

b. **Property, Plant, and Equipment.** In 1984, the company purchased manufacturing equipment, a power shear and a punch press, for a total of $32,000 in cash. Also, the company sold an eight-year-old punch press for $2,500 in cash. The machine had cost $11,500 new, but it was fully depreciated to its salvage value of $1,000 by year-end 1983.

c. **Long-Term Bank Note Payable.** The 8%, $60,000 bank note, originally issued on February 1, 1976, requires semiannual interest payments on January 31 and July 31 of each year. Because the note is secured by the land and building, no principal payments are required until maturity on January 31, 1986. However, Ed Kent repaid one-half of the face value of the note on July 31, 1984.

d. **Inventories.** Inventories consisted of the following:

	12/31/83	12/31/84
Raw materials and supplies	$19,600	$18,200
Work-in-process	9,800	11,300
Finished product	2,200	1,500
Total	$31,600	$31,000

The amounts shown were determined by a physical count of inventories on hand at year end. Purchases of raw materials and supplies on account totaled $51,600 in 1984. Payments to suppliers on accounts payable totaled $53,300 during the year.

e. **Insurance.** The company has a fire and casualty insurance policy on the factory and its contents including inventories and equipment. The premium on this policy is paid annually on June 1 and provides coverage through May of the following year. In 1984, the company renewed the policy and paid a premium of $4,800 There were no other insurance policies owned by the company during 1983 or 1984.

f. Wages. Lake Michigan Gasket Company paid $61,400 to employees for wages during 1984, including $1,200 accrued in 1983. Ed Kent determined that the company owed $600 to employees for accrued wages at year end. He noted that all wages applied to direct labor costs or to maintenance of plant and equipment.

g. Other Expenditures. Other cash expenditures incurred during the year included $9,000 for factory overhead (primarily for utilities) and $14,400 for selling and administrative expenses.

h. Dividends. The company paid cash dividends of $22,000 to shareholders during 1984.

j. Depreciation. Depreciation of plant and equipment totaled $14,500 in 1984. Of this amount, $12,100 related to manufacturing assets and the remainder related to office equipment.

Required

1. Describe the operating cycle of Lake Michigan Gasket Company. At each stage in this cycle, explain how the events that transpire are recorded in the accounting system.
2. Prepare journal entries to record the transactions that occurred during 1984. Post these journal entries to the ledger (T) accounts.
3. Prepare an income statement and a balance sheet for 1984.
4. Note that both cash and working capital decreased considerably in 1984. Given the net income for the year, how would you explain the decrease in cash to Ed Kent?

EXHIBIT 1
Lake Michigan Gasket Company
Statement of Financial Position,
December 31, 1983

Assets

Current assets	
Cash	$ 33,900
Accounts receivable	16,100
Prepaid Insurance	2,500
Inventories	31,600
Total current assets	84,100
Property, plant, and equipment	192,000
Less: Accumulated depreciation	42,000
Total assets	$234,100

Liabilities and Owners' Equity

Current liabilities	
Accounts payable	$ 20,300
Accrued wages payable	1,200
Accrued interest payable	2,000
Total current liabilities	23,500
Long-term bank note payable	60,000
Total liabilities	83,500
Common stock	90,000
Retained earnings	60,600
Total liabilities and owners' equity	$234,100

Case 1–5

The Haloid Company

The Haloid Company manufactured and marketed photographic products for office and industrial applications, including photocopying machines and paper, photocopy chemicals, photographic papers, and negative materials for the graphic arts. In 1955, the company purchased xerography patents and patent applications from the Battelle Development Corporation, a wholly owned subsidiary of Battelle Memorial Institute. Products based on these patents became so successful that the company changed its name to Xerox a few years later.

Exhibits 1 and 2 present Haloid's comparative consolidated balance sheets and income statements for 1954 and 1955.

Required

1. Accounting terminology is not uniform across firms and is particularly subject to change over time. Identify unfamiliar terms in these statements and speculate as to the current description of the item.
2. Compute Haloid's working capital at the end of 1954 and 1955.
3. During 1955, the company retired fully depreciated plant and equipment that had originally cost $277,125.61. What amount of property, plant, and equipment did Haloid purchase in 1955?
4. Prepare a journal entry to record depreciation and amortization of plant and equipment in 1955.
5. Haloid follows the standard practice of including among current liabilities that portion of long-term debt that is due to be repaid within one year. Given that there was no additional long-term borrowing during the year, compute the amount of long-term debt repaid in 1955.
6. Compute the amount of dividends paid in cash in 1955.

This case was prepared from published financial statements of The Haloid Company.

EXHIBIT 1
The Haloid Company
Comparative Consolidated Balance Sheet

	December 31	
	1955	*1954*
Assets		
Current Assets:		
Cash on hand and demand deposits	$ 1,971,120.97	$ 2,585,311.43
Notes and accounts receivable: Trade (less provision for doubtful notes and accounts: 1955—$106,693.87; 1954—$88,212.80)	2,723,128.53	2,247,203.18
Inventories:		
Finished goods, work in process, raw materials and supplies (Note 1)	3,911,119.49	3,292,699.69
Other current assets	65,099.68	72,200.51
Total current assets (Note 6)	$ 8,670,468.67	$ 8,197,414.81
Investment:		
Mortgage receivable	$ 6,138.02	$ 6,954.38
Property, Plant and Equipment (Note 2):		
At cost	$ 8,594,424.29	$ 6,960,629.65
Less: Reserves for depreciation and amortization	2,728,887.29	2,123,318.31
Net property, plant and equipment	$ 5,865,537.00	$ 4,837,311.34
Intangibles:		
Patents (nominal cost) (Note 12)	$ 1.00	$ 1.00
Formulae (nominal cost)	1.00	1.00
Total intangibles	$ 2.00	$ 2.00
Deferred Charges:		
Unexpired insurance premiums and deposits	$ 56,226.06	$ 56,517.54
Research development costs largely recoverable upon completion of military and other contracts	162,376.11	70,832.87
Other deferred charges	58,591.88	63,666.57
Total deferred charges	$ 277,194.05	$ 191,016.98
Total Assets	$14,819,339.74	$13,232,699.51

EXHIBIT 1 *(Continued)*

	December 31	
	1955	1954
Liabilities and Capital		
Current Liabilities:		
Accounts payable: Trade	$ 884,748.54	$ 690,120.62
Accrued liabilities:		
Salaries, wages and commissions	126,451.21	91,866.09
Estimated provision for taxes based on		
income (Note 3)	1,461,000.83	1,199,191.11
Miscellaneous	282,002.88	149,914.68
Other current liabilities:		
Dividends payable	115,682.85	102,826.40
Payment due within one year on long-term debt (below)	5,474.64	5,234.18
Employees' pension and profit-sharing trust funds (Note 4)	445,025.18	291,853.26
Miscellaneous	153,623.53	154,892.56
Total current liabilities (Note 6)	$ 3,474,009.66	$ 2,685,898.90
Executive Compensation Earned, Payment Deferred (Note 5)	203,470.58	84,547.28
Long-Term Debt:		
Notes payable (Note 6)	3,000,000.00	3,000,000.00
Mortgage payable (less amount payable within one year: 1955—$5,474.64; 1954—$5,234.18) (Note 2)	2,353.08	7,827.72
Commitments and Contingent Liabilities (Notes 7, 8, 10 and 12)	—	—
Total Liabilities	$ 6,679,833.32	$ 5,778,273.90
Rental Income Prepaid: Less Expenses Applicable Thereto (Note 9)	$ 180,832.05	$ 208,287.69
Capital and Surplus:		
Common stock: Par value of $5.00 each share (Notes 6, 11 and 12):		
Authorized 1955—1,500,000 shares; 1954—600,000 shares		
Issued and outstanding 1955—771,222 shares; 1954—257,074 shares	$ 3,856,110.00	$ 1,285,370.00
Unallocated capital:		
Excess of par value of preferred stock converted over par value of common stock issued (Note 11)	—	2,014,895.00
Surplus:		
Paid-In (Notes 11 and 12)	900,166.05	1,456,011.05
Earned (Note 6)	3,202,398.32	2,489,861.87
Total Capital and Surplus	$ 7,958,674.37	$ 7,246,137.92
Total Liabilities and Capital (Notes 7, 8, 10 and 12)	$14,819,339.74	$13,232,699.51

EXHIBIT 2
The Haloid Company
Comparative Consolidated Income Profit and Loss Statement

	Year Ended December 31	
	1955	1954
Net Sales, Equipment Rentals and Royalties	$21,390,653.22	$17,318,403.21
Cost of Sales (Notes 1 and 2)	13,213,335.69	10,860,796.38
Gross Profit from Sales	$ 8,177,317.53	$ 6,457,606.83
Shipping, Selling, and Administrative and General Expenses	$ 5,082,098.25	$ 4,059,901.92
Profit-Sharing and Pension Plans	520,922.42	361,652.73
Total	$ 5,603,020.67	$ 4,421,554.65
Net Operating Income	$ 2,574,296.86	$ 2,036,052.18
Other Income Less Other Income Charges	68,115.64	43,429.49
Net Income Before Provision for Taxes	$ 2,642,412.50	$ 2,079,481.67
Provision for Taxes:		
Federal and Canadian taxes	$ 1,375,000.00	$ 1,090,000.00
State taxes	105,000.00	105,000.00
Total	$ 1,480,000.00	$ 1,195,000.00
Net Income to Surplus (Notes 2,9, and 10)	$ 1,162,412.50	$ 884,481.67

Case 1–6

Polaroid Corporation

Polaroid Corporation is engaged in the manufacture and sale of instant photographic products. The company is a pioneer in the field of self-developing photographic film and cameras and other related products developed by Dr. Edwin H. Land.

Polaroid's 1976 and 1977 consolidated balance sheets and consolidated statements of earnings are presented in Exhibits 1 and 2.

Required

1. In 1977, Polaroid reported that the proceeds from the sale of property, plant, and equipment totaled $758,000. These assets had originally cost the company $3,828,000, but they were carried at book value of $1,531,000 at the time they were sold. Prepare a journal entry to record the sale of property, plant, and equipment.

2. What amount of property, plant, and equipment was purchased or constructed in 1977?

3. What amount of depreciation of property, plant, and equipment was recorded in 1977?

4. Compute the amount of cash collected from customers during 1977. State any assumptions you think are necessary.

5. Polaroid reported that inventories included "finished goods" of $87,038,000 in 1976 and $85,139,000 in 1977. Compute the cost of goods manufactured in 1977.

6. What amount of taxes did Polaroid pay in cash during 1977?

7. Determine the amount of dividends declared in 1977.

This case was prepared from published financial statements of the Polaroid Corporation.

EXHIBIT 1
Polariod Corporation
Consolidated Balance Sheet
(in thousands)

	December 31	
	1977	*1976*
Assets		
Current Assets:		
Cash, including time deposits of $80,680 ($47,206 in 1976)	$ 91,869	$ 53,942
Marketable securities, at cost which approximates market	121,153	204,930
Receivables, less allowances of $9,202 ($6,603 in 1976)	295,202	203,454
Inventories (Note 4)	294,271	255,782
Prepaid expenses	38,838	33,319
Total current assets	$ 841,333	$751,427
Property, Plant and Equipment, At Cost:		
Land	7,597	6,991
Buildings	132,489	124,170
Machinery and equipment	346,460	316,013
Construction in process	40,652	15,093
Gross property, plant and equipment	$ 527,198	$462,267
Less accumulated depreciation	301,305	264,078
Net property, plant and equipment	$ 225,893	$198,189
Total Assets	$1,067,226	$949,616
Liabilities and Stockholders' Equity		
Current Liabilities:		
Notes payable to banks (Note 5)	$ 49,993	$ 30,726
Payables and accruals (Note 6)	139,180	100,135
Federal, state and foreign income taxes	51,888	63,518
Total current liabilities	$ 241,061	$194,379
Stockholders' Equity:		
Common stock, $1 par value, authorized 36,000,000 shares, issued 32,855,475 shares	32,855	32,855
Additional paid-in capital	121,999	121,999
Retained earnings	671,311	600,383
Total stockholders' equity	$ 826,165	$755,237
Total Liabilities and Stockholders' Equity	$1,067,226	$949,616

EXHIBIT 2
Polaroid Corporation
Consolidated Statement of Earnings
(in thousands, except per share data)

	Year Ended December 31	
	1977	*1976*
Net Sales	$1,061,945	$950,032
Cost of Sales	575,729	511,786
Selling, Advertising, Research, Engineering, Distribution and Administrative Expenses (Note 2)	337,298	294,937
Total Costs	$ 913,027	$806,723
Profit from Operations	148,918	143,309
Other Income, Including Interest Income of $14,567 ($12,535 in 1976)	19,017	14,442
Interest Expense	6,424	3,336
Earnings Before Income Taxes	$ 161,511	$154,415
Federal, State and Foreign Income Taxes (Note 3)	69,227	74,725
Net Earnings: $2.81 per Share ($2.43 in 1976)	$ 92,284	$ 79,690

REVENUE RECOGNITION AND RECEIVABLES

Case 2–1

Sperry and Hutchinson Company

The Sperry and Hutchinson Company, a diversified manufacturing and financial services firm, is best known for its promotional services featuring S & H Green Stamps. In this line of business, the company sells trading stamps to licensees—mostly grocery stores and service stations—that, in turn, award the stamps to customers. The customers then return the stamps to S & H redemption centers where the stamps can be exchanged for housewares, appliances, sporting goods, and other consumer products.

The following paragraph from the company's "summary of significant accounting policies" describes Sperry and Hutchinson's policy for revenue recognition and stamp redemptions:

This case was prepared from published financial statements of Sperry and Hutchinson Company.

The company records stamp service revenue and provides for cost of redemptions at the time stamps are furnished to licensees. The liability for stamp redemptions is adjusted each year based upon current operating experience and the cost of merchandise and related redemption service expenses required to redeem 95% of the outstanding stamps issued prior to 1979 and 90% of the outstanding stamps issued thereafter (see Note 1). The company will continue to review periodically the appropriateness of its estimated redemption rates based on future redemption experience and statistical evaluations. Company evaluations have indicated that approximately 50% of the stamps expected to be redeemed are not presented for redemption within one year; consequently, this portion of the liability for stamp redemptions is classified as a long-term liability.

Note 1 to the company's 1979 financial report provided the following explanation for the change in the estimated redemption rate:

For many years prior to 1979, the company prepared its financial statements and its Federal income tax returns on the basis of an estimate that 95% of the trading stamps issued by the company would ultimately be redeemed. The company has based its use of this redemption estimate on the actual redemption experience of the company since inception and, in recent years, on statistical evaluations of stamp redemption patterns. However, on the basis of recent special statistical evaluations, the company has now concluded that in recent years there has been a decline in the redemption rate from the historical 95% rate. In order to reflect this decline, the company will prepare its financial statements for 1979 and subsequent years on the basis that 90% of the trading stamps issued by the company after 1978 will ultimately be redeemed.

As a result of this change in the redemption estimate, net earnings of the company for 1979 were increased by $5,187,000 ($.57 per primary share and $.52 per fully diluted share), after providing for related income taxes of $4,909,000.

Sperry and Hutchinson's consolidated balance sheets and statements of earnings for 1978 and 1979 are presented in Exhibits 1 and 2.

Required

1. Describe the operating cycle for the Sperry and Hutchinson Green Stamp operations.

2. Assume that Sperry and Hutchinson recognizes revenues when trading stamps are sold to licensees. Explain how the accounting system would record sales of trading stamps and stamp redemptions.

3. Repeat question 2 assuming that Sperry and Hutchinson recognizes revenues when stamps are redeemed.

4. Evaluate Sperry and Hutchinson's revenue recognition policy. Do you think the company's performance is accurately portrayed? Why or why not?

EXHIBIT 1

Consolidated Balance Sheet

The Sperry and Hutchinson Company

(Amounts Expressed in Thousands Except Share-Related Amounts)	December 29, 1979	December 30, 1978
Assets		
Current assets		
Cash and cash equivalents (Note 3)	$ 43,680	$ 43,105
Marketable securities, at cost, which approximates market (Note 2)	45,300	40,818
Notes and accounts receivable (less allowance for uncollectible amounts of $6,295 and $5,595)	130,183	132,855
Premiums receivable from assureds (less allowance for uncollectible amounts of $703 and $634) (Note 3)	74,284	59,329
Inventories (Notes 1 and 4)	129,498	125,791
Future Federal tax benefits (Note 7)	24,916	20,621
Prepaid expenses	6,791	5,933
Total current assets	**454,652**	428,452
Investments in marketable securities (Note 2)		
Debt obligations (at cost)	93,581	70,544
Equity securities (at market)	21,143	14,211
Investments in unconsolidated subsidiaries (Note 9)	13,440	53,345
Future Federal tax benefits (Note 7)	23,820	22,811
Long-term notes receivable (less allowance for uncollectible amounts of $599 and $706)	13,236	10,345
Property, improvements and equipment		
Land	7,433	7,647
Buildings, equipment and leasehold improvements	205,654	200,389
Less accumulated depreciation and amortization	113,471	109,197
	99,616	98,839
Intangible and other assets (Note 5)	94,513	93,427
Total assets	**$814,001**	**$791,974**

	December 29, 1979	December 30, 1978
Liabilities and Stockholders' Equity		
Current liabilities		
Notes due to banks and other current obligations	$ 4,142	$ 3,738
Accounts payable and accrued liabilities	109,244	96,628
Premiums payable to insurance companies (Note 3)	85,947	68,363
Federal, state and local taxes (Note 7)	16,509	17,069
Dividends payable	2,636	2,623
Liability for stamp redemptions (Notes 1 and 7)	149,258	141,605
Total current liabilities	**367,736**	330,026
Long-term liabilities, less current portions		
Liability for stamp redemptions (Notes 1 and 7)	149,258	141,605
Debt (Note 6)	44,479	44,804
Other	4,429	3,187
	198,166	189,596
Commitments and contingencies (Note 8)		
Stockholders' equity (Notes 9 and 10)		
Capital stock		
6% cumulative preferred, par value $100, authorized 50,860 shares; issued 2,300 shares in 1979 and 1978	230	230
Cumulative preference, no par value, authorized 2,000,000 shares; issued 506,141 shares in 1979 and 507,484 in 1978, $3 cumulative convertible preference, $3 stated value	1,518	1,523
Common, par value $1, authorized 30,000,000 shares; issued 11,044,609 shares in 1979 and 11,015,428 in 1978	11,045	11,015
Capital surplus	24,430	24,943
Retained earnings	267,095	290,783
Less net depreciation on marketable equity securities (Note 2)	4,883	3,955
Less treasury stock (at cost)	51,336	52,187
Total stockholders' equity	**248,099**	272,352
Total liabilities and stockholders' equity	**$814,001**	**$791,974**

EXHIBIT 2

Consolidated Statement of Earnings

The Sperry and Hutchinson Company

(Amounts Expressed in Thousands Except Per Share Amounts)	1979	1978	1977
Sales and revenues			
Net sales, revenues and commissions	**$809,448**	$798,329	$696,309
Investment income* (Note 2)	**9,672**	7,119	2,549
Net earnings of unconsolidated subsidiaries	**1,887**	1,692	1,861
Total sales and revenues	**821,007**	807,140	700,719
Costs and expenses			
Cost of goods sold, redemption and other costs	**555,186**	558,244	499,435
Marketing and administrative expenses	**213,328**	195,749	160,770
Interest expense	**4,746**	4,725	3,777
Total costs and expenses	**773,260**	758,718	663,982
Earnings from continuing operations before provision for income taxes	**47,747**	48,422	36,737
Provision for income taxes (Note 7)	**20,411**	22,018	16,602
Earnings from continuing operations	**27,336**	26,404	20,135
Discontinued operations (Note 9)	**1,679**	4,022	2,458
Earnings before extraordinary item	**29,015**	30,426	22,593
Extraordinary item			
Net earnings (Note 1)	**29,015**	30,426	22,593
Preferred and preference dividends	**1,470**	1,699	1,815
Earnings applicable to common stock after preferred and preference dividends	**$ 27,545**	$ 28,727	$ 20,778
Earnings from continuing operations per common share			
Primary	**$2.85**	$2.74	$2.04
Fully diluted	**$2.75**	$2.69	$2.04
Net earnings per common share			
Primary	**$3.03**	$3.18	$2.31
Fully diluted	**$2.92**	$3.11	$2.30
Average number of shares outstanding			
Primary	**9,079**	9,026	9,012
Fully diluted	**9,918**	9,720	9,706
Cash dividends declared per share of common stock	**$1.00**	$1.00	$1.00
*Excluding increase (decrease) in depreciation of market value of marketable equity securities	**$ 767**	$ 746	$ (1,594)

Case 2–2

Alaska Gold Company

Alaska Gold Company was incorporated in 1974 as a subsidiary of UV Industries, Inc. The company is engaged in mining its own existing gold reserves, developing additional reserves, and exploring for gold and other mineral reserves all within the State of Alaska. In addition, the company sells waste gravel, a by-product of its gold mining operations, for use in the construction industry.

The most important economic variable that Alaska Gold must contend with is the market price of gold. Because gold is a monetary metal, in addition to being used in a variety of industrial applications, its price is determined by a number of factors, all of which are beyond the control of the company. As a result, the rapid and often significant fluctuations in the price of gold ultimately affect the profitability of the company.

In Alaska Gold's *1977 Annual Report* to shareholders, company president William R. Kastelic summarized the problem as follows:

> Sharp fluctuations in the price of gold has made forward planning difficult. The subtle relationship between the market price at any given time and the International Monetary Fund's policy of selling gold from its inventory together with the possibility of sales of gold by the United States Government as well as the attitude of the dominant powers toward paper currencies are among the factors which influence and create uncertainties. Our production goals from time to time are necessarily based upon the prevailing price of gold and its near term prospects.

Operations

Alaska Gold Company's gold placer mining operation is located near Nome, Alaska. Placer gold consists of gold particles concentrated in sand, gravel, or other detrital material. The gold has been eroded from the land mass by the sea, redistributed by surf action in beach deposits, and then covered by later deposits of gravel, sand, and clay. These gravel deposits are permanently frozen and rest on limestone bedrock.

The frozen gravel must be thawed prior to dredging. This is accomplished by forcing water into the ground through pipes that extend to the bedrock. Thawing precedes dredging operations by at least one year so that an adequate quantity of gravel is available for dredging at all times.

The gold is mined by floating dredges. Buckets attached as a continuous belt scoop the gold-bearing gravel and carry it upward at the bow end of the dredge. The gravel is then dumped into a hopper from which it passes to a screen. Waste gravel is discharged from the stern by a conveyor belt. The gold travels through the

---

This case was prepared from published financial statements of Alaska Gold Company.

screen and is then recovered by a mercury amalgam in riffled sluices. The amalgam is later heated to separate the gold from the mercury. The gold product is then shipped to a refiner who refines it to remove impurities and returns it to the company.

Because of the climate in Alaska, gold mining operations are seasonal. The dredging operation is conducted during the six months from May through October; the thawing operation is conducted from May through August. During the remainder of the year, necessary dredge repairs and maintenance are completed, and preparations are made for the subsequent mining season.

Exploration and Development

Alaska Gold Company's estimated gold reserves as of December 31, 1977 totaled 1,164,400 troy ounces, contained in approximately 123,346,000 cubic yards of gravel within a 1,280-acre area. Reserves are estimated by prospect drilling and by calculating the gold content of the gravel.

The company spent $50,000 during 1975 on prospect drilling. This effort developed 7,282,600 cubic yards of gravel containing estimated reserves of 61,600 ounces of gold. There was no prospect drilling during either the 1976 or 1977 season.

Gold Production and Sales

The following table summarizes Alaska Gold Company's gold production and sales efforts from 1975 through 1977:

	1975	1976	1977
Gravel dredged (cubic yards)	1,414,923	1,194,620	1,369,398
Gold produced (troy ounces)	12,632	14,320	11,563
Gold sales (troy ounces)	—	—	38,515
Gold inventory (troy ounces)	12,632	26,952	—

Alaska Gold Company did not sell any gold during 1975 or 1976. During 1977, the company sold 38,515 ounces, including the inventory held at December 31, 1976 and all the company's 1977 production. The decision not to sell in 1975 or 1976 was based on the price of gold, as Mr. Kastelic explained:

You will recall that the gold price reached a low of $103 in August, 1976. In light of what we then considered a precipitous drop in the price of gold, it was decided to retain our 1976 [and 1975] gold production in inventory awaiting a better market. With the upward movement in the price of gold, the company started selling its inventory toward the end of February 1977.

The continuation of the upward trend in the price of gold which started in 1973 indicates a hopeful future for the company. Our gold reserves remain substantial. We continue to look forward to a recognition of the fundamental importance of gold in a society which some believe has over-extended its use of paper currencies. It is likely that with the passage of time, gold will continue to be regarded by some as a hedge against future inflation and the resulting inherent uncertainties.

Balance sheets and income statements for the three years ended December 31, 1975, 1976, and 1977 are provided in Exhibits 1 and 2 along with the summary of significant accounting policies (Exhibit 3).

Required

1. Describe the operating cycle of Alaska Gold Company. At what stage in this cycle does the company incur costs of gold production? When is cash collected from customers? When does the company recognize revenues?

2. Ignoring the constraints imposed by generally accepted accounting principles, at what stage in its operating cycle should Alaska Gold Company recognize revenues? Why?

3. How does Alaska Gold Company account for "thawing costs"? Is this appropriate? Why?

4. Assume that Alaska Gold Company recognizes revenues from gold mining at the time that production is completed. Also assume that inventories are valued at fair market value rather than at historical cost. Restate the company's income statements for 1975, 1976, and 1977 to reflect these assumptions.

5. Evaluate the income statements prepared in question 4 in comparison with the statements prepared and published by the company. Which approach provides a clearer presentation of the firm's operating performance? Which set of statements provides a better matching of revenues and expenses?

6. Alaska Gold Company's common stock is traded on the Pacific Stock Exchange. If the company published the statements prepared in question 4, how would its stock price be affected?

EXHIBIT 1
Alaska Gold Company
Balance Sheets, 1975–1977

For the Years Ended December 31.

	1977	1976	1975
Assets			
Current assets			
Cash	$ 34,611	$ 127,082	$ 157,783
Accounts receivable	35,609	48,314	41,802
Inventories			
Gold, at cost (market value:			
1976: $3,606,517			
1975: $1,711,000)	—	2,856,511	1,262,524
Materials and supplies	2,396,834	3,130,849	2,620,409
Prepaid expenses	83,824	15,747	15,418
Total current assets	2,550,878	6,178,503	4,097,936
Insurance claim receivable	—	—	1,229,817
Properties, plant, and equipment, net	11,605,907	10,365,511	7,300,146
Deferred charges			
Thawing costs	3,680,996	2,602,620	1,437,817
Other	146,136	171,366	145,783
Total assets	$17,983,917	$19,318,000	$14,211,499
Liabilities and Stockholders' Equity			
Current liabilities			
Accounts and loans payable	$ 348,427	$ 127,365	$ 163,279
Accrued expenses			
Insurance	6,094	136,190	—
Other	38,230	11,442	22,498
Total current liabilities	392,751	274,997	185,777
Term loans payable to UV Industries	13,893,181	14,984,754	8,507,238
Stockholders' equity			
Common stock, par value $0.10	500,000	500,000	500,000
Additional paid-in capital	4,896,926	4,896,926	4,896,926
Retained earnings	(1,698,941)	(1,338,677)	121,558
Total liabilities and stockholders' equity	$17,983,917	$19,318,000	$14,211,499

EXHIBIT 2
Alaska Gold Company
Statements of Income and Retained Earnings, 1975-1977

	1977	1976	1975
Revenues from sales of gold	$5,838,018	$ —	$ —
Cost of gold sales	4,990,286	—	—
Gross margin	$ 847,732	$ —	$ —
Other income (expense), net	(1,207,996)	(1,482,935)	144,258
Income (loss) before income taxes	(360,264)	(1,482,935)	144,258
Provision (credit) for income taxes	—	(22,700)	22,700
Net income (loss)	(360,264)	(1,460,235)	121,558
Retained earnings, beginning of year	(1,338,677)	121,558	—
Retained earnings, end of year	($1,698,941)	($1,338,677)	$121,558
Earnings (loss) per share	($0.07)	($0.29)	$0.02

EXHIBIT 3
Alaska Gold Company
Notes to Financial Statements

Summary of Significant Accounting Policies

Inventories

Inventories of gold, materials, and supplies are carried at the lower of average cost or market. Inventory costs include materials, labor costs, and mining costs, including depreciation of equipment and amortization of deferred thawing costs.

Thawing Costs

Expenditures relating to thawing mineral bearing gravel in preparation for dredging operations are deferred and amortized on the units-of-production basis over the estimated yards of gravel benefited.

Dredge Preparation Costs

Expenditures relating to preparing the dredges for the following operating season are deferred and charged to operations of that season. The cost of significant repairs to the dredges are deferred and are charged to operations over the expected life of such repairs.

Prospect Drilling Costs

Expenditures relating to prospect drilling are charged to income as incurred.

Properties, Plant, and Equipment

Substantially all of the company's depreciable assets are long-lived assets employed in the dredging and thawing operations and are depreciated on the units of production method. Maintenance, minor repairs, and renewals are charged to operations as incurred; major repairs and renewals are deferred to be charged off against future operations. Upon retirement or sale, the cost of the assets disposed of and the related accumulated depreciation, depletion, or amortization are removed from the accounts, and any resulting gain or loss is credited or charged to operations.

Case 2–3

Thousand Trails, Inc.

Thousand Trails is a member-based outdoor family entertainment service company. The company acquires, develops, and operates membership campground resorts ("preserves") in scenic areas within 100 miles of metropolitan centers along the West Coast (refer to Exhibit 1). The company's preserves generally include features such as 1,000-square-foot full-service campsites, planned recreational programs, adult and family clubhouses, tennis and sports courts, swimming pools, playground facilities, and nature trails. Buildings and campsites are designed to blend in with the natural surroundings. The objective is to provide the ideal camping experience for the recreational vehicle (RV) camper at a convenient location.

Thousand Trails was founded in 1972. Since then it has established itself as one of the fastest-growing companies in the United States. Family memberships have grown from 104 in 1974 to 21,800 as of March 1981 (see Exhibit 2). The first preserves developed were in Washington State with later expansion into Oregon and California. By 1981, 5.5% of all RV owners in Washington had purchased memberships. The company estimates that if a 5.5% market share could be obtained in California, the company's membership list would swell to over 100,000 families.

Operations

Thousand Trails selects sites for preserves according to established criteria for development potential. The company has its own design and construction company that ensures uniformity and a high level of quality control. The average development cost for each preserve has been just over $2 million.

Membership sales occur only at one of the company's preserve locations after a tour of the facilities, which includes a video presentation of the other facilities available for use. Prospective members are solicited through referrals from other members, direct-mail promotions, and media advertising in major metropolitan areas within a short drive of preserve locations. Membership referrals result in the most cost-effective sales for the company. Of the approximately 50,000 new member prospects who toured a preserve in 1980, 37% were referrals. Of these, about one-third purchased a membership. Approximately 41% of the prospects responded to some form of direct-mail advertising, but only 1 out of 10 such individuals who visited a preserve in 1980 actually purchased a membership.

As of 1981, the price of an unlimited membership was $5,595. Unlimited membership entitles the member's family to use all existing and future preserves in the Thousand Trails system. Regional memberships were $4,595. Exhibit 2 reflects the trend in the average price per membership over the past five years. In addition

---

This case was prepared from published financial statements of Thousand Trails, Inc.

to the cost of the membership, members pay annual dues, which averaged $160 in 1980.

Memberships are offered on a cash or installment basis. On installment sales, the company requires a minimum down payment of 10%, with installments payable over periods from 24 to 72 months. During 1980, the company increased the interest rate charged on installment sales from 12% to 15%. At the end of 1980, 2.2% of the membership contracts receivable were more than 30 days past due.

Future Plans

Exhibit 3 lists the location and size of the 14 existing operating preserves as of year-end 1980. The company limits memberships to 10 per developed campsite. This implies a total membership potential from existing preserves of about 75,000. Since Thousand Trails has strategically covered the major market areas along the West Coast, the company is now studying the feasibility of expanding into Texas and the Midwest. In addition, the company is considering placing on-site lodging at some preserves to accommodate the noncamper market.

Financial Data

Thousand Trails' income statement, balance sheet, and selected notes to the financial statements are presented in Exhibits 4, 5, and 6. The company's balance sheet reveals the capital-intensive nature of preserve acquisition and development. The company has financed its rapid expansion by borrowing heavily. Most of this debt consists of real estate contracts and capital leases secured by preserve properties.

As indicated, the company is one of the fastest-growing companies in the country. Revenues have risen from $7.7 million in 1977 to approximately $45 million in 1981, and net profits have grown from $1.1 million to an estimated $5.9 million in the same period of time. These revenues and profit figures represent compound annual growth rates of 55% and 52%, respectively.

Required

1. What percentage of total operating revenues is attributable to preserve operations? Thousand Trails sets a maximum limit on the number of memberships sold per preserve. What happens to revenues and earnings as this limit is approached?

2. Revenues from installment sales can be recognized at the point of sale or at the point of cash collection. Assume that Thousand Trails sells a membership for $5,595 and that the new member agrees to pay $1,200 down and make three annual payments of $1,465 plus 12% interest on the outstanding balance. Also assume that Thousand Trails assigns a cost of $1,500 to the membership. What amount of gross profit would the company report in each period if revenues from this contract were recognized at (a) the point of sale? (b) the point of cash collection?

3. For fiscal 1980, Thousand Trails reported "cash sales of memberships and down payments on membership contracts" in the amount of $15,410,000. Prepare a journal entry to record membership sales for the year.

4. The "provision for doubtful accounts" in the income statement has been decreasing in absolute and percentage terms over the 1978-1980 period. Why? Compute the amount of customer accounts written off during 1980 as uncollectable.

5. Evaluate Thousand Trails' accounting for membership contracts receivable. When is revenue recognized? What costs are matched against these revenues?

EXHIBIT 1

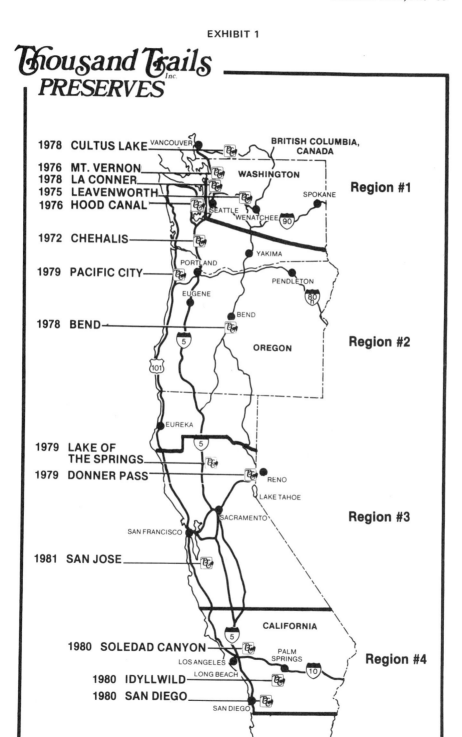

Thousand Trails PRESERVES

1978 CULTUS LAKE

1976 MT. VERNON
1978 LA CONNER
1975 LEAVENWORTH
1976 HOOD CANAL

1972 CHEHALIS

1979 PACIFIC CITY

1978 BEND

1979 LAKE OF THE SPRINGS
1979 DONNER PASS

1981 SAN JOSE

1980 SOLEDAD CANYON

1980 IDYLLWILD
1980 SAN DIEGO

VANCOUVER
BRITISH COLUMBIA, CANADA
WASHINGTON
SPOKANE
SEATTLE
WENATCHEE
90
Region #1

PORTLAND
YAKIMA
PENDLETON
80
EUGENE
BEND
5
101
OREGON
Region #2

EUREKA
5
RENO
LAKE TAHOE
SACRAMENTO
Region #3
SAN FRANCISCO

CALIFORNIA
5
PALM SPRINGS
LOS ANGELES
LONG BEACH
10
Region #4
SAN DIEGO

EXHIBIT 2
Thousand Trails, Inc.
Membership Growth, 1976–1981

	1976	1977	1978	1979	1980	Est. 1981
Outstanding memberships (year end)	1,117	3,575	7,664	12,926	20,675	30,000
Average price per membership	$1,900	$2,725	$3,375	$ 3,825	$ 4,400	$ 5,200

EXHIBIT 3
Thousand Trails, Inc.
Size and Location of Existing Preserves

Location	Year Acquired	Acreage	Total Planned	Campsites Existing	Campsites Approved
Chehalis, Wash.	1973	218	600	425	600
Leavenworth, Wash.	1975	135	400	275	275
Hood Canal, Wash.	1976	199	252	40	252
Mt. Vernon, Wash.	1976	260	500	275	275
La Conner, Wash.	1978	108	500	268	500
Cultus Lake, B.C., Canada	1978	84	530	400	530
Bend, Ore.	1978	156	530	330	530
Pacific City, Ore.	1978	108	251	149	251
Donner Pass, Calif.	1979	238	500	310	310
Lake of the Springs, Calif.	1979	754	1,000	285	560
Soledad Canyon, Calif.	1980	230	1,100	—	—
Idyllwild, Calif.	1980	120	450	105	286
San Diego, Calif.	1980	88	534	234	234
San Jose, Calif.	1980	62	300	140	140
Totals			7,447	3,236	4,743

EXHIBIT 4

Consolidated Statements of Earnings

	1980	1979	1978
	Year ended December 31,		
SALE OF MEMBERSHIPS	$33,950,000	$21,396,000	$14,341,000
COSTS ATTRIBUTABLE TO MEMBERSHIP SALES:			
Marketing expenses	15,323,000	8,159,000	5,957,000
Preserve land and improvement costs	4,825,000	2,832,000	2,044,000
General and administrative expenses	5,760,000	3,980,000	1,828,000
Provision for doubtful accounts	824,000	886,000	1,146,000
	26,732,000	15,857,000	10,975,000
INCOME FROM MEMBERSHIP SALES	7,218,000	5,539,000	3,366,000
PRESERVE OPERATIONS:			
Membership dues and preserve revenues	2,916,000	1,559,000	680,000
Less –			
Preserve maintenance and operations expense	(2,533,000)	(1,193,000)	(596,000)
General and administrative expenses	(524,000)	(498,000)	(433,000)
LOSS FROM PRESERVE OPERATIONS	(141,000)	(132,000)	(349,000)
OTHER INCOME (EXPENSE):			
Interest income	2,530,000	1,267,000	642,000
Interest expense (Note G)	(1,332,000)	(1,470,000)	(932,000)
Gain on sale of property held for investment	437,000	122,000	
Other income	24,000	50,000	16,000
	1,659,000	(31,000)	(274,000)
EARNINGS BEFORE DEFERRED INCOME TAXES	8,736,000	5,376,000	2,743,000
DEFERRED INCOME TAXES	4,200,000	2,586,000	1,263,000
NET EARNINGS	$ 4,536,000	$ 2,790,000	$ 1,480,000
NET EARNINGS PER SHARE:			
Primary	$1.69	$1.17	$.66
Fully diluted	$1.42	$1.17	$.66

EXHIBIT 5

Consolidated Balance Sheets

Assets	December 31,	
	1980	1979
CURRENT ASSETS:		
Cash	$ 632,000	$ 4,131,000
Notes, contracts and accounts receivable –		
Current portion of membership contracts	6,078,000	3,481,000
Notes and other accounts receivable	438,000	450,000
	6,516,000	3,931,000
Less allowance for doubtful accounts	(254,000)	(201,000)
	6,262,000	3,730,000
Prepaid expenses	681,000	153,000
TOTAL CURRENT ASSETS	7,575,000	8,014,000
CONTRACTS RECEIVABLE, less current portion:		
Membership contracts receivable	18,429,000	11,324,000
Real estate contracts	889,000	939,000
Notes and other accounts receivable	180,000	66,000
	19,498,000	12,329,000
Less allowance for doubtful accounts	(771,000)	(655,000)
	18,727,000	11,674,000
OPERATING PRESERVES:		
Land	7,299,000	4,679,000
Improvements	22,359,000	10,677,000
	29,658,000	15,356,000
Less costs applicable to membership revenues	(11,362,000)	(6,602,000)
	18,296,000	8,754,000
PRESERVES UNDER DEVELOPMENT, at cost	2,311,000	
INVESTMENT IN REAL ESTATE, at cost	2,222,000	2,609,000
CONSTRUCTION AND OPERATING EQUIPMENT, net of accumulated depreciation of $863,000 and $426,000	2,133,000	1,556,000
OTHER ASSETS, at cost	1,303,000	1,673,000
	$52,567,000	$34,280,000

EXHIBIT 5 *(Continued)*

Liabilities and Shareholders' Equity

December 31,

	1980	1979
CURRENT LIABILITIES:		
Notes payable to bank	$ –	$ 194,000
Accounts payable	594,000	441,000
Accrued salaries	848,000	738,000
Prepaid membership dues	598,000	365,000
Other liabilities	412,000	145,000
Accrued payroll and business taxes	238,000	207,000
Deferred income taxes	2,098,000	1,012,000
Current portion of long-term debt	2,967,000	3,848,000
TOTAL CURRENT LIABILITIES	7,755,000	6,950,000
DEFERRED INCOME TAXES	6,360,000	3,244,000
LONG-TERM DEBT, less current portion	24,342,000	16,979,000
COMMITMENTS AND CONTINGENCIES (Note F)		
SHAREHOLDERS' EQUITY:		
Common stock, no par value –		
Authorized, 5,000,000 shares		
Issued, 2,984,593 and 2,539,256 shares	6,162,000	2,280,000
Retained earnings	7,950,000	4,829,000
Treasury stock, 1,254 shares, at cost	(2,000)	(2,000)
	14,110,000	7,107,000
	$52,567,000	$34,280,000

EXHIBIT 6

Note A—Significant Accounting Policies:

General

The Company operates outdoor recreational facilities (preserves) in the Western United States and Canada. All significant intercompany transactions and balances have been eliminated in the accompanying financial statements.

Revenue recognition

The Company sells memberships for cash or on installment contracts. Revenues are recorded in full upon execution of membership agreements. Installment sales require a down payment of at least 10% of the sales price. All marketing costs and an allowance for estimated contract collection losses (based on historical loss occurrence rates) are recorded currently.

Members are assessed annual dues which are used for preserve maintenance and operations, members' services and allocated general and administrative expenses. The Company establishes dues at rates intended to fully provide for such expenses when active memberships sold reach approximately 40% of total memberships available for sale. Membership agreements provide for annual adjustment of dues to reflect increases in the Consumer Price Index.

Preserve operating costs in excess of those necessary for preserve operations and member services are incurred to provide support for the Company's marketing program. Accordingly, those costs which management considers to be primarily related to membership sales are included in marketing expenses as follows —

December 31, 1978 $384,000
December 31, 1979   296,000
December 31, 1980   611,000

Operating preserves

Operating preserve land and improvement costs, including estimated costs to complete preserves in accordance with the Company's development plans, are aggregated by geographical region and are charged to costs and expenses based on the relationship of memberships sold to total memberships available for sale in each region. The maximum number of memberships which will be sold in a geographical region is determined based on members' historical use of the Company's preserve facilities in that region. The Company plans to sell ten memberships for each campsite. Preserve utilization statistics are reviewed on a regular basis and revision of total planned memberships available for sale is made as necessary. As of December 31, 1980, the Company had approximately 20,700 members which represented approximately 30% of the total memberships available for sale on operating preserves.

The Company generally incurs indebtedness in connection with the acquisition of preserve land and improvements. It is the Company's policy to reduce such indebtedness in a proportion at least equal to the ratio that memberships sold bears to total memberships available for sale. The Company capitalizes interest as a component of the cost of significant improvements of preserve properties.

EXHIBIT 6 *(Continued)*

Preserves under development

Costs related to preserves under development are classified as operating preserve land and improvements in the appropriate geographical region when development has been completed to the extent that the preserve is reflected in the Company's marketing program as available for use by members.

Investment in real estate

Land acquired in excess of that necessary for operating preserves or preserves under development is classified as investment in real estate. Real estate contiguous to operating preserves is infrequently used but is generally available for use by members until disposition or further development. Certain parcels of the real estate contiguous to operating preserves are subject to land use permits required in connection with development of the preserves. Prior to disposition or development of such parcels, the Company will be required to obtain waivers or modifications of such restrictions from local governmental authorities.

Depreciation

Depreciation is provided on the straight-line method over the assets' respective useful lives.

Income taxes

Deferred income taxes result from use of the installment method of reporting gross profit on installment sale of memberships for tax purposes. Benefits from tax credits are reflected as reductions of current income taxes or the provision for deferred income taxes.

Note B—Membership Contracts Receivable:

Membership contracts receivable bear interest at an average rate of 13.5% and are written with initial terms of 24 to 72 months (average term of 47 months). The Company has no obligation to refund monies received or provide further services to members in the event a membership is cancelled for nonpayment of contract obligations or annual dues.

Substantially all membership contracts receivable are pledged as collateral for debt, as described in Note C.

Membership contracts provide for aggregate annual principal payments as follows—

Year ending December 31,	
1981	$6,078,000
1982	6,396,000
1983	5,857,000
1984	3,799,000
1985	1,764,000
1986	613,000

Case 2–4

Otis Elevator Company

Otis Elevator is the leading producer of elevator and escalator systems in the world and operates in over 120 countries outside the United States. In addition to the production, installation, and maintenance of a complete line of passenger elevators, the company also produces, sells, and services industrial elevators, dumbwaiters, fork lift trucks, small motorized personnel carriers, overhead crane and hoisting devices, and railroad signal equipment.

A description of the company's accounting for revenues was provided among the notes to the company's 1975 financial statements:

Revenue Accounting

Elevator and escalator installation and modernization contracts are recorded in the consolidated statements of income on the completed contract method. Cost of contracts in progress includes standard cost of manufactured components, actual installation cost and apportioned administrative and sales overhead cost. Capitalized administration and sales overhead costs of the current year on contracts in progress are recorded as other revenue. Service contracts and orders are recorded in income as earned. Sales of industrial trucks and material handling equipment are recorded in the consolidated statements of income as completed contracts upon shipment to customers.

Cost of Contracts in Progress

Contracts in progress include apportioned administrative and sales overhead costs which at December 31, 1975 and 1974 amounted to $45,093,000 and $45,186,000, respectively. The portion of administrative and sales overhead costs applicable to uncompleted contracts and recorded as other revenue in 1975 and 1974 amounted to $29,282,000 and $27,950,000, respectively.

Exhibits 1, 2, and 3 present the five-year financial summary, the 1975 balance sheet, and the 1975 income statement of Otis Elevator. (Note that in 1975, the company became a majority-owned subsidiary of United Technologies Corporation.)

Required

1. Compute the amount of costs incurred in 1975 on contracts completed or in progress.
2. Compute the ratio of "revenues from contracts completed" to "cost of contracts completed" for 1975. Assume that the same "profit margin" applies to contracts *not completed* at the beginning and end of 1975. What would

---

This case was prepared from published financial statements of Otis Elevator Company. It is based on a case written by Professor Robert G. May of the University of Texas at Austin.

have been the effect on income statement and balance sheet amounts *if* the company had used the percentage of costs completed as a basis for recognizing revenue. Ignore taxes.

3. From information in financial statements (including the five-year financial summary) and your analysis in the preceding exercise, evaluate which method —percentage of completion or completed contract—appears to best reflect the financial condition of Otis Elevator.

4. Evaluate the inclusion of "apportioned administrative and sales overhead cost" in the asset account "Cost of contracts in progress."

EXHIBIT 1
Otis Elevator Company
Five-Year Financial Summary
(in thousands, except per share data)

	1975	1974	1973	1972	1971
New Orders Received:					
North American elevator	$ 377,068	$ 422,258	$ 387,497	$ 345,906	$ 337,117
International elevator	708,656	708,888	595,084	426,727	359,512
Industrial trucks	77,004	87,443	96,307	79,540	59,486
Diversified being terminated	2,638	9,767	14,550	29,393	14,236
World total	$1,165,366	$1,228,356	$1,093,438	$ 881,566	$ 770,351
New sales	$ 652,374	$ 804,430	$ 733,364	$ 582,195	$ 503,656
Service	512,992	423,926	360,074	299,371	266,695
World total	$1,165,366	$1,228,356	$1,093,438	$ 881,566	$ 770,351
Contracts Completed:					
North American elevator	$ 433,838	$ 424,829	$ 410,034	$ 331,128	$ 323,477
International elevator	627,689	551,752	454,010	354,241	312,268
Industrial trucks	83,098	91,155	86,859	69,870	65,076
Diversified being terminated	8,594	8,485	10,999	31,926	7,461
World total	$1,153,219	$1,076,221	$ 961,902	$ 787,165	$ 708,282
Gross Margins:					
North American elevator	$ 123,083	$ 121,145	$ 121,626	$ 106,340	$ 102,798
International elevator	237,950	192,328	157,055	104,740	80,974
Industrial trucks	13,372	24,222	22,945	18,654	16,388
Diversified being terminated	(7,288)	(1,948)	(2,944)	(2,708)	(1,397)
World total	$ 367,117	$ 335,747	$ 298,682	$ 227,026	$ 198,763

Billings and Backlogs:					
Contracts and orders billed	$1,230,918	$1,108,942	$1,004,568	$ 839,067	$ 789,633
Unbilled contracts	$ 684,998	$ 784,201	$ 667,815	$ 551,945	$ 509,446
Uncompleted contracts	$1,329,926	$1,370,139	$1,229,870	$1,048,334	$ 953,933
Summary of Operations:					
Contracts completed and other revenues	$1,192,023	$1,111,579	$ 991,625	$ 811,496	$ 732,295
Cost of contracts completed	824,906	775,832	692,943	584,470	533,532
Gross margins	367,117	335,747	298,682	227,026	198,763
Other cost (substantially selling, general and administrative expense)	246,715	215,921	185,993	145,160	126,665
Income before provisions for interest expense, income taxes & minority interest	120,402	119,826	112,689	81,866	72,098
Less: Interest expense	23,414	19,039	16,898	15,461	14,904
Provision for income taxes	46,852	50,169	50,077	32,844	30,054
Minority interest	9,569	7,089	5,363	5,293	2,346
Net income	$ 40,567	$ 43,529	$ 40,351	$ 28,268	$ 24,794
Primary earnings per share	$ 5.02	$ 5.43	$ 5.02	$ 3.50	$ 3.05
Fully diluted per share	$ 4.59	$ 4.97	$ 4.61	$ 3.28	$ 2.88
Dividends declared per share	$ 2.20	$ 2.20	$ 2.10	$ 2.00	$ 2.00
Percentage return on completions	3.5%	4.0%	4.2%	3.6%	3.5%
Percentage return on equity	13.8	16.3	16.0	12.1	10.9
Number of stockholders	17,787	23,780	21,183	22,678	22,456
Shares of common stock—average outstanding	8,081,838	8,013,402	8,041,249	8,070,522	8,126,681

EXHIBIT 2
Otis Elevator Company
Consolidated Balance Sheets
(in thousands)

	Dec. 31, 1975	Dec. 31, 1974
Assets		
Current Assets:		
Cash	$ 31,676	$ 36,479
Short-term investments (at cost—1975, $9,539; 1974, $579, approximates market) and interest-bearing deposits	50,574	10,583
Receivables (net of allowances—1975, $11,236; 1974, $10,204)	276,201	282,062
Inventories	281,915	299,174
Cost of contracts in progress	565,774	513,774
Prepayments (deferred tax benefits—1975,$1,761; 1974, $4,481)	8,620	13,102
	$1,214,760	$1,155,174
Less billings on contracts in progress	628,347	585,585
Total current assets	$ 586,413	$ 569,589
Long-Term Receivables (Installment accounts: 1975, $6,291; 1974, $2,913)	14,167	10,979
Long-Term Investments	7,401	8,348
Total	$ 21,568	$ 19,327

Property, Plant and Equipment

	1975		1974	
	Cost	Accum. Dep.	Cost	Accum. Dep.
Land	$ 15,997	$ —	$ 19,069	$ —
Buildings	123,920	36,578	115,474	34,743
Equipment	151,942	80,458	141,965	75,314
Total	$291,859	$117,036	$276,508	$110,057

	Dec. 31, 1975	Dec. 31, 1974
Net Property, Plant and Equipment	174,823	166,451
Deferred Charges (unamortized purchase costs—1975, $4,324; 1974, $5,736)	6,988	8,842
Total Assets	$ 789,792	$ 764,209

EXHIBIT 2 *(Continued)*

	Dec. 31, 1975	Dec. 31, 1974
Liabilities and Stockholders' Equity		
Current Liabilities:		
Short-term borrowings (international—1975, $36,616; 1974, $50,684)	$ 36,616	$ 57,184
Current maturities of long-term debt	5,269	7,993
Accounts payable	79,099	98,651
Accrued liabilities	85,601	69,469
Income taxes	22,661	28,798
Dividends payable	4,751	4,436
Total current liabilities	$ 233,997	$ 266,531
Long-Term Debt (international—1975, $26,299; 1974, $53,141)	118,701	132,131
Provision for Pension and Severance Indemnities	21,051	17,135
Incentive Compensation Allotments	3,959	3,735
Deferred Taxes	5,105	2,697
Other (deferred unrealized foreign exchange gains— 1975, none; 1974, $2,647)	7,217	5,397
Deferred Income	6,744	—
Total Liabilities	$ 396,774	$ 427,626
Minority Interests in Subsidiary Companies	42,772	36,354
Stockholders' Equity:		
Common stock—authorized 15,000,000 shares—par value $3.125		
Issued: 1975—8,940,432 shares; 1974—8,376,598 shares	27,939	26,177
Additional paid-in capital	31,748	6,487
Earnings retained	297,787	275,294
Total	$ 357,474	$ 307,958
Less cost of common shares held in treasury (1975— 182,099 shares; 1974—195,472 shares)	7,228	7,729
Total Stockholders' Equity	$ 350,246	$ 300,229
Total Liabilities and Stockholders' Equity	$ 789,792	$ 764,209

EXHIBIT 3

Otis Elevator Company

Consolidated Statements of Income and Earnings Retained

(in thousands, except per share data)

	Year Ended December 31	
	1975	1974
Revenues:		
Contracts completed (1975, $1,153,219 and 1974, $1,076,221) and other revenue	$1,182,501	$1,104,171
Interest income	9,522	7,408
Total	$1,192,023	$1,111,579
Costs and Expenses:		
Cost of contracts completed	824,906	775,832
Selling, general and administrative expense	237,021	215,502
Interest expense	23,414	19,039
Foreign exchange	1,549	(799)
Miscellaneous—net	8,145	1,218
Total	$1,095,035	$1,010,792
Income Before Provision for Income Taxes and Minority Interests	96,988	100,787
Provision for Income Taxes	46,852	50,169
	$ 50,136	$ 50,618
Less Income Applicable to Minority Interests	9,569	7,089
Net Income (primary earnings per share: 1975, $5.02; 1974, $5.43)		
(fully diluted basis: 1975, $4.59; 1974, $4.97)	40,567	43,529
Earnings Retained at Beginning of Year	275,294	249,457
	315,861	292,986
Less Cash Dividends Declared ($2.20 per share in 1975 and 1974)	18,074	17,692
Earnings Retained at End of Year	$ 297,787	$ 275,294

Case 2-5

Prentice-Hall, Inc.

Prentice-Hall is a leading publisher of textbooks, periodicals, and audiovisual aids for educational purposes. The company's consolidated income statements and balance sheets for 1979 and 1980 appear in Exhibits 1 and 2.

A. Marketable Securities

The notes to Prentice-Hall's December 31, 1980 financial statements contained the following paragraph:

> Marketable securities are carried at the lower of aggregate cost or market. To adjust their carrying value to approximate market, equity securities included in the portfolio have been reduced by unrealized losses (net of unrealized gains). During 1980, the allowance for decline in market value of equity securities was reduced by $679,000 primarily due to the realization of losses of $640,000. Charges against income for unrealized losses in 1979 and 1978 were $522,000 and $361,000, respectively.

Required

1. Explain what is meant by "unrealized losses." How are these different from realized losses? When are these losses recognized? When are gains recognized?
2. Prepare journal entries to record the transactions affecting the marketable securities account during 1980.

B. Receivables

Prentice-Hall's short-term receivables consist of trade receivables and rental contracts receivable. The following paragraph from the notes to the financial statements pertains to the company's trade receivables.

> For financial reporting purposes, provision is made at the time of sale for the estimated effect of sales returns where right-of-return privileges exist. Returns of books from customers are accepted in accordance with standard industry practice. The full amount of the returns allowance (estimated sales to be returned net of inventory costs and reductions in royalties) is shown as a reduction of trade receivables in the accompanying financial statements.

The notes also contained the following summary of short-term receivables:

This case was prepared from published financial statements of Prentice-Hall, Inc.

	1980	1979
Trade receivables	$91,812,000	$88,234,000
Allowance for returns	(15,619,000)	(14,194,000)
Allowance for doubtful accounts	(6,332,000)	(6,126,000)
Net trade receivables	69,861,000	67,914,000
Rental contracts receivable	25,232,000	18,750,000
Total current receivables	$95,093,000	$86,664,000

Required

1. Assume that trade receivables determined to be uncollectable in 1980 totaled $6,448,000. What entry did Prentice-Hall make to write off these accounts?

2. What amount of doubtful accounts did Prentice-Hall deduct from income during fiscal 1980? How did the company determine this amount?

3. How is Prentice-Hall's accounting for the "allowance for returns" different from the "allowance for doubtful accounts?

4. Assume that sales returns accepted by the company during 1980 totaled $35,946,000. Also assume that inventory costs amount to 50% of sales and royalties are another 5%. What entry did Prentice-Hall make to record these returns? What entry was made during 1980 to record a provision for estimated returns?

EXHIBIT 1

PRENTICE-HALL, INC. AND SUBSIDIARIES

STATEMENTS OF CONSOLIDATED INCOME AND RETAINED EARNINGS

(Dollars in Thousands, Except Per Share Data)	YEAR ENDED DECEMBER 31		
	1980	1979	1978
Sales and other revenue	$353,413	$281,552	$254,912
Cost of operations:			
Cost of sales	130,739	104,838	94,353
Selling, general, and administrative expenses	160,727	126,219	108,649
Total cost of operations	291,466	231,057	203,002
Income from operations	61,947	50,495	51,910
Other:			
Interest expense	(7,311)	(832)	(212)
Gain on sales of land—installment basis	1,168	545	238
Other income—net	1,201	1,064	792
Total other	(4,942)	777	818
Income before income taxes	57,005	51,272	52,728
Income taxes (Notes 1 and 8):			
Federal and foreign	15,300	20,875	23,370
State and local	3,900	3,600	3,600
Deferred	7,000	(1,025)	(970)
Total income taxes	26,200	23,450	26,000
Net income	30,805	27,822	26,728
Retained earnings at beginning of year (Note 2)	130,570	116,543	102,467
Cash dividends—per share, $1.50 in 1980; $1.39 in 1979; $1.27 in 1978	(14,868)	(13,795)	(12,652)
Retained earnings at end of year	$146,507	$130,570	$116,543
Net income per share of common stock	$3.11	$2.80	$2.68

EXHIBIT 2

PRENTICE-HALL, INC. AND SUBSIDIARIES

CONSOLIDATED BALANCE SHEETS

ASSETS

(Dollars in Thousands)	DECEMBER 31	
	1980	1979
Current Assets:		
Cash	$ 3,212	$ 4,802
Marketable securities and certificates of deposit at market		
(cost: 1980—$1,284; 1979—$4,572) (Note 1)	1,080	3,689
Receivables (Notes 1 and 5)	95,093	86,664
Finished goods inventories	50,196	44,061
Paper, supplies, and other inventories	10,805	11,425
Prepaid expenses	10,394	11,427
Deferred income tax benefits (Notes 1 and 8)	5,891	9,675
Total Current Assets	**176,671**	171,743
Property and Equipment—at cost (less accumulated		
depreciation: 1980—$54,828; 1979—$44,962)		
(Notes 1 and 6)	**77,398**	70,055
Other Assets:		
Receivables (Notes 1 and 5)	25,073	12,598
Advances to authors (Note 1)	8,495	7,818
Excess of cost over net value of assets acquired (Note 1)	8,524	6,041
Cash value of life insurance (less insurance		
policy loans: 1980—$1,416; 1979—$407)	212	1,200
Total Other Assets	**42,304**	27,657
TOTAL	**$296,373**	$269,455

EXHIBIT 2 *(Continued)*

LIABILITIES AND STOCKHOLDERS' EQUITY

(Dollars in Thousands)	DECEMBER 31	
	1980	1979
Current Liabilities:		
Notes payable—banks (Note 4)	**$ 1,000**	$ 7,500
Accounts payable	**8,145**	12,161
Accrued royalties	**17,257**	15,560
Other accrued expenses (Note 7)	**27,592**	21,496
Federal and foreign income taxes	**14,309**	10,689
Unexpired subscriptions	**7,910**	7,005
Advance subscription payments (Note 1)	**15,971**	14,908
Total Current Liabilities	**92,184**	89,319
Long-Term Liabilities:		
Long-term borrowings (Note 3)	**33,283**	30,813
Future service costs of rental contracts (Note 1)	**5,826**	2,742
Deferred gain on sales of land	**1,392**	2,046
Deferred income taxes payable (Note 1)	**4,678**	1,462
Total Long-Term Liabilities	**45,179**	37,063
Stockholders' Equity (Notes 2 and 10):		
Common stock—authorized 15,000,000 shares of		
$.33-1/3 par value; issued, 10,429,888 shares	**3,477**	3,477
Capital surplus	**21,447**	21,447
Retained earnings	**146,507**	130,570
Total	**171,431**	155,494
Less treasury stock at cost, 518,100 shares	**12,421**	12,421
Stockholders' Equity	**159,010**	143,073
TOTAL	**$296,373**	$269,455

Case 2–6

Caesars New Jersey, Inc.

Exhibits 1, 2, and 3 are from the *1981 Annual Report* of Caesars New Jersey, Inc. (CNJ), the owner and operator of the Caesars Boardwalk Regency Hotel and Casino in Atlantic City, New Jersey. The company is an 85%-owned subsidiary of Caesars World, Inc. (CWI).

A. Accounts Receivable

The "Provision for doubtful accounts" increased from $3,850,000 to $8,429,000 between 1980 and 1981, while casino revenues changed very little. Also note that the "Allowance for doubtful accounts" increased from $3,566,000 to $10,009,000 during the same period. While CNJ does not disclose how it determines its allowance for doubtful accounts, it is likely that the company uses the percentage-of-sales method, with an adjustment at the end of the period based upon the aging-of-accounts-receivable method.

Required

1. How much of accounts receivable was written off in 1981 as uncollectable? In other words, what was the total amount of specific receivables removed from the books due to the determination that they would never be paid?

2. Is there any indication that bad-debt experience has been any worse than expected?

3. While it is common in the casino industry to recognize revenue even when credit is extended to customers, it would seem prudent to ask what would happen to the financial statements if recognition of revenue were deferred until accounts were collected. What would be the effect on 1981 revenues if revenues were recognized at the point of cash collection?

B. Preopening Costs

Note 1a (see Exhibit 3) describes some difficulties CNJ is having with the New Jersey Casino Control Commission. The Casino Control Commission found that the chairman and vice chairman of the board (of both Caesars World, Inc., and Caesars New Jersey, Inc.) were not qualified to be associated with Caesars New Jersey, Inc. As a consequence, the note indicates that Caesars World may withdraw from gaming activities in New Jersey.

This case was prepared by Professor Eric Noreen of the University of Washington from published financial statements of Caesars New Jersey, Inc.

Required

1. Do you think it is appropriate for CNJ to continue to defer preopening costs (described in Note 1e) and other charges (described in Note 3)? Defend your position.

EXHIBIT 1

CAESARS NEW JERSEY, INC.
AND SUBSIDIARY
(a subsidiary of Caesars World, Inc.)

CONSOLIDATED
BALANCE SHEETS

July 31, 1981 and 1980	1981	1980
	(In Thousands)	
ASSETS		
Current assets:		
Cash .... $	7,616	$ 6,303
Short-term investments at cost, which approximates market value	2,375	2,000
Accounts receivable, net of allowance for doubtful accounts of $10,009 and $3,566		
in 1981 and 1980, respectively	14,661	13,008
Inventories	614	644
Prepaid expenses and other current assets	2,376	2,265
Total current assets	27,642	24,220
Restricted cash from sale of common stock and warrants (Note 10)		12,566
Property and equipment at cost, net of accumulated depreciation and		
amortization (Notes 2, 7 and 8)	122,578	118,156
Deferred pre-opening costs, net of accumulated amortization	3,467	7,775
Deferred charges and other assets, net of accumulated amortization (Note 3)	8,717	9,455
	$162,404	$172,172
LIABILITIES AND SHAREHOLDERS' EQUITY		
Current liabilities:		
Notes payable to banks (Note 5) .... $	30,100	
Current portion of long-term debt (Note 7)	5,038	$ 3,634
Current portion of obligations under capital leases (Note 8)	1,752	1,565
Accounts payable and accrued expenses (Note 6)	20,004	20,797
State income taxes	714	3,322
Due to parent (Notes 4 and 9)	4,774	40,470
Total current liabilities	62,382	69,788
Long-term debt, net of current portion (Note 7)	17,449	25,132
Obligations under capital leases, net of current portion (Note 8)	38,851	40,506
Deposits payable	227	227
Deferred income taxes (Note 4)	4,855	5,961
Contingent obligation to repurchase common stock (Note 10)		10,243
Commitments and contingencies (Note 11)		
Shareholders' equity (Notes 5, 9, 10 and 12)		
Common stock, $.10 par value; authorized 30,000,000 shares;		
issued and outstanding, 16,025,260 shares and 15,976,258 shares, respectively ...	1,603	1,598
Capital in excess of par	16,494	6,005
Retained earnings	20,543	12,712
	38,640	20,315
	$162,404	$172,172

See notes to consolidated financial statements.

EXHIBIT 2

CAESARS NEW JERSEY, INC.
AND SUBSIDIARY
(a subsidiary of Caesars World, Inc.)

CONSOLIDATED STATEMENTS OF EARNINGS

Years ended July 31,	1981	1980	1979
	(In Thousands Except Per Share Data)		
Revenues:			
Casino	$197,738	$198,384	$11,384
Rooms	12,888	12,555	1,442
Food and beverage	30,089	28,839	3,577
	240,715	239,778	16,403
Less: Promotional allowances	(21,221)	(18,266)	(992)
	219,494	221,512	15,411
Other income	4,271	5,340	1,493
	223,765	226,852	16,904
Costs and expenses:			
Casino	91,670	81,974	8,572
Rooms	4,799	6,563	757
Food and beverage	24,271	22,559	3,322
Music and entertainment	6,431	6,947	1,086
Selling, general and administrative (Note 9)	42,552	46,676	6,840
Interest (Note 9)	14,904	15,346	7,011
Less: Interest capitalized			(3,118)
Provision for doubtful accounts	8,429	3,850	10
Depreciation and amortization	8,682	6,308	896
Amortization of pre-opening costs	4,308	4,308	844
	206,046	194,531	26,220
Income (loss) before income taxes (credits)	17,719	32,321	(9,316)
Income taxes (credits) (Note 4)	9,888	16,194	(6,338)
Net income (loss)	$ 7,831	$ 16,127	$(2,978)
Net income (loss) per common and common equivalent share	$ .48	$ .97	$(.20)
Number of shares used in computation (Note 1h)	16,447	16,710	15,207

See notes to consolidated financial statements.

EXHIBIT 3

CAESARS NEW JERSEY, INC.
AND SUBSIDIARY
(a subsidiary of Caesars World, Inc.)

NOTES TO
FINANCIAL STATEMENTS

NOTE 1.
SUMMARY OF ACCOUNTING POLICIES
AND DESCRIPTION OF BUSINESS:

a. Description of business and principles of consolidation: Caesars New Jersey, Inc. (the "Company"), a New Jersey corporation, was incorporated on July 13, 1978 and immediately acquired all of the stock of Boardwalk Regency Corporation ("BRC"). The Company was formed by Caesars World, Inc. ("CWI") to conduct CWI's hotel and casino activities in New Jersey and engage in other activities directly or indirectly related to gaming. CWI had previously formed BRC in 1977 under the name Desert Palace of New Jersey, Inc. The Company is an 85% owned subsidiary of Caesars World, Inc.

The Company, through BRC, operates Caesars Boardwalk Regency Hotel/Casino ("CBR") in Atlantic City, New Jersey. In addition, through BRC, the Company leases a second property in Atlantic City, New Jersey (the "Indiana Avenue Property") on which the Company is considering construction of another hotel and casino facility but has suspended these efforts, at least until resolution of the problems regarding BRC's casino license.

From June 26, 1979 until October 25, 1980, BRC operated its casino under a temporary permit issued by the New Jersey Casino Control Commission (the "CCC"). On October 25, 1980, BRC was granted a license to operate that casino. However, during the licensing process, the CCC found the Chairman and Vice Chairman of the Board of the Company and of CWI not qualified to be officers, directors or stockholders of the Company, BRC or CWI. Before the CCC would license BRC, it required that the Chairman and Vice Chairman take leaves of absence from their positions as officers and directors of CWI (but not its subsidiaries outside New Jersey), the Company and BRC and required the Company and CWI to agree that, until November 26, 1980 (subsequently extended until determination of court appeals), the Chairman and Vice Chairman would not

be entitled to any benefits conferred by securities of the Company and CWI owned by them, including the right to receive interest and dividends. The Chairman had been on a similar leave of absence since May 1979 because of an agreement he made in order to obtain consent of the New Jersey Division of Gaming Enforcement to the issuance to BRC of a temporary permit.

Following the actions described above, the CCC issued a license to BRC subject to the condition that, by November 26, 1980, CWI either (a) notify the CCC of its intent to continue to operate a casino in New Jersey, in which case the Chairman and Vice Chairman must stop being officers, directors or employees of CWI or any of its subsidiaries (including those outside New Jersey) and CWI must submit a plan and timetable as to how the Chairman and Vice Chairman would dispose of their approximately 2% stock interest in the Company and their approximately 17% stock interest in CWI, or (b) notify the CCC that it will withdraw from the casino industry in New Jersey, in which case it must submit a plan and timetable as to how it would accomplish that. The Supreme Court of New Jersey subsequently suspended the time by which CWI would have to fulfill the conditions to the BRC casino license until adjudication of appeals from the determinations of the CCC.

The Company, BRC and CWI, as well as the Chairman and Vice Chairman of the Board, appealed the determination regarding the qualifications of the Chairman and Vice Chairman and the conditions imposed on BRC's license. The Appellate Division of the New Jersey Superior Court affirmed substantial portions of the decision of the CCC, but held that the CCC could not prohibit the Chairman and Vice Chairman from being involved in CWI's nongaming activities outside New Jersey. The three companies and the Chairman and Vice Chairman have appealed to the New Jersey Supreme Court from the decision of

EXHIBIT 3 *(Continued)*

the Appellate Division, and the CCC and the Division of Gaming Enforcement have appealed from the finding that the Chairman and Vice Chairman may be involved in CWI's nongaming activities outside New Jersey.

CWI has not decided whether, if its appeals are not successful, CWI will withdraw from the gaming industry in New Jersey, or whether CWI will try to cause the Chairman and Vice Chairman to sever their relationships with CWI. However, most of the directors of CWI have indicated that, if they were currently required to make a decision, they would favor withdrawing from the gaming industry in New Jersey on some reasonable basis.

The consolidated financial statements include the accounts of Caesars New Jersey, Inc. and its subsidiary after elimination of all material intercompany balances and transactions. Certain reclassifications have been made to conform to the fiscal 1981 presentation.

b. Accounting for casino revenue and promotional allowances: In accordance with common industry practice, the Company recognizes as casino revenue the net win from gaming activities, which is the difference between gaming wins and losses. The retail value of accommodations, food and beverages furnished without charge to customers is included in gross revenues and then deducted as promotional allowances. Other promotional items are treated as casino expenses.

c. Inventories: Inventories are stated at the lower of cost or market; cost is determined on a first-in, first-out basis.

d. Property and equipment: Property and equipment, excluding leased properties under capital leases, are stated at cost less accumulated depreciation and amortization. For financial reporting purposes, the Company has capitalized certain leased properties and equipment. Depreciation and amortization are provided for in amounts sufficient to relate the cost of depreciable assets to operations over

their estimated service lives on the straight-line basis while accelerated methods are used for tax purposes.

Amounts capitalized as leased properties under capital leases include land (Indiana Avenue Property) which is not subject to amortization, and hotel/casino facilities and equipment (Caesars Boardwalk Regency Property) which are being amortized.

e. Deferred pre-opening costs and capitalization of interest: The Company deferred the pre-opening costs of its hotel/casino facility prior to its substantial completion on May 24, 1979, and commenced amortization of these costs over a three-year period from that date. The cost of the hotel/casino facility includes interest on funds borrowed to finance its construction.

f. Casino licensing costs: Costs of obtaining a casino license incurred prior to October 25, 1980 were deferred and are being amortized over a three-year period from that date.

g. Income taxes: The Company and its subsidiary are included in CWI's consolidated federal income tax return. Income taxes and credits reflected in the accompanying financial statements are based on the terms of a tax reimbursement agreement entered into with CWI (see Note 4). Deferred income taxes are provided for those items for which the period of reporting for income tax purposes is different from the period of reporting for financial statement purposes.

Investment tax credits are accounted for by the flow-through method, which recognizes the credits as reductions of income tax expense in the year utilized.

h. Earnings (loss) per share: Earnings (loss) per common and common equivalent share are computed on the basis of the weighted average number of shares outstanding during the respective periods, including, when dilutive, warrants and outstanding stock options using the treasury stock method.

EXHIBIT 3 *(Continued)*

CAESARS NEW JERSEY, INC.
AND SUBSIDIARY
(a subsidiary of Caesars World, Inc.)

NOTE 2.
PROPERTY AND EQUIPMENT, NET:

	1981	1980
	(In Thousands)	
Land	$ 11,585	$ 5,348
Buildings and improvements	46,661	42,445
Leasehold improvements	1,433	1,175
Furniture, fixtures and equipment	15,176	13,381
Tenants' rights acquired	1,177	1,177
Construction in progress — Caesars Boardwalk Regency	1,908	3,146
Construction in progress — plans, permits and other — Indiana Avenue property	2,423	2,654
Leased properties under capital leases:		
Land	9,055	9,055
Buildings	34,703	34,703
Furniture and equipment	12,647	12,910
	136,768	125,994
Less: Accumulated depreciation and amortization	14,190	7,838
	$122,578	$118,156

NOTE 3.
DEFERRED CHARGES AND OTHER ASSETS:

	1981	1980
	(In Thousands)	
Casino licensing costs, net of accumulated amortization	$4,908	$4,972
Deposits[a]	2,743	3,080
Other	1,066	1,403
	$8,717	$9,455

(a) *Included is a $2,500,000 security deposit which the Company has given under the Indiana Avenue Property lease. Under the terms of the lease, $2,000,000 of the security deposit is returnable in installments when major specified improvements have been completed. The remaining $500,000 is returnable upon the expiration (or termination) of the lease, or when the Company exercises its option to purchase the property. The Company has the option to purchase the leased property in the future under certain terms (Note 8).*

3

INVENTORIES AND LONG-LIVED ASSETS

Case 3–1

Perry Drug Stores

Using $200 of his own capital, Jack Robinson opened his first drugstore on Perry Street in Pontiac, Michigan, in 1957. Sales have increased each year, and no stores have ever been closed. The company was operating 18 stores when it issued its first public stock offering in early 1973. Since then, the company has expanded to over 110 stores in five states. More than 70 stores are located in the southeastern quadrant of Michigan's lower peninsula, making Perry the state's largest drugstore chain.

Perry's growth philosophy has stressed the opening of stores in suburban shopping centers. The typical Perry store covers 15,000 square feet of floor space as opposed to 8,000 to 10,000 square feet for traditional drugstores. In addition to the usual pharmacy services, these larger units offer an expanded array of merchandise not normally found in traditional drugstores, including household and automotive supplies, small appliances, phonograph records, convenience foods, and alcoholic beverages.

During fiscal 1980, Perry continued its expansion program while instituting

This case was prepared from published financial statements of Perry Drug Stores.

new controls on operating expenses. In July, the company acquired DeKoven Drug Company, a Chicago-based firm that operated 26 stores in Illinois, Nebraska, Texas, and Oklahoma. As part of an overall plan to reduce operating expenses, Perry installed a new electronic inventory control system consisting of a microcomputer and portable hand-held scanners that interface with the main computer at the distribution center. This system reduced clerical labor for ordering merchandise by 75 percent and cut inventory replacement time from three days to two. This reduces inventory holding and shipping costs.

Yet, despite its growth and cost-cutting efforts, Perry's earnings declined in 1980 as explained by Jack Robinson in a letter to shareholders:

> Higher interest costs and accelerating inflation combined in fiscal 1980 to deny Perry Drug Stores a fifth consecutive year of record earnings. LIFO-measured fiscal 1980 earnings declined 5.5% to $2,363,000 from $2,501,000 in 1979. Net income on a per share basis amounted to $1.51 against $1.62 the year before.
>
> There was also a heavy impact on earnings of the LIFO method of inventory valuation. Under this method, current costs are matched against revenues. In periods of rising costs, utilization of LIFO results in greater cost of goods sold and therefore lower earnings than the FIFO basis. The LIFO charge against net income in 1980 was 55% greater than in 1979.

Throughout the 1980 annual report to shareholders, management emphasized the effect of LIFO on profits (for one example, see Exhibit 1). In addition, the notes to the consolidated financial statements included the following description of inventories:

Inventories

Inventories, consisting of general merchandise and prescription drugs, are stated at the lower of cost or market. As of October 31, 1980 and 1979, the last-in, first-out (LIFO) method was used to determine cost for [substantially all] inventories. Inventories valued on LIFO at October 31, 1980 and 1979, respectively, were $4,589,500 and $3,210,500 lower than the amounts that would have been reported using FIFO.

Perry Drug Stores' consolidated statements of earnings and balance sheets for fiscal 1979 and 1980 appear in Exhibits 2 and 3.

Required

1. Compute the amount of merchandise inventories purchased during fiscal 1980. How would the use of FIFO for inventory valuation affect this amount? Explain.
2. Compute the amount of earnings before income taxes that Perry would have reported had FIFO been used to value all inventories.

3. Assuming a 46% federal income tax rate, what would have been reported for 1980 net income if Perry had used FIFO to value both beginning and ending inventories? How would the use of FIFO have affected Perry's 1980 federal income tax bill?

4. Perry Drug Stores adopted the LIFO method in 1974. Assuming a 46% federal income tax rate, what amount of retained earnings would Perry have reported in its 1980 balance sheet if FIFO had always been used?

5. If you were in the position to choose· Perry's inventory valuation method, which method (LIFO, FIFO, or any other) would you select? Be prepared to defend your choice.

EXHIBIT 1

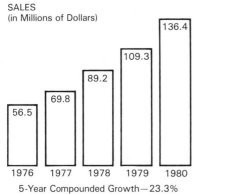

SALES
(in Millions of Dollars)

56.5 — 1976
69.8 — 1977
89.2 — 1978
109.3 — 1979
136.4 — 1980

5-Year Compounded Growth—23.3%

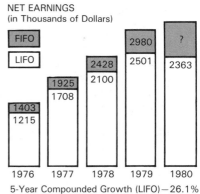

NET EARNINGS
(in Thousands of Dollars)

FIFO / LIFO

Year	FIFO	LIFO
1976	1403	1215
1977	1925	1708
1978	2428	2100
1979	2980	2501
1980	?	2363

5-Year Compounded Growth (LIFO)—26.1%

EXHIBIT 2

Consolidated Statements of Earnings

Fiscal Years Ended October 31

IP perry

	1980	1979
REVENUES:		
Net sales	$136,426,694	$109,275,332
Other revenues	234,746	392,672
Total revenues	136,661,440	109,668,004
COST AND EXPENSES:		
Cost of goods sold	94,906,983	75,915,824
Warehouse, store operating and administrative expenses	36,753,788	29,093,494
Interest	1,182,029	521,081
Total cost and expenses	132,842,800	105,530,399
EARNINGS BEFORE INCOME TAXES	3,818,640	4,137,605
PROVISION FOR INCOME TAXES	1,456,000	1,637,000
NET EARNINGS	$ 2,362,640	$ 2,500,605
AVERAGE NUMBER OF SHARES OUTSTANDING	1,565,175	1,545,881
NET EARNINGS PER SHARE	$1.51	$1.62

EXHIBIT 3

 Consolidated Balance Sheets
October 31

ASSETS	1980	1979
CURRENT ASSETS:		
Cash.	$ 550,210	$ 922,546
Accounts receivable, trade	2,002,998	1,373,905
Inventories	30,064,405	21,796,693
Prepayments and other	1,815,130	1,405,649
Total current assets.	34,432,743	25,498,793
PROPERTY AND EQUIPMENT:		
Land and land improvements	1,054,196	1,044,697
Building	5,758,371	5,602,642
Fixtures and equipment	7,127,951	5,258,977
Automotive equipment	1,675,922	1,308,269
Leasehold improvements.	3,287,964	2,303,430
	18,904,404	15,518,015
Less-Accumulated depreciation and amortization	3,459,939	2,596,061
	15,444,465	12,921,954
INTANGIBLE AND OTHER ASSETS:		
Intangible assets, net of accumulated amortization of		
$83,065 in 1980 and $63,369 in 1979	530,649	396,731
Land contract receivable, net of current portion of $102,250	185,900	306,750
Other assets.	939,151	430,954
	1,655,700	1,134,435
	$51,532,908	$39,555,182
LIABILITIES AND SHAREHOLDERS' EQUITY		
CURRENT LIABILITIES:		
Notes payable to bank, unsecured.	$ —	$ 3,000,000
Current portion of long-term debt and obligation under capital lease	307,952	281,500
Accounts payable	14,893,595	10,826,079
Accrued liabilities	1,775,002	830,311
Accrued income taxes	101,676	40,987
Total current liabilities.	17,078,225	14,978,877
LONG-TERM DEBT, less current portion	8,520,050	2,372,500
LONG-TERM OBLIGATION UNDER CAPITAL LEASE, less current portion	4,565,000	4,639,000
DEFERRED TAXES	988,000	826,000
SHAREHOLDERS' EQUITY:		
Preferred stock	—	—
Common stock.	85,743	77,402
Paid-in capital.	8,236,008	6,529,932
Retained earnings	12,059,882	10,131,471
Total shareholders' equity	20,381,633	16,738,805
	$51,532,908	$39,555,182

Case 3–2

Farmer Brothers Company

Roy F. Farmer, president and chairman of the board of Farmer Brothers Company, opened the company's *1977 Annual Report* with the following summary of operations:

> The much publicized Brazilian frost of July, 1976, and the shortage of coffee which it allegedly created, was used by producing countries to drive the cost of green coffee to record highs. This situation, combined with our use of the last-in, first-out method of costing which channels the latest and most expensive purchases into cost of goods sold and applies those costs against sales made at prices based on earlier and lower costs, resulted in a pre-tax loss of $11,745,859 for fiscal 1977.

The Company

Farmer Brothers roasts and packages coffee and processes spices and other restaurant supplies at its main facilities in Torrance, California. In addition, the company manufactures a complete line of coffee-brewing equipment at its Brewmatic Division plant in Los Angeles. Farmer Brothers operates through four divisions and a subsidiary:

> The Restaurant and Institutional Sales Division, through its 62 branches, distributes coffee and other supplies to restaurants, hotels, and other institutions.
>
> The Custom Coffee Plan Division distributes coffee and other merchandise through branches in California and Texas.
>
> The Spice Products Division is engaged in the sale of spices to a variety of industrial food producers.
>
> The Brewmatic Division manufactures coffee-brewing equipment for use by the Restaurant and Institutional Sales Division and for sale within the United States. Sales are also made to Brewmatic International.
>
> Brewmatic International is a wholly owned subsidiary that distributes coffee-brewing equipment to the Canadian and overseas markets.

1977 Operations

Farmer Brothers reported record-high sales revenues for fiscal 1977 even though the quantity of coffee sold decreased from 40,628,328 pounds in 1976 to 39,544,583 pounds in fiscal 1977. The record sales were precipitated by a freeze in coffee-growing regions of Brazil in 1976 that severely damaged the coffee crop

---

This case was prepared from published financial statements of Farmer Brothers Company.

and caused green coffee prices to rise sharply. As a result of aberrations in the coffee market and Farmer Brothers' use of LIFO inventory accounting, the company reported a loss of $5,986,259 for fiscal 1977 despite the record-high revenues. The company's annual report included the following analysis:

> The continuing escalation of green coffee costs through most of fiscal 1977 was directly responsible for the large losses incurred by the company. During the period between January 1, 1977 and March 15, 1977, green coffee costs rose from $2.00 to $3.40 per pound. Farmer Bros. Co., in order to remain competitive, was forced to absorb a portion of the additional cost; consequently, our selling prices did not reach a level which would produce reasonable gross profit margins until May, 1977. Because the company utilizes the Last-In-First-Out method of accounting for coffee costs, its latest purchases are channeled directly into costs of goods sold and are applied against sales which were made at prices based on earlier and lower priced green coffee purchases. The combination of the LIFO method of accounting and the delay in increasing selling prices produced heavy losses during the third quarter. Fourth quarter operations resulted in the recovery of 8 million of the 19 million dollar pretax loss incurred in the first 9 months. The recovery can be attributed to two factors. First, at March 31, 1977, in anticipating the replacement of [liquidated] LIFO inventory, the company used $3.00 per pound as an estimated cost. Management, however, did not replenish the inventory at the time green coffee was priced at $3.00 per pound but waited and made its purchases at an average price of $2.32 per pound. The difference between the $3.00 estimate and the $2.32 actual cost accounted for approximately $4,750,000 of the fourth quarter profit. Second, the increase in selling prices raised our gross margins to a more reasonable level and this accounted for $3,940,000 in fourth quarter profits, while the addition of 1.9 million pounds of coffee to our LIFO base served to reduce the fourth quarter profit and increase the loss for fiscal 1977.

Information concerning Farmer Brothers' inventories was obtained from the notes to the 1977 financial statements and is presented in Exhibit 1. Also, the company's consolidated balance sheets and statements of earnings (and loss) for fiscal 1976 and 1977 are presented in Exhibits 2 and 3.

Required

1. Cost of goods sold, as stated in Farmer Brothers' 1977 income statement, includes $93,884,710 for the cost of 39,544,583 pounds of coffee sold through the Restaurant and Institutional Sales and Custom Coffee Plan divisions. Compute the following amounts:
   a. average cost per pound of coffee in inventory at June 30, 1976
   b. average cost per pound of coffee in inventory at June 30, 1977
   c. average cost per pound of coffee sold during fiscal 1977
   d. average cost per pound of coffee purchased during fiscal 1977
   Explain why these average costs differ. Be specific.
2. Assume that Farmer Brothers' management wished to report a larger profit

(or smaller loss) in fiscal 1977 without switching to FIFO. What would you recommend?

3. Management's "Report on Operations" in the *1977 Annual Report* included the following statement:

> The corporation again increased its LIFO coffee inventory base, adding approximately 2 million pounds to the previous base of 17,800,000 pounds. The LIFO base is now at a level which, in the opinion of management, will enable it to freely adjust its inventory purchases to coincide with changes in economic conditions.

Assume that as of June 30, 1977, the price of green coffee was $2.25 per pound. Also assume that management expected that coffee prices would drop to $2.00 per pound in the first quarter of fiscal 1978. Determine the benefits and costs of increasing coffee inventories at year end. How would this cost-benefit trade-off change if coffee prices were expected to drop to $1.40?

EXHIBIT 1
Farmer Brothers
Inventories, 1976-1977

	1977		1976	
	Pounds	*Cost**	*Pounds*	*Cost**
Coffee	19,677,532	$ 9,920,842	17,800,000	$ 7,706,245
Allied products	—	5,400,394	—	5,594,160
Brewmatic equipment	—	2,505,611	—	2,134,388
		$17,826,847		$15,434,893

*Coffee and allied products inventories are stated at cost, utilizing the LIFO method, not exceeding market value. All other inventories are stated at cost under the FIFO method, not exceeding market value. Current cost of coffee and allied products inventories exceeded the cost based on the LIFO method by $40,800,000 and $12,700,000 at June 30, 1977 and 1976, respectively.

EXHIBIT 2
Farmer Bros. Co.
Consolidated Balance Sheet

	June 30	
	1977	*1976*
Assets		
Current Assets:		
Cash	$ 2,228,019	$ 587,965
Marketable securities, at cost (approximates market)	3,599,154	3,101,902
Accounts receivable, less allowance for doubtful accounts of $480,000 in 1977 and $375,000 in 1976	13,434,729	7,976,904
Federal and State income taxes receivable	5,973,213	1,422,582
Inventories	17,826,847	15,434,893
Prepaid expenses	679,860	460,541
Total current assets	$43,741,822	$28,984,787
Properties and Equipment, At Cost, Less Accumulated Depreciation	10,009,444	8,731,176
Cash Surrender Value of Life Insurance	787,868	753,783
Other Assets	1,023	6,952
	$54,540,157	$38,476,698
Liabilities		
Current Liabilities:		
Accounts payable, including accrued items	$21,219,262	$11,144,547
Short-term borrowings	12,887,518	—
Deferred taxes	115,267	105,422
Total current liabilities	$34,222,047	$11,249,969
Long-Term Liabilities:		
Notes payable	626,156	626,156
Deferred taxes	31,024	166,169
	$34,879,227	$12,042,294
Shareholders' Equity		
Capital Shares:		
Common	1,968,037	1,968,037
Additional Paid-in Capital	1,290,687	1,290,687
Retained Earnings	16,402,206	23,175,680
	$19,660,930	$26,434,404
	$54,540,157	$38,476,698

EXHIBIT 3
Farmer Bros. Co.
Consolidated Statement of Income and (Loss)

| | Year Ended June 30 | |
	1977	1976
Sales	$135,271,053	$87,156,483
Cost of Goods Sold	124,267,341	64,799,214
Gross Profit	$ 11,003,712	$22,357,269
Selling Expense	19,615,507	17,752,185
General and Administrative Expense	3,485,365	2,962,941
	$ 23,100,872	$20,715,126
Income (Loss) from Operations	(12,097,160)	1,642,143
Other Income, Net	351,301	444,268
Income (Loss) Before Provision (Credit) for Taxes	(11,745,859)	2,086,411
Provision (Credit) for Taxes on Income	(5,759,600)	1,098,039
Net Income (Loss)	$ (5,986,259)	$ 988,372
Net Income (Loss) per Average Common Share Outstanding	$(3.04)	$.50

Case 3–3

Oscar Mayer and Company

Oscar Mayer, known best as the largest producer of hot dogs, bacon, and bologna in the United States, produces a wide variety of other processed meats. Founded in 1883 as a small neighborhood meat market, the company has grown into a billion-dollar, international operation. It has developed a reputation for innovation in processing, packaging, and marketing its products.

The following note concerning Oscar Mayer's inventories appeared in the company's *1978 Annual Report*:

Inventories consist of the following:

	October 28, 1978	October 29, 1977
Manufactured product	$ 36,539,000	$26,528,000
Raw materials	24,700,000	22,662,000
Supplies	39,897,000	35,312,000
	101,136,000	84,502,000
LIFO reserve	(35,625,000)	(23,838,000)
	$ 65,511,000	$60,664,000

The LIFO method of valuing inventories, first adopted in 1940, normally charges cost of products sold with current costs, which results in a more accurate matching of revenue and costs. However, the effect of this method on the balance sheet is to value inventories at historical costs, which may bear no relation to current cost. The historical LIFO cost of inventories was less than current cost by the amounts reflected in the LIFO reserve.

In an inflationary period, the FIFO method of valuing inventories places an unrealistically low value on cost of product sold because inventory is charged to operations at amounts below current replacement prices. Resulting "inventory profits" are unrealistic since inventories must be replenished at current higher prices. In addition, taxes must be paid on the inventory profits resulting in a depletion of capital. The LIFO method normally does not produce such inventory profits and conserves capital in a period of rising prices.

Required

1. What are "inventory profits"? What happens to these "inventory profits" if the LIFO method is used?

2. If Oscar Mayer and Company had used current costs to value inventories in-

---

This case was prepared from published financial statements of Oscar Mayer and Company.

stead of LIFO, what amount of unrealized holding gains would the company have reported in its 1978 balance sheet?

3. Oscar Mayer reported cost of products sold of $1,156,452,000 in 1978. What amount would have been reported if the company had used current costs to value inventories?

4. The note stated that "The LIFO method of valuing inventories . . . normally charges cost of products sold with current costs, which results in a more accurate matching of revenue and costs." Comment. Would this statement be true if inventory prices were falling?

Case 3–4

Control Data Corporation

Control Data Corporation (CDC), founded in 1957, produces large, high-speed, digital computer systems as well as compatible peripheral equipment and software. From its inception, CDC grew rapidly, reflecting industry growth and the company's aggressive product development and marketing strategy. By 1964, sales, rentals, and service income had grown to over $131 million, giving CDC the third largest market share in the industry.

In 1965, CDC reported record sales and earnings as discussed by company President William C. Norris in his letter to shareholders:

> During the past year, we moved forward on many fronts. While our sales and earnings fell short of our ambitious goals, the business still showed reasonable growth. Our organization again made substantial growth, both in capabilities and numbers of people. There were major achievements with respect to the design, manufacture and introduction of new products. Our research and development effort was substantially increased. Our business backlog at year-end was up approximately 60% over the backlog one year earlier.
>
> Sales, rental and service income of Control Data Corporation and its subsidiaries amounted to $160 million for the year ended June 30, 1965, as compared with $131 million in the same period last year. Net earnings for the year ended June 30, 1965 were $7,912,961 as compared with $6,018,121 for last year. The earnings per share were $1.06 versus $0.84 last year.

Rental and service income represented a growing portion of CDC's total revenues (see Exhibit 1). By the mid-1960s computer leasing had become common practice in the industry. CDC began renting computer systems to customers in 1960, and by 1965 the company reported that 55% of the systems delivered were rentals. As a result of this trend, CDC announced a change in its accounting policies for leased computers in the *1965 Annual Report*. Company Treasurer Allan L. Rudell explained:

> Approximately 55% of the Company's orders booked in fiscal year 1965 were lease orders, compared with 40% in the previous year, and this significant change to lease business is also reflected in the backlog at the close of the year. This means that approximately 55% of the Company's marketing, development and programming efforts were expended in obtaining lease orders from which the rental revenues will be spread over the next several years. To charge off all of such expenses in the year incurred results in an understatement of the current year's earnings and a consequent overstatement of the income to be derived in the future from those leases. The apparent pattern is that our business is changing, and an increasing percentage of our backlog of orders is represented by leases. Although we cannot foresee the

---

This case was prepared from published financial statements of Control Data Corporation. The case was suggested by a case written by Professor Richard F. Vancil of Harvard University.

future with certainty, we believe that we should plan that this trend will continue.

The occurrence of this change in our business dictated that we change our accounting practices to more properly match costs with related revenues.

The first change made was in our depreciation policy on leased computers from the four year double declining balance method to four years straight line. Under the four year double declining balance method 50% of the cost of the leased equipment was charged to income during the first twelve months after installation as compared with 25% under the straight line method. This change was announced in the third quarter report to stockholders and became effective January 1, 1965. The change in depreciation was a change in method only; no change was made in the depreciable life (four years) so the equipment still becomes fully depreciated as soon as, or sooner than, that of other companies in the computer industry. Without this accounting change earnings for fiscal year 1965 would have been reduced by $0.16 per share.

The second accounting change was the deferment of a portion of product development costs, systems application, programming and marketing expenses associated with the specific computer models for which lease orders were secured during the fiscal year. These deferred costs are being amortized over the periods during which the rental income is received, but not to exceed three years. Although this accounting change was made as of July 1, 1964 the profits reported for fiscal year 1965 were determined as though this accounting change had been in effect for all prior years. This required that we reduce fiscal year 1965 earnings by the amount of amortization that would have been applicable thereto had comparable costs been deferred in prior years. Without this accounting change the earnings for fiscal year 1965 would have been reduced by $0.30 per share.

Our incoming orders for fiscal year 1965 increased approximately 40% and our backlog as of June 30 increased approximately 60% over the previous year, again with a much larger portion in rentals. This means that this improved performance for the past year would not have been reflected in the profit and loss statement without the recognition that certain current development, application and support costs apply to the Company's firm lease contracts and should therefore be charged against future rental income.

The effects of these changes in accounting policy on the financial statements was detailed in the notes to CDC's consolidated financial statements.

Changes in Accounting Practices

In order to more closely match costs against related revenues, the Company retroactively as of July 1, 1964 adopted a policy of deferring, for amortization over a three year period, allocated portions of certain product and software development costs, systems application costs and marketing expenses most directly related to the acquisition of lease orders. Comparable costs and expenses charged off as incurred in previous years which would have been unamortized under the new policy as of the beginning of the year were reinstated with a credit (net of deferred income taxes) to retained earnings. The change to this accepted alternative method of accounting had the effect, after appropriate charges for amortization of both the current and previous years' deferrals, of increasing net earnings for the year ended June 30, 1965 by approximately $2,180,000 ($0.30 per share). Had the prior year's figures been restated to give effect to this change, net earnings for the year ended June 30, 1964 would have been increased by approximately $1,050,000 ($0.15 per share).

As of January 1, 1965, the Company changed from an accelerated method of recording depreciation of computing systems and related equipment to the straight line method with no change in estimated lives of the assets. This change in method resulted in an increase of $1,210,000 in net earnings ($0.16 per share) for the year ended June 30, 1965. Had this change in depreciation method been made as of January 1, 1964, it would have resulted in an increase of approximately $980,000 in net earnings ($0.14 per share) for the year ended June 30, 1964.

In the case of both of the foregoing changes, the former methods of accounting or computation will continue to be used for income tax purposes. Accordingly, appropriate provisions have been made for related income tax deferments which will be charged with the increase in income taxes in future years when amounts charged against earnings in the accounts exceed amounts deductible for tax purposes.

CDC's consolidated balance sheets and statements of earnings are presented in Exhibits 2 and 3.

Required

1. What alternative accounting policies were available to CDC at the time that these changes were considered? Which alternative would you recommend?

2. Estimate the amount of depreciation expense CDC would have reported in 1965 had the company not changed accounting policies.

3. Evaluate management's decision to change accounting policies. Can you think of any reasons for the change besides those presented by management?

EXHIBIT 1
Control Data Corporation
Eight-Year Trend in Selected Financial Statistics, 1958-1965

	1958	1959	1960	1961	1962	1963	1964	1965
Net sales	$625,756	$4,588,174	$9,442,933	$18,062,074	$32,128,792	$44,861,576	$105,452,868	$127,820,209
Rentals and service income	—	—	222,357	1,721,671	8,905,217	18,249,825	25,618,729	32,652,953
Research and development expenditures	50,691	16,406	355,152	1,707,524	2,615,039	5,129,463	12,323,106	16,551,437
Expenditures for property, plant, and equipment	326,987	26,000	1,643,000	4,161,000	13,756,000	18,363,000	29,754,951	53,165,461
Depreciation of property, plant, and equipment	31,000	53,000	235,000	1,377,000	5,181,000	8,852,000	13,614,000	14,388,000
Amortization of patents and deferred lease costs*	—	—	—	—	—	13,000	177,000	3,264,000
Stockholders' equity	650,284	1,828,512	4,318,143	9,793,256	23,390,474	29,468,412	61,252,358	98,318,632

*Amortization of deferred lease costs included in 1965 statistics only.

EXHIBIT 2

CONTROL DATA CORPORATICN AND SUBSIDIARIES

CONSOLIDATED BALANCE SHEET

As of June 30, 1965 and 1964

ASSETS	1965	1964
Current assets:		
Cash	$ 5,999,200	$ 4,569,164
Marketable securities, at cost (approximately market value)	12,968,493	—
Receivables:		
Trade accounts	28,546,498	20,230,921
Unbilled receivables and accrued costs and estimated earnings on contracts in process (note 3)	18,892,707	27,953,820
Other	328,055	629,105
Total receivables	47,767,260	48,813,846
Inventories (note 4):		
Work in process	38,339,668	34,456,348
Raw materials and purchased parts	20,493,952	14,145,998
Total inventories	58,833,620	48,602,346
Prepaid expenses	927,769	941,070
Total current assets	126,496,342	102,926,426
Long-term contracts receivable	4,027,000	—
Investments in other companies, at cost	927,839	1,085,844
Property, plant and equipment, at cost less depreciation and amortization (note 2):		
Land	2,454,620	852,478
Buildings and improvements	6,271,928	6,798,998
Leased computing systems	65,042,674	32,626,135
Machinery and equipment	24,127,533	16,274,838
Construction in progress (approximate cost to complete $240,000)	2,067,638	648,097
	99,964,393	57,200,546
Less allowance for depreciation and amortization	33,420,106	24,094,753
Net property, plant and equipment	66,544,287	33,105,793
Deferred charges and other assets:		
Development, systems application and acquisition costs related to leases, less amortization (note 2)	8,444,131	—
Patents at purchase cost, less amortization	498,450	663,422
Recoverable foreign taxes and deposits	692,164	—
Prepaid rent, etc.	800,364	657,969
Total deferred charges and other assets	10,435,109	1,321,391
	$208,430,577	$138,439,454

See accompanying notes to consolidated financial statements.

EXHIBIT 2 *(Continued)*

LIABILITIES	1965	1964
Current liabilities:		
Notes payable to banks...	$ —	$ 4,415,281
Current maturities of long-term debt.................................	1,460,726	1,355,500
Customer advances..	2,630,217	6,245,801
Accounts payable...	9,283,606	8,743,971
Accrued taxes..	8,132,395	13,336,112
Other accrued liabilities...	6,979,470	4,355,620
Total current liabilities......................................	28,486,414	38,452,285
Long-term debt, less current maturities (note 5):		
Equipment purchase contract due in monthly installments to November 15, 1966...	639,996	2,210,736
5% sinking fund debentures, due May 1, 1985..........................	40,000,000	—
3¾% convertible subordinated debentures, due February 1, 1989..	35,000,000	35,000,000
Other mortgages and notes..	268,610	1,259,770
Total long-term debt.......................................	75,908,606	38,470,506
Reserve for product and service warranties...........................	112,526	172,172
Minority interest in foreign subsidiary...............................	92,203	92,133
Deferred income taxes (note 2)......................................	5,512,196	—
Stockholders' equity (notes 5, 6, 8, and 9):		
Cumulative preferred stock of $50 par value per share. Authorized 500,000 shares.		
Issued and outstanding—4% convertible preferred stock, 489,448 shares at June 30, 1965............................	24,472,400	—
Common stock of $0.50 par value per share. Authorized 15,000,000 shares.		
Issued and outstanding—7,384,689 shares at June 30, 1965 and 7,208,377 shares at June 30, 1964...........................	3,692,345	3,604,188
Additional paid-in capital..	49,821,106	46,608,080
Retained earnings (note 7)	21,664,969	12,372,278
	99,650,820	62,584,546
Deduct cost of 52,500 shares of Control Data Corporation common stock held by subsidiary....................................	1,332,188	1,332,188
Total stockholders' equity...................................	98,318,632	61,252,358
Contingent liabilities and commitments (note 10)		
	$208,430,577	$138,439,454

EXHIBIT 3

CONTROL DATA CORPORATION AND SUBSIDIARIES
CONSOLIDATED STATEMENT OF EARNINGS

Years ended June 30, 1965 and 1964	1965	1964
Net sales	$127,820,209	$105,452,868
Rentals and service income	32,652,953	25,618,729
	160,473,162	131,071,597
Cost of sales	73,493,195	60,600,862
Cost of rentals and service	21,416,092	18,255,758
	94,909,287	78,856,620
Gross profit	65,563,875	52,214,977
Selling, administrative and general expenses	32,070,568	23,148,789
Research and development expenses	13,915,618	12,323,106
	45,986,186	35,471,895
Operating profit	19,577,689	16,743,082
Other income	319,812	187,072
	19,897,501	16,930,154
Interest and other deductions	3,334,540	1,714,801
Earnings before income taxes	16,562,961	15,215,353
Federal, state and foreign income taxes, estimated	8,650,000	9,197,232
Net earnings (note 2)	$ 7,912,961	$ 6,018,121
Net earnings per share of common stock, after preferred stock dividends and proforma interest adjustment of $40,289 in 1964 (note 2)	$ 1.06	$ 0.84

Note: Depreciation and amortization of fixed assets and deferred charges included above in costs and expenses (note 2):

	1965	1964
Depreciation of property, plant and equipment	$14,387,829	$13,613,623
Amortization of patents and in 1965 deferred costs related to leases	3,264,233	177,055
	$17,652,062	$13,790,678

ACCOUNTANTS' REPORT
The Board of Directors, Control Data Corporation:

We have examined the consolidated balance sheet of Control Data Corporation and subsidiaries as of June 30, 1965 and the related consolidated statements of earnings, retained earnings and additional paid-in capital for the year then ended. Our examination was made in accordance with generally accepted auditing standards, and accordingly included such tests of the accounting records and such other auditing procedures as we considered necessary in the circumstances. It was not practicable to confirm accounts receivable from Government departments and agencies by direct communication with them but we satisfied ourselves as to such accounts by means of other auditing procedures.

As explained in note 2 to the consolidated financial statements, certain development and application costs and marketing expenses, heretofore charged off as incurred, have been deferred and are being amortized over a period of three years. Also, as of January 1, 1965, the Company changed from an accelerated method of recording depreciation of computing systems and related equipment to the straight-line method with no change in estimated lives. The effect of these changes was to increase net earnings for the year ended June 30, 1965 by approximately $3,390,000.

In our opinion, such financial statements present fairly the consolidated financial position of Control Data Corporation and subsidiaries at June 30, 1965 and the results of their operations for the year then ended, in conformity with generally accepted accounting principles which, except for the changes which significantly increased net earnings as described in the preceding paragraph, have been applied on a basis consistent with that of the preceding year.

Minneapolis, Minnesota
August 16, 1965

PEAT, MARWICK, MITCHELL & CO.

Case 3–5

COMSERV Corporation

Headquartered in Eagen, Minnesota, COMSERV is a leading independent supplier of computer software products for the manufacturing industry. COMSERV designs, constructs, markets, and supports a family of advanced manufacturing, accounting, and production software systems—the AMAPS products. As of the beginning of 1983, approximately 300 manufacturing facilities worldwide (including Bausch & Lomb, Gillette, Parke-Davis, Parker Brothers, and Warner-Lambert) used AMAPS software to plan, schedule, monitor, and control the intricate network inherent in day-to-day operations. The company also designs, constructs, and markets educational products (primarily software) useful to customers for training employees to use the AMAPS system.

A. Computer Software Construction Costs

COMSERV capitalizes the costs related to the enhancement, improvement, and adaptations of its existing computer software products and amortizes these costs primarily over four to six years. Most computer companies expense all costs related to research and development including computer software construction costs, yet COMSERV "management believes that its treatment of software construction costs is well supported by generally accepted accounting principles, and views the AMAPS products as major corporate assets with proven future value" (*COMSERV Corporation 1982 Annual Report*, p. 24). The note below is included among the summary of the company's accounting policies:

Computer Software and Educational Courseware Construction Costs

The Company owns various proprietary computer software products that it licenses to customers and operates in its computer services facility. Certain costs related to the enhancement, improvement, and adaptation to particular requirements of the Company's existing proprietary software are capitalized and are being amortized primarily on a straight-line basis over the estimated period of benefit, which is generally six years for software designed to operate on IBM-compatible mainframe computer equipment, and four years for all other software. The costs of purchased software are capitalized and amortized on the same basis. The costs incurred in the search for or evaluation of product or process alternatives or in the design of pre-production models or in conceptual formulation or translation of knowledge into designs for new or significantly improved software products are charged to research and development expense as incurred. Costs related to software deemed to have an impaired future value are written off immediately or amortized over the remaining estimated period of benefit once this becomes apparent. Net software construction costs amounted to $9,634,616 and $5,060,840 at December 31, 1982, and 1981, respectively.

This case was prepared from published financial statements of COMSERV Corporation.

The Company designs and constructs educational courseware that aids customers in effectively utilizing the Company's software products. These courseware constructions costs are capitalized and are being amortized over the estimated period of benefit, which is four years. Net educational courseware construction costs amounted to $1,711,488 and $536,380 at December 31, 1982, and 1981, respectively.

Included in Exhibits 1 and 2, respectively, are COMSERV's Consolidated Balance Sheets and Statements of Operations (income statements).

Required

1. No computer software or educational courseware assets were sold or retired in 1982. Prepare journal entries to record: (a) amortization of computer software and educational courseware construction costs during 1982; and (b) additions to computer software and educational courseware construction costs during 1982.
2. Estimate the effect on the 1982 balance sheet and income statement if COMSERV had expensed (instead of capitalizing) its computer software and educational courseware construction costs.
3. Which approach (expense or capitalize) do you favor for computer software and educational courseware construction costs? Prepare specific arguments to support your position.

B. Property and Equipment

Also included in the summary of significant accounting policies is a description of COMSERV's accounting for property and equipment:

Property and Equipment

Property and equipment are carried at cost. Certain items of equipment acquired under capital lease agreements, which are essentially financing arrangements, have been capitalized and are reflected in the accompanying consolidated balance sheets as assets under property and equipment and as related obligations under long-term debt.

Depreciation of computer equipment, and furniture, fixtures, and equipment, including assets under capital leases, is computed on the straight-line method based on estimated useful lives of five or eight years. Prior to 1981 all property and equipment was being depreciated over eight years. After 1980, computer equipment has been depreciated over five years to more accurately reflect its economic life. The effect of this change is not material to the financial statements. Leasehold improvements are amortized over the useful lives of the assets or the terms of the leases, whichever is less.

In February 1982, COMSERV acquired 81 acres of land for $2,030,000, upon which it is building its new corporate headquarters. The total cost was estimated to be approximately $14,000,000. The company expected to move to the new facility in April 1983.

Additions to property and equipment, including construction in progress, totaled $15,894,406. Property and equipment sold or retired in 1982 had a net book value of $50,130.

Required

1. Prepare journal entries to record property and equipment acquired and retired in 1982. Assume retired equipment was sold for $10,000. Ignore taxes.
2. Prepare a journal entry to record depreciation and amortization of property and equipment in 1982. Where does depreciation and amortization of property and equipment likely appear in the 1982 income statement?
3. Discuss the depreciation policies COMSERV uses for financial reporting.

C. Capitalization of Interest Costs

Starting with Statement No. 34 (October 1979), the Financial Accounting Standards Board began requiring capitalization of interest costs associated with expenditures for the acquisition or construction of certain assets. To qualify for interest capitalization, the underlying asset must require a period of time before it is ready for its intended use. Interest cannot be capitalized on inventories that are routinely produced. COMSERV's summary of significant accounting policies includes a description of capitalized interest related to construction of its new headquarters building:

Capitalization of Interest Costs

In 1982, the Company applied Statement of Financial Accounting Standards No. 34, Capitalization of Interest Costs, to its accounting for construction in progress on its new headquarters building. This statement requires that interest costs related to certain long-term construction projects be capitalized rather than charged directly to expense. Accordingly, of total interest costs of $1,478,842 incurred in 1982, $470,323 was capitalized. There were not significant construction projects that would have required interest to be capitalized in 1981 or 1980.

Required

1. Prepare the journal entry to record interest expensed and capitalized in 1982.
2. Prior to 1979, it was common practice for firms to expense all interest costs. What would have been "income before income taxes" if all interest was expensed?
3. Discuss the pros and cons of the Financial Accounting Standards Board's decision to require capitalization of interest costs on projects under construction.

EXHIBIT 1

COMSERV CORPORATION AND SUBSIDIARIES

CONSOLIDATED BALANCE SHEETS

ASSETS December 31	1982	1981
Current assets:		
Cash, including time deposits	$ 7,578,434	$ 6,836,350
Short-term investments, at cost (approximates market)	—	308,000
Trade accounts receivable, less allowance for doubtful accounts of $453,000 and $320,000, respectively	7,098,252	4,142,179
Unbilled accounts receivable (Note 3)	3,925,395	2,482,581
Interest receivable	294,576	464,464
Prepaid expenses and other current assets	729,275	520,484
Total current assets	19,625,932	14,754,058
Computer software and educational courseware construction costs (Note 1)	15,282,654	7,790,838
Less accumulated amortization	3,936,550	2,193,618
	11,346,104	5,597,220
Property and equipment, at cost (Note 1):		
Computer equipment	8,243,492	4,409,037
Office furniture, fixtures, and equipment	2,231,144	1,408,703
Leasehold improvements	697,809	614,031
	11,172,445	6,431,771
Less accumulated depreciation and amortization	2,726,274	1,356,744
	8,446,171	5,075,027
Construction in progress (Note 4)	11,112,064	72,496
	19,558,235	5,147,523
Other long-term assets (Note 5)	2,772,500	371,264
	$53,302,771	$25,870,065

See accompanying notes to consolidated financial statements.

EXHIBIT 1 *(Continued)*

COMSERV CORPORATION AND SUBSIDIARIES

CONSOLIDATED BALANCE SHEETS

LIABILITIES AND COMMON STOCKHOLDERS' EQUITY — December 31	1982	1981
Current liabilities:		
Current portion of long-term debt	$ 456,988	$ 339,527
Accounts payable	3,373,016	1,879,591
Income taxes payable	12,000	81,000
Accrued liabilities (Note 6)	2,026,310	1,805,355
Deferred revenue, principally advance payments	3,143,218	1,300,731
Total current liabilities	9,011,532	5,406,204
Deferred income taxes	3,526,000	2,444,800
Long-term debt (Note 8)	21,439,687	1,298,290
Common stockholders' equity (Notes 8, 9, and 10):		
Common stock, $.10 par value. Authorized 10,000,000 shares; issued 3,264,349 shares and 3,240,233 shares at December 31, 1982 and December 31, 1981	326,435	324,023
Additional paid-in capital	12,888,595	13,029,788
Retained earnings	6,438,391	3,886,284
	19,653,421	17,240,095
Less: Unearned compensation	317,442	508,897
Cost of 15,000 common shares held in treasury	10,427	10,427
Total common stockholders' equity	19,325,552	16,720,771
Commitments (Note 11)		
	$53,302,771	$25,870,065

See accompanying notes to consolidated financial statements.

EXHIBIT 2

COMSERV CORPORATION AND SUBSIDIARIES
CONSOLIDATED STATEMENTS OF OPERATIONS

Year ended December 31	1982	1981	1980
Revenues	$25,075,499	$17,667,477	$10,703,503
Costs and expenses:			
Operating costs	7,011,258	5,727,232	3,526,699
Selling expenses	8,102,694	5,635,140	3,623,340
General and administrative expenses	4,423,141	2,698,992	1,257,151
Amortization of computer software and educational courseware construction costs	1,742,932	719,882	469,593
Provision for doubtful accounts	291,000	185,000	165,451
Total costs and expenses	21,571,025	14,966,246	9,042,234
Operating income	3,504,474	2,701,231	1,661,269
Other income (expense):			
Interest income	1,219,127	1,052,093	72,870
Interest expense (Note 1)	(1,008,519)	(125,170)	(172,008)
Miscellaneous	(68,975)	—	(121,000)
Total other income (expense), net	141,633	926,923	(220,138)
Income before income taxes	3,646,107	3,628,154	1,441,131
Income taxes (Note 2)	1,094,000	1,415,000	538,000
Net income	$ 2,552,107	$ 2,213,154	$ 903,131
Earnings per common share and common stock equivalent (Note 1)	$ .76	$ .71	$ .45
Weighted average number of common shares and common stock equivalents outstanding	3,346,457	3,117,237	1,988,772
Earnings per common share assuming full dilution (Note 1)	$ .76	$ .71	$ .42
Weighted average number of common shares and common stock equivalents outstanding assuming full dilution	4,024,481	3,126,025	2,178,638

See accompanying notes to consolidated financial statements.

LONG-TERM BONDS

Case 4–1

Dyco Petroleum Corporation

Dyco Petroleum was incorporated in Minnesota in June of 1971. The company engages in oil and gas exploration and production.

A. May 1983 Debt Issue

The announcement in Exhibit 1 appeared in *The Wall Street Journal* in early May 1983. The "tombstone" announced a $50,000,000 debt issue maturing on May 1, 1988. The purpose of this issue was to repay existing bank loans. Dyco Petroleum has a December 31 fiscal year.

Required

1. What is meant by "Price 99⅛% plus accrued interest from May 1, 1983"?
2. Given the information in the announcement, what amount of proceeds did Dyco receive from this debt issue?
3. What effective interest rate is implicit in the stated price of these notes?

4. Ignore the issue price stated in the tombstone and assume that these notes were issued at par. Prepare journal entries to record: (a) the issuance of these notes on May 1, 1983; (b) the November 1 coupon payment; and (c) the year-end accrual of interest.

5. Assume that the notes were issued at a price that reflected an effective annual interest rate of 12%. Prepare journal entries to record: (a) the issuance of these notes on May 1, 1983; (b) the November 1 coupon payment; and (c) the year-end accrual of interest.

6. Assume that the notes were priced to reflect an effective interest rate of 14%. What journal entries would have been necessary to record: (a) the May 1 debt issue; (b) the November 1 coupon payment; and (c) the year-end interest accrual?

B. Restrictive Covenants

According to *Moody's Industrial Manual*,* as of December 31, 1982, long-term debt outstanding of $85,289,200 consisted of:

1. $80,000,000 87% of the prevailing prime rate unsecured revolving loan; beginning December 31, 1983, monthly payments aggregating $12,000,000 annually for 5 years are required.
2. $3,114,200 11½ % convertible subordinated debentures. Convertible into common at $29 per share.
3. $2,175,000 secured loan-noncurrent portion.

Agreement contains various restrictive covenants which are subject to waiver by the lenders. The more significant restrictions are (1) working capital must be maintained such that current assets exceed current liabilities after adjustment for short-term borrowings and the current portion of nonproducing oil and gas leases; (2) a tangible net worth of not less than $38,000,000 must be maintained; (3) cash dividends are restricted to 15% of Co.'s net earnings for the preceding 12 months; and (4) should Co. fail in any year to raise at least $45,000,000 of funds from participants in its oil and gas programs, Co. will grant to the banks a security interest in its producing oil and gas properties.

The subordinated debentures are convertible at any time prior to maturity into shares of common stock at a conversion price of $29 per share. The debentures are redeemable at the option of Co.

Required

1. Note that the first three restrictions listed above are based on financial accounting numbers. What actions might management take to avoid technical default should the company approach violation of a loan covenant?

Moody's Industrial Manual, 1983, Vol. 1 (A-I); Moody's Investors Service, Inc., New York, NY, p. 2783.

Moody's Manuals provide financial data on selected corporations, including those who have debt or equity issues traded on major U.S. stock exchanges.

2. Why are restrictions (such as those in effect on 12/31/82) written into lending agreements? What benefits, if any, do stockholders receive from such restrictive covenants?

3. The accounting methods used in lending agreements are typically restricted to generally accepted accounting principles. How might this fact affect accounting standard setters at the Financial Accounting Standards Board?

EXHIBIT 1

This announcement is neither an offer to sell nor a solicitation of an offer to buy these securities.
The offer is made only by the Prospectus.

$50,000,000

Dyco Petroleum Corporation

13% Senior Subordinated Notes due 1988

(Interest payable May 1 and November 1)

Price 99⅛%

plus accrued interest from May 1, 1983

Copies of the Prospectus are obtainable in any State from only such of the undersigned and such other dealers as may lawfully offer these securities in such State.

Drexel Burnham Lambert
INCORPORATED

Dain Bosworth
INCORPORATED

Blyth Eastman Paine Webber
INCORPORATED

The First Boston Corporation

Dillon, Read & Co. Inc.

E. F. Hutton & Company Inc.

Kidder, Peabody & Co.
INCORPORATED

Lazard Frères & Co.

Prudential-Bache
SECURITIES

L. F. Rothschild, Unterberg, Towbin

Salomon Brothers Inc

Shearson/American Express Inc.

Smith Barney, Harris Upham & Co.
INCORPORATED

Dean Witter Reynolds Inc.

Piper, Jaffray & Hopwood
INCORPORATED

Bateman Eichler, Hill Richards
INCORPORATED

Boettcher & Company

Montgomery Securities

Sutro & Co.
INCORPORATED

Charter Investment Group, Inc.

Seidler Amdec Securities Inc.

May 6, 1983

Case 4–2

Federated Department Stores, Inc.

Federated is one of the largest mercantile organizations in the United States. Its principal divisions include department stores (e.g., Bloomingdale's, Bullock's, Filene's, I. Magnin, and Sanger Harris) as well as discount, grocery, and specialty stores.

A. Accounting for Bond Discounts

The announcement in Exhibit 1 appeared in the financial press in May 1983. The bonds were callable for 110.38% of their face value. Federated has a January 31 fiscal year end.

Required

1. Assume that these bonds were issued on May 1, 1983, and mature on May 1, 2013. Coupon payments are made semi-annually on November 1 and May 1. Prepare a journal entry to record the bond issue.
2. Prepare a journal entry to record the November 1, 1983, coupon payment using "straight-line" amortization of the bond discount.
3. The effective annual interest rate on this bond issue was approximately 10.653%. Record the November 1 coupon payment using the "effective interest" method to amortize the bond discount. Note: do not round off the interest rate.
4. Holding other factors constant, what effect does a call privilege have on the issue price of the bonds?

B. Bond Ratings

In 1909, John Moody originated a system of gradations (or ratings) whose purpose is to inform investors of the relative investment qualities of bonds. Exhibit 2 provides a description of these ratings. *Moody's Bond Record** presented the following average yields for industrial bonds in May 1983:

Aaa	Aa	A	Baa
10.91%	11.46%	11.86%	12.12%

**Moody's Bond Record*, June 1983, Vol. 50, No. 6, Moody's Investors Service, Inc., New York, NY, p. 2.

Required

1. Estimate the May 1983 Moody's bond rating for:
   a. Federated's sinking fund debentures described in Exhibit 1.
   b. Dyco's senior subordinated notes described in Case 4-1, Exhibit 1.
2. What form of risk do bond ratings purport to measure? Speculate as to why the ratings for Dyco's and Federated's debt issues differ.

EXHIBIT 1

$100,000,000

Federated Department Stores, Inc.

10⅝% Sinking Fund Debentures Due 2013

Price 99.75%

(Plus accrued interest from May 1, 1983)

Copies of the Prospectus and the related Prospectus Supplement may be obtained in any State only from such of the several Underwriters, including the undersigned, as may lawfully offer the securities in such State.

Lehman Brothers Kuhn Loeb
Incorporated

The First Boston Corporation

Merrill Lynch White Weld Capital Markets Group
Merrill Lynch, Pierce, Fenner & Smith Incorporated

Morgan Stanley & Co.
Incorporated

Salomon Brothers Inc

May 6, 1983

EXHIBIT 2
Key to Moody's Corporate Ratings

Aaa

Bonds which are rated *Aaa* are judged to be of the best quality. They carry the smallest degree of investment risk and are generally referred to as "gilt edge." Interest payments are protected by a large or by an exceptionally stable margin and principal is secure. While the various protective elements are likely to change, such changes as can be visualized are most unlikely to impair the fundamentally strong position of such issues.

Aa

Bonds which are rated *Aa* are judged to be of high quality by all standards. Together with the *Aaa* group they comprise what are generally known as high grade bonds. They are rated lower than the best bonds because margins of protection may not be as large as in *Aaa* securities or fluctuation of protective elements may be of greater amplitude or there may be other elements present which make the long term risks appear somewhat larger than in *Aaa* securities.

A

Bonds which are rated *A* possess many favorable investment attributes and are to be considered as upper medium grade obligations. Factors giving security to principal and interest are considered adequate but elements may be present which suggest a susceptibility to impairment sometime in the future.

Baa

Bonds which are rated *Baa* are considered as medium grade obligations, i.e., they are neither highly protected nor poorly secured. Interest payments and principal security appear adequate for the present but certain protective elements may be lacking or may be characteristically unreliable over any great length of time. Such bonds lack outstanding investment characteristics and in fact have speculative characteristics as well.

Ba

Bonds which are rated *Ba* are judged to have speculative elements; their future cannot be considered as well assured. Often the protection of interest and principal payments may be very moderate and thereby not well safeguarded during both good and bad times over the future. Uncertainty of position characterizes bonds in this class.

B

Bonds which are rated *B* generally lack characteristics of the desirable investment. Assurance of interest and principal payments or of maintenance of other terms of the contract over any long period of time may be small.

Caa

Bonds which are rated *Caa* are of poor standing. Such issues may be in default or there may be present elements of danger with respect to principal or interest.

Ca

Bonds which are rated *Ca* represent obligations which are speculative in a high degree. Such issues are often in default or have other marked shortcomings.

C

Bonds which are rated *C* are the lowest rated class of bonds and issues so rated can be regarded as having extremely poor prospects of ever attaining any real investment standing.

Note: Moody's applies numerical modifiers, *1, 2,* and *3* in each generic rating classification from *Aa* through *B* in its corporate bond rating system. The modifier 1 indicates that the security ranks in the higher end of its generic rating category; the modifier 2 indicates a mid-range ranking; and the modifier 3 indicates that the issue ranks in the lower end of its generic rating category.

Source: Moody's Bond Record, June 1983, Vol. 50, No. 6. Moody's Investors Service, Inc., New York, NY, p. 1.

Case 4–3

J. C. Penney Company

Exhibit 1 is an announcement (sometimes called a tombstone) that appeared in major business journals in late April 1981. It announced two long-term instruments: zero coupon notes due in 1989 and 6% coupon bonds due in 2006. While issuing deep discount bonds was consistent with a recent trend, the zero coupon note received considerable attention. It is not difficult to understand why any borrower would like to avoid paying interest, but who would want to purchase such a bond?

Required

1. "A bond with no interest sounds like a car with no motor" (*Forbes*, May 25, 1981). Why would J. C. Penney be interested in issuing zero (or 6%) coupon notes when the prevailing interest rates were 12% or higher?

2. What type of lender would want to purchase zero coupon notes?

3. What is the effective yield to maturity of the zero (6%) coupon bonds? Assume that the bonds mature in April 1989 (2006) and that interest is compounded semiannually. Do you think this rate should be above or below prevailing market rates for a coupon bond issued at par?

4. Prepare a journal entry to record the sale of these bonds on April 30, 1981. What entries will J. C. Penney have to make during 1981 to record interest and accruals?

5. What type of company would most likely benefit from issuing deep discount or zero coupon bonds?

EXHIBIT 1

This advertisement is neither an offer to sell nor a solicitation of offers to buy any of these securities. The offering is made only by the Prospectus.

April, 1981

$400,000,000

J.C. Penney Company, Inc.

$200,000,000

Zero Coupon Notes Due 1989

Price 33.247%

plus accrued amortization of original issue discount from May 1, 1981

$200,000,000

6% Debentures Due 2006

Price 42.063%

plus accrued interest from May 1, 1981

Copies of each Prospectus may be obtained from any of the several underwriters, including the undersigned, only in States in which such underwriters are qualified to act as dealers in securities and in which the Prospectus may legally be distributed.

The First Boston Corporation

Goldman, Sachs & Co.		Merrill Lynch White Weld Capital Markets Group
		Merrill Lynch, Pierce, Fenner & Smith Incorporated
Bache Halsey Stuart Shields	Bear, Stearns & Co.	Blyth Eastman Paine Webber
Incorporated		Incorporated
Dillon, Read & Co. Inc.	Donaldson, Lufkin & Jenrette	Drexel Burnham Lambert
	Securities Corporation	Incorporated
E. F. Hutton & Company Inc.	Kidder, Peabody & Co.	Lazard Frères & Co.
	Incorporated	
Lehman Brothers Kuhn Loeb		L. F. Rothschild, Unterberg, Towbin
Incorporated		
Shearson Loeb Rhoades Inc.		Smith Barney, Harris Upham & Co.
		Incorporated
Warburg Paribas Becker	Wertheim & Co., Inc.	Dean Witter Reynolds Inc.
A. G. Becker		

Case 4-4

Sunshine Mining Company

Sunshine Mining Company ("Sunshine") is the largest primary producer of silver in the United States. Copper, antimony, and small amounts of gold are also extracted from their mines in the Coeur d'Alene mining district in Northern Idaho. In 1982, a new mine in the Silver Peak, Nevada, area was brought into production, and development of a mine in the East Tintict District of Utah continues, with production expected to begin late in 1984.

Sunshine is a vertically integrated firm exclusively engaged in the mining, refining, and marketing of precious metals. In the past, most of Sunshine's output was in the form of metal-bearing ore concentrates that were shipped to other firms for refining and final sale. However, Sunshine's current strategy is to gear up their refining and marketing operations so they can refine all they mine and sell all they refine.

Sunshine Bullion Company has been formed to produce and market silver bullion in the form of one-ounce, ten-ounce, and one-hundred-ounce SUNSHINES®. Although most SUNSHINES® sales have been on a wholesale basis to coin dealers, banks, and brokerage firms, the company hopes to begin to tap what they perceive to be "a substantially untapped enormous market" for individual investor silver bullion. They recently introduced their first limited edition proof set.

Sunshine is a single product company, and it has no control over the price of that single product. The cost of producing silver is relatively fixed, and these costs are not easily adjusted to meet market conditions. In June of 1982, the price of silver dropped to a low of $4.98, which was well below the firm's cost of production. It was therefore decided to close the mine, pending improvement in the silver market. A number of employees were laid off, and the only activity at the mine consisted of maintenance and development to prepare for an expected improvement in the silver market late in 1982 or early in 1983. The mine was reopened on December 6, 1982, and was back in full production by the first quarter of 1983.

Despite the poor results in 1982, when a loss of $22.5 million was reported, the firm's management remains committed to their chosen course of specialization. Management believes that SUNSHINES® will become the recognized, established norm for millions of Americans to invest in silver bullion and that the price of silver will level out at a price well above their cost of production, resulting in a vast improvement in the profitability of the firm.

A. Bond Issue

On February 15, 1983, Sunshine sold $30,000,000 of 8% silver indexed bonds due February 15, 1995. Each $1,000 face value bond is payable at maturity or redemption at the greater of $1,000 or an amount equal to the market price of 50 ounces

---

This case was prepared from published financial statements of Sunshine Mining Company.

of silver ("indexed principal amount"). If the indexed principal amount is greater than $1,000, the company, at its option, may deliver silver bullion to bondholders electing to accept silver in satisfaction of the indexed principal amount. Note that bondholders always have the option of receiving cash.

Assume the following:

a. Bond issuance costs were approximately 2.5% of the face value of the issue.

b. Bonds were sold at par.

c. Coupon interest is paid semi-annually on August 15 and February 15.

d. The company has a December 31 fiscal year end.

Required

1. What entries would be used to record events related to these bonds in 1983?

2. If the market discount rate for this type of investment was 9% at the time of issue, what entries would have been made in 1983? (Use the effective interest amortization method.)

3. Assume that on February 15, 1995, the specified market price of silver was $21.75 per ounce. Also assume that 30% of the bondholders elected to take the indexed principal amount in silver bullion instead of the cash equivalent.

    a. Prepare the journal entry to record the extinguishment of the debt, assuming the bonds were issued at par and no bonds were redeemed by Sunshine prior to maturity.

    b. How can you determine the actual yield received by those holding the bond to maturity? (Set up appropriate equations using all information available. You do not have to solve for the specific yield.)

B. Operating Leverage

Financial leverage involves the use of fixed cost debt financing as a substitute for owner financing. Another form of leverage, operating leverage, occurs whenever a company has fixed production costs which are relatively insensitive to volume of output. To some degree, management can influence the level of operating leverage by trading off fixed and variable costs of production.

The Chairman's letter in the 1982 Annual Report contained the following statement:

> The profitability of your company, being a direct function of silver prices, is also highly leveraged. . . . If silver prices move from $15/oz. to $20/oz., the price of silver has increased 33%, but because our cost of production is relatively fixed, the entire additional revenue goes to profits and the profitability of Sunshine Mining will increase by almost 100%.

Required

1. Assume Sunshine would have sold all of its 1982 production (2,228,500 ounces) at either price mentioned by the chairman. Estimate the fixed cost of silver production implicit in his statement.

2. If silver prices move from $10.80 to $48.70 per ounce (the low and high prices of silver in 1980), estimate the percentage increase in the profitability of Sunshine.

3. The price of silver can also go down. If the price moves from $11.21 to $4.98, as happened in the first six months of 1982, estimate the percentage decrease in the profitability of Sunshine.

4. What can management do to protect Sunshine from the effects of downward movements in the price of silver?

Case 4–5

Masco Corporation

Masco Corporation is a diversified manufacturing company with over 70 manufacturing facilities located in 11 countries. The company's product line includes faucets, plumbing fittings, builders' hardware, and other home improvement products, as well as energy-related and other industrial and specialty products. Based on 1981 results, Masco ranked among the 500 largest U.S. industrial corporations.

Masco's stated corporate objective is "consistent and predictable growth." The company seeks to develop "proprietary" products in "selected market segments" to achieve and maintain positions of leadership. Financially, Masco's goal is to "increase earnings per share, on average, 15–20 percent or more annually through internal growth and selected acquisitions."

In 1982, Masco reported its twenty-sixth consecutive year of increased earnings. Richard A. Manoogian, company president, discussed the company's success in a letter to shareholders:

> To have reported increased earnings in 1982 during a period when every one of our major markets was experiencing a recession was also a positive achievement. Net income in 1982 was $92.2 million or $1.78 per share, representing increases from the previous year of 4 percent and 3 percent, respectively. In all candor, however, our results for the year prompted mixed emotions. Sales declined 2 percent to $855.7 million and operating profits declined approximately 10 percent.
>
> Net income for the year increased, even though operating profits declined, with the benefit of $.28 per share extraordinary income from the retirement of debentures. High interest rates during the year provided us with an opportunity to retire approximately $61 million of our outstanding debentures at a substantial discount from their face value. Most of these debentures were acquired by Masco in exchanges for common stock, resulting in tax-free profits to the Company. The net effect was a substantial reduction in our outstanding debt with a corresponding increase in shareholders' equity. This strengthening of our balance sheet enabled us to maintain a strong financial position later in the year when the opportunity arose to acquire several outstanding companies.

The notes to Masco's 1982 financial statements contained the following description of the debenture retirements:

Extraordinary Income

During 1982, the Company issued 2.1 million shares of common stock to retire $48.0 million of the 8⅞ percent debentures due 2001 in nontaxable transactions, and an additional $12.8 million of these debentures were retired

---

This case was prepared from published financial statements of Masco Corporation.

for cash of $9.7 million in taxable transactions. These retirements of debentures resulted in extraordinary income of $14.5 million, net of taxes of $1.3 million.

The notes also contained the following information concerning long-term debt:

Long-Term Debt

	(In Thousands) At December 31	
	1982	1981
Notes, 12¼%, due 1985	$100,000	$100,000
Notes payable to banks under revolving-credit agreements	200,000	75,000
Debentures, 8⅞%, due 2001	14,170	75,000
Convertible subordinated Debentures, 4½%, due 1988	—	16,306
Other	58,367	41,294
	$372,537	$307,600

The 12¼ percent notes due 1985 may be redeemed at 100 percent on or after May 1, 1983, at the Company's option.

The bank agreements run to December 31, 1985, at which time they may be converted to term loans payable in eight equal semi-annual installments beginning May, 1986; interest is payable at floating rates based on Company options which include prime and rates based on the London Inter-bank Offered Rate and certificates of deposit rate. During 1982, the Company entered into additional revolving-credit and term-loan agreements of $100 million with a group of banks, of which $25 million had been borrowed at December 31, 1982; the terms of these agreements are identical to those discussed above.

In December, 1982, the Company redeemed its outstanding 4½ percent Convertible Subordinated Debentures due 1988.

Certain borrowing agreements contain limitations on additional borrowings and restrictions on cash dividend payments; at December 31, 1982, the amount of retained earnings not restricted for cash dividends approximated $123 million under these provisions.

Masco's 1981 and 1982 consolidated balance sheets and statements of income for 1980–1982 are presented in Exhibits 1 and 2.

Required

1. Record the retirement of the 8⅞% debentures in a journal entry.
2. What interest rate is implicit in the price Masco paid to retire these debentures?

3. Why has Masco reported the gain from retirement of debentures as extraordinary income? Do you agree with this classification? Why or why not?

4. Evaluate Masco's decision to retire the 8⅞% debentures before the 2001 maturity date. What are the costs and benefits of this decision?

EXHIBIT 1

MASCO CORPORATION and Consolidated Subsidiaries

CONSOLIDATED BALANCE SHEET
December 31, 1982 and 1981

ASSETS	1982	1981
Current Assets:		
Cash and marketable securities	$ 203,347,000	$137,545,000
Receivables	163,379,000	143,408,000
Inventories	243,623,000	214,529,000
Prepaid expenses	11,414,000	10,633,000
Total current assets	621,763,000	506,115,000
Investments in Partially Owned Companies	41,602,000	41,531,000
Receivables and Investments, Related-Party	36,883,000	9,509,000
Other Assets	171,433,000	105,176,000
Property and Equipment	350,478,000	277,682,000
	$1,222,159,000	$940,013,000

LIABILITIES and SHAREHOLDERS' EQUITY

	1982	1981
Current Liabilities:		
Notes payable	$ 123,894,000	$ 23,175,000
Accounts payable	34,170,000	31,761,000
Income taxes	28,607,000	26,193,000
Accrued liabilities	48,539,000	43,548,000
Total current liabilities	235,210,000	124,677,000
Long-Term Debt	372,537,000	307,600,000
Deferred Income Taxes	25,020,000	15,476,000
Shareholders' Equity	589,392,000	492,260,000
	$1,222,159,000	$940,013,000

EXHIBIT 2

MASCO CORPORATION and Consolidated Subsidiaries

CONSOLIDATED STATEMENT OF INCOME
for the years ended December 31, 1982, 1981 and 1980

	1982	1981	1980
Net sales	$855,740,000	$876,530,000	$766,440,000
Cost of sales	557,110,000	571,400,000	496,913,000
Gross profit	298,630,000	305,130,000	269,527,000
Selling, general and administrative expenses	150,440,000	139,910,000	116,505,000
Operating profit	148,190,000	165,220,000	153,022,000
Other expense (income), net:			
Interest expense	40,210,000	39,874,000	38,743,000
Other income, net	(27,070,000)	(25,394,000)	(22,611,000)
	13,140,000	14,480,000	16,132,000
Income before income taxes and extraordinary income	135,050,000	150,740,000	136,890,000
Income taxes	57,410,000	62,420,000	59,710,000
Income before extraordinary income ($1.50 per share in 1982)	77,640,000	88,320,000	77,180,000
Extraordinary income from retirement of debentures	14,510,000	–	–
Net income	$ 92,150,000	$ 88,320,000	$ 77,180,000
Earnings per share	$1.78	$1.73	$1.51

5

LEASES, PENSIONS, AND INCOME TAXES

Case 5–1

Pay 'n Save Corporation

Pay 'n Save Corporation was founded in 1947 as a single drugstore in Seattle, Washington. By the end of 1981, the company operated 233 stores in 10 western states. The company's retail operations are organized into three divisions: drugs, home center, and apparel.

Pay 'n Save's 1980 and 1981 consolidated balance sheets and consolidated statements of income and retained earnings appear in Exhibits 1 and 2. In addition, the following information concerning Pay 'n Save's leased property was obtained from the notes to the financial statements:

Leased Property

The company leases a majority of its stores, as well as transportation and data processing equipment. Generally, the store leases provide for minimum rentals (which, in some cases, include payment of taxes and insurance), plus con-

---

This case was prepared from published financial statements of Pay 'n Save Corporation.

tingent rentals (based upon a percentage of the stores' sales in excess of a stipulated minimum). The majority of lease agreements cover periods from 20 to 30 years, with three to five renewal options of five years each. However, the company has a number of leases covering shorter periods, with fewer renewal options.

Contingent rentals including taxes and insurance paid on capital leases were $2,769,000 in 1981, $2,794,000 in 1980 and $2,575,000 in 1979. Sublease rental income received from buildings under capital leases was $846,000 in 1981, $782,000 in 1980 and $776,000 in 1979.

Future minimum rental payments under capital leases together with present value of net minimum lease payments are as follows:

For the Fiscal Years	Amount (Thousands of Dollars)
1982	$ 12,945
1983	12,967
1984	12,988
1985	12,942
1986	12,726
Thereafter	206,428
Total minimum rental payments	$270,996
Less: Estimated executory costs (primarily taxes and insurance)	(5,242)
Less: Amount representing interest	(163,139)
Present value of obligations under capital leases at January 31, 1981	102,615
Less: Current portion	(1,836)
Long-term obligations under capital leases	$100,779
Future sublease rentals	$ 1,992

Future minimum rental payments under operating leases are as follows:

For the Fiscal Years	Amount (Thousands of Dollars)
1982	$ 8,604
1983	8,190
1984	8,063
1985	7,784
1986	7,492
Thereafter	111,703
Total minimum rental payments	$151,836
Future sublease rentals	$ 663

Rental expenses under operating leases is as follows:

For the Fiscal Years	1981	1980	1979
		(Thousands of Dollars)	
Minimum rentals	$ 8,709	$6,861	$5,954
Contingent rentals	1,668	1,707	1,303
Sublease rentals	(353)	(301)	(249)
	$10,024	$8,267	$7,008

Required

A. **Leases**

1. During the fiscal year ended January 31, 1981, Pay 'n Save entered into several lease agreements that were classified as capital leases in the financial statements. The present value of future minimum lease payments under these new leases totaled $24,360,000. Prepare a summary journal entry to record these lease agreements.

2. Pay 'n Save reported that interest expenses amounting to $9,989,000 in 1981 resulted from the capitalization of leases. Prepare a journal entry to record lease payments on capital leases for 1981.

3. What entries were necessary to record amortization of leased property and the expiration of capital lease agreements in 1981.

4. Prepare a journal entry to record lease payments on operating leases for 1981.

B. **Income Taxes**

1. Pay 'n Save reported that "Deferred income tax expense results from the capitalization of store leases." Explain how capitalizing leases results in deferred income tax expenses.

2. Prepare a journal entry to record income tax expense for 1981.

EXHIBIT 1

Consolidated Balance Sheet
Assets

	January 31, 1981	February 2, 1980
	(thousands of dollars)	
CURRENT ASSETS		
Cash and temporary investments	$ 4,555	$ 3,525
Notes receivable	1,809	1,041
Accounts receivable	6,132	4,644
Recoverable store location expenditures	8,485	1,868
Inventories	171,460	141,245
Prepaid insurance and miscellaneous	1,861	1,095
Total current assets	194,302	153,418
PROPERTY, PLANT, AND EQUIPMENT, at cost		
Buildings and land improvements	27,749	11,345
Furniture, fixtures, and equipment	65,669	50,757
Leasehold improvements	15,311	13,515
	108,729	75,617
Less — Accumulated depreciation and amortization	39,097	31,882
	69,632	43,735
Land	10,977	9,848
Construction in progress	2,638	3,440
Buildings under capital leases, less accumulated amortization of $20,640,000 (1981) and $17,171,000 (1980)	89,861	69,713
Total property, plant, and equipment	173,108	126,736
OTHER ASSETS		
Notes receivable	3,038	3,926
Investment in common stock	755	687
Deferred income taxes	5,205	4,435
Cash value of life insurance and other	367	461
Total other assets	9,365	9,509
EXCESS OF COST OVER NET ASSETS OF ACQUIRED COMPANIES	3,593	3,703
	$380,368	$293,366

The accompanying notes are an integral part of these financial statements.

Liabilities

	January 31, 1981	February 2, 1980
	(thousands of dollars)	
CURRENT LIABILITIES		
Short-term indebtedness	$62,534	$22,762
Accounts payable	41,190	34,176
Withheld and accrued taxes	4,539	4,498
Accrued salaries and bonuses	5,991	4,803
Accrued rent, pension, and other expenses	7,129	6,061
Federal and state income taxes	5,873	5,404
Current maturities of long-term indebtedness	1,145	868
Current maturities of obligations under capital leases	1,836	1,500
Total current liabilities	130,237	80,072
NON-CURRENT LIABILITIES		
Long-term indebtedness, less current maturities	10,645	10,770
Obligations under capital leases, less current maturities	100,779	78,333
Total non-current liabilities	111,424	89,103
STOCKHOLDERS' EQUITY		
Capital stock — authorized 10,000,000 shares without par value, outstanding 5,498,571 (1981) and 5,480,582 (1980)	36,008	35,761
Retained earnings	102,699	88,430
Total stockholders' equity	138,707	124,191
	$380,368	$293,366

EXHIBIT 2

Consolidated Statement of Income and Retained Earnings

For the fiscal years

	1981	1980	1979
	(thousands of dollars)		
SALES AND OTHER REVENUE			
Net sales	$823,390	$709,064	$618,731
Interest and other income	2,067	2,416	2,466
	825,457	711,480	621,197
COSTS AND EXPENSES			
Cost of merchandise sold	580,196	500,421	434,439
Operating and administrative expenses	195,762	165,515	144,287
Interest	15,106	10,182	8,992
	791,064	676,118	587,718
Income before federal and state income taxes	34,393	35,362	33,479
Provision for federal and state income taxes	15,395	16,049	16,280
Net income for the year	18,998	19,313	17,199
Retained earnings at beginning of year	88,430	73,062	59,133
Cash dividends — $.86 (1981), $.72 (1980) and $.60 (1979)	(4,729)	(3,945)	(3,270)
Retained earnings at end of year	$102,699	$ 88,430	$ 73,062
Net income per common and common equivalent share	$3.46	$3.52	$3.14

The accompanying notes are an integral part of these financial statements.

Case 5–2

American Seating Company

American Seating Company produces furniture for school classrooms, stadium bleachers, auditorium and theater seating, seating for automobiles, trucks, and buses, and other institutional furniture. The company has manufacturing plants in Grand Rapids, Michigan, and Champaign, Illinois. In addition, the Joerns Furniture Company, a wholly owned subsidiary located in Stevens Point, Wisconsin, manufacturers furniture for the health care industry.

During the Financial Accounting Standards Board's (FASB) deliberations on lease accounting, American Seating, like most lessees, was opposed to suggested rules requiring capitalization of certain leases. In the summer of 1974, the FASB distributed a discussion memorandum on lease accounting that outlined the various options available to the board and requested comments from interested parties. American Seating responded in a letter from John J. Donnelly, Jr., vice president of finance:

> You have requested comments on the FASB Discussion Memorandum regarding leases. We are very much interested in the matter of reporting of leases in financial statements of lessees.
>
> Many companies have a number of off-balance-sheet leases which are structured into covenants of their loan agreements. Mandatory capitalization of leases could create a potential default under those agreements.
>
> We favor full disclosure of lease obligations in the notes to the financial statements but oppose capitalization of leases, especially retroactive capitalization. We urge the Financial Accounting Standards Board to adopt that position.

After lengthy deliberations, the FASB adopted Statement No. 13 in November 1976. This statement called for retroactive capitalization of certain leases which had previously been treated as operating leases.

American Seating Company's 1978 balance sheet is presented in Exhibit 1. Also, notes relating to long-term obligations and lease commitments are provided in Exhibits 2 and 3.

Required

A. Lease Obligations as Reported

American Seating reports that the company is obligated under leases that are classified into three different categories: capital leases, noncapitalized financing leases, and operating leases (see note 13 in Exhibit 2).

1. Explain the distinction among capital leases, noncapitalized financing leases, and operating leases.

This case was prepared from published financial statements of American Seating Company.

2. Assume that any new leases entered into during 1978 were signed on December 31. What entries did American Seating make to record transactions relating to capital leases?

3. What entries did the company make to record lease payments for non-capitalized financing leases during 1978?

4. What entries did the company make to record lease payments for operating leases during 1978?

B. Effects of Capitalizing Leases

Assume that American Seating had complied with the provisions of FASB Statement No. 13 in 1978 by capitalizing all noncapitalized financing leases.

1. Determine the account balances that would have been reported at December 31, 1978 for the following accounts: assets held under capital leases, accumulated amortization of leased assets, and lease obligations.

2. What entries would have been made by the company to record lease payments and lease-related expenses for noncapitalized financing leases had these leases been capitalized.

3. What effect would capitalizing all noncapitalized financing leases have on working capital? on long-term obligations? on unrestricted retained earnings?

4. In recent years, there has been considerable discussion in the financial press about the potential "economic consequences" of accounting policy regulations such as FASB Statement No. 13. What economic effects would technical default on existing loan agreements have on American Seating?

5. What other "economic consequences" might a mandatory accounting change impose upon a company such as American Seating?

EXHIBIT 1
American Seating Company
Consolidated Balance Sheet

December 31	1978	1977
Assets		
Current Assets:		
Cash (Note 5)	$ 1,563,578	$ 1,712,750
Certificates of deposit	–	500,069
Accounts and notes receivable, less allowance		
of $219,000 and $365,000 for possible losses	17,375,417	14,103,242
Inventories (Note 2)	20,973,278	18,655,556
Assets relating to discontinued operations		
(Note 10)	152,210	1,463,499
Prepaid expenses (Note 12)	1,472,029	1,273,974
Total current assets	$41,536,512	$37,709,090
Property and Equipment, Net (Note 3)	12,964,786	10,601,239
Deferred Costs and Other Assets (Notes 4 and 10)	1,253,741	782,269
Other Assets of Discontinued Operations (Note 10)	–	1,183,835
	$55,755,039	$50,276,433
Liabilities		
Current Liabilities:		
Notes payable (Note 5)	$ 4,900,000	$ –
Accounts payable	3,986,322	4,811,883
Accrued income taxes: (Note 12)		
Current	399,077	127,617
Deferred	906,000	823,000
Other accrued taxes	674,959	602,852
Accrued compensation and pensions	3,612,546	3,066,958
Other accruals	451,956	671,778
Provision for loss on disposal of laboratory		
furniture business (Note 10)	–	142,000
Current maturities of long-term obligations	1,234,000	500,000
Total current liabilities	$16,164,860	$10,746,088
Long-term Obligations (Note 6)	9,731,000	10,675,000
Deferred Income Taxes (Note 12)	2,523,000	2,287,000
Unamortized Actuarial Gain	98,780	123,475
	$28,517,640	$23,831,563
Commitments and Contingencies (Notes 11, 13, and 14)		
Stockholders' Equity (Note 7)		
Preferred Stock (Note 8)	2,682,560	2,682,560
Common Stock, $5 Par–Shares Authorized		
4,000,000; Issued 885,505 and 872,005 (Note 9)	4,427,525	4,360,025
Additional Paid-in Capital	830,306	767,869
Retained Earnings (Note 6)	19,297,008	18,634,416
Total Stockholders' Equity	$27,237,399	$26,444,870
	$55,755,039	$50,276,433

EXHIBIT 2
American Seating Company
Note 13—Lease Commitments

The Company's principal leases cover manufacturing, sales office and warehouse space, as well as data processing and manufacturing equipment and automobiles. Non-capitalized financing leases consist primarily of sale lease-back arrangements for the Grand Rapids foundry and the Joerns Furniture Company plant and equipment in Stevens Point, Wisconsin. Noncancelable operating leases are principally for showroom and manufacturing space and data processing equipment. Certain leases contain renewal and purchase options and some require the Company to pay property taxes, insurance and other expenses.

The Financial Accounting Standards Board (FASB), in November, 1976, issued Statement No. 13 which requires recording as an asset and a liability all capital (financing-type) leases, as defined, which are entered into after December 31, 1976. At December 31, 1978 assets include $316,932 and liabilities include $290,000 relating to capitalized automobile financing leases. Amortization of these leased assets has been included with depreciation expense. At December 31, 1977, such leases were not material, and as such, were not capitalized by the Company.

The FASB requires retroactive capitalization, no later than January 1, 1981, of financing leases entered into prior to 1977. The Securities and Exchange Commission's Accounting Series Release No. 225 suggests that financial statements filed with the SEC for fiscal years ending after December 24, 1978 reflect early application of the accounting requirements of Statement No. 13, unless a violation or probable future violation of a restrictive clause in an existing loan indenture or other agreement would result. Such early application of the accounting requirements of the FASB would result in noncompliance with certain covenants in the Company's debt instruments and therefore it is not retroactively capitalizing financing leases at this time.

Total rental expense charged to operations is summarized as follows:

	1978	1977
Non-capitalized financing leases	$ 685,000	$ 830,000
Operating leases	869,000	736,000
	$1,554,000	$1,556,000

The following summary of non-capitalized financing-type leases presents the approximate amounts of the assets and liabilities that would have been included in the balance sheet had these leases been capitalized.

Classes of Property	Asset Balance at December 31		Present Value of Future Rentals at December 31	
	1978	1977	1978	1977
Land and Buildings	$2,790,000	$2,790,000	$2,453,000	$2,508,000
Equipment	4,108,000	4,108,000	3,355,000	3,506,000
Automobiles	124,000	579,000	14,000	308,000
Total	7,022,000	7,477,000	$5,822,000	$6,322,000
Less accumulated amortization	2,204,000	1,967,000		
Net property and equipment	$4,818,000	$5,510,000		

In calculating the present values as of December 31, 1978, a range of interest rates from 6.2% to 15.2% was used, the weighted average of which was 7.2%.

Future minimum rental commitments for all noncancelable leases as of December 31, 1978 are as follows:

	Operating Leases	Capitalized Financing Leases	Non-capitalized Financing Leases
1979	$279,000	$161,000	$ 649,000
1980	124,000	125,000	637,000
1981	73,000	43,000	600,000
1982	70,000	—	592,000
1983	28,000	—	585,000
1984–1988	4,000	—	3,020,000
1989–1993	—	—	1,972,000
1994–1998	—	—	1,868,000
Total minimum payments	$578,000	329,000	9,923,000
Less amount representing interest		39,000	4,101,000
Present value of net minimum lease payments		$290,000	$5,822,000

EXHIBIT 2 *(Continued)*

If all non-capitalized financing leases had been capitalized, the related assets amortized on a straight-line basis and interest cost accrued on the basis of the outstanding lease obligations, net income for 1978 and 1977 would have been reduced as indicated below:

	1978	1977
Additions to expense:		
Amortization	$421,000	$531,000
Interest expense	427,000	472,000
Less: Reversal of reported rent expense	(685,000)	(830,000)
	163,000	173,000
Less: Tax effect	80,000	85,000
Reduction of net income	$ 83,000	$ 88,000
Per common share	$ .09	$ .08

EXHIBIT 3
American Seating Company
Note 6—Long-Term Obligations

	1978	1977
8¼% Notes, payable 1979 through 1988	$ 6,500,000	$ 6,500,000
6⅝% Notes, payable through 1987	4,175,000	4,675,000
Obligations under capitalized leases	290,000	—
Total	10,965,000	11,175,000
Less current maturities	1,234,000	500,000
Long-term obligations	$ 9,731,000	$10,675,000

Aggregate maturities of long-term obligations during the next five years (in thousands) are:

1979	1980	1981	1982	1983
$1,234	$1,216	$1,140	$1,100	$1,100

Among other things, the various loan agreements contain covenants with respect to working capital, total indebtedness, additional borrowings, repurchase of stock and payment of dividends. One agreement also requires the Company to eliminate all short-term indebtedness for at least 60 consecutive days during each 15-month period. The amount of unrestricted earnings at December 31, 1978 was $1,014,000.

Case 5–3

Ford Motor Company

Ford Motor Company is the second largest automobile producer in the world and the sixth largest U.S. industrial corporation. Although automotive products account for more than 90% of the company's sales, in recent years Ford has diversified into nonautomotive areas, including aerospace and defense systems, agricultural and industrial tractors, electrical and electronic systems, and steel, glass, paint, plastic, and vinyl products.

In 1981, Ford's newest product line—the "Escort"—was the best selling car in the United States and the world. Yet despite the success of the Escort, the company's U.S. market share declined from 17.3% in 1980 to 16.6% in 1981. As a result of this decline and the weak worldwide automotive market, 1981 was the second consecutive year that Ford reported losses in excess of $1 billion.

Employment, Payrolls, and Benefit Programs

Ford employs approximately 200,000 people in the United States and over 400,000 people worldwide. The company's worldwide payroll totaled $9.4 billion in 1981. Ford's U.S. labor costs, including payroll and benefit programs, averaged just under $40,000 per employee.

The company has two principal retirement plans covering U.S. employees. The "Ford-UAW Retirement Plan" covers hourly employees represented by the United Auto Workers, and the "General Retirement Plan" provides retirement benefits to substantially all other employees in the United States. Retirement benefits paid to more than 87,000 retired employees and their beneficiaries totaled $489 million in 1981.

Ford's accounting policies, as reported in the 1981 annual report, provides for the following treatment of retirement plan costs:

Retirement Plan Costs

Current service costs are accrued and funded currently. As of January 1, 1980, unamortized prior service costs are amortized and funded over a period of not more than 30 years from the later of January 1, 1980 or the date such costs were established (see Note 3).

Note 3 to the 1981 financial statements provides more detailed information:

Note 3. Employee Retirement Plans

Amendments made in 1979 to the Ford-UAW Retirement Plan and to the General Retirement Plan provided for additional benefits that increase retirement plan costs each year through 1982.

This case was prepared from published financial statements of Ford Motor Company.

The assumed rate of return used in determining retirement plan costs for the two principal U.S. retirement plans was 8% for 1981, 7% for 1980 and 6% for 1979. In 1981, the change recommended by the independent actuary in the assumed rate of return resulted in a reduction in fourth-quarter and full-year 1981 retirement plan costs of approximately $85 million (54¢ a share). In 1980, changes recommended by the independent actuary in the assumed rate of return and in other actuarial rates and a change in the amortization of certain prior service costs resulted in a reduction of 1980 retirement plan costs of approximately $165 million ($1.05 a share).

The values of accumulated benefits and net assets for the Company's U.S. defined benefit plans are presented below:

	December 31	
	1981	1980
	(in Millions)	
Actuarial value of accumulated plan benefits		
Vested	$6,830	$6,085
Nonvested	1,380	1,595
Total value	$8,210	$7,680
Fair market value of net assets available for plan benefits	$6,170	$6,200

The actuarial values of accumulated plan benefits were computed using a rate of return of 8% at year-end 1981 and 7% at year-end 1980. The value of accumulated plan benefits at year-end 1981 increased from year-end 1980 primarily because of retirement experience and the inclusion in 1981 of scheduled increases in benefits through August 22; the increase in the assumed rate of return was a partial offset.

Ford's consolidated statements of income and consolidated balance sheets are provided in Exhibits 1 and 2.

Required

1. Define the following terms:
   a. current service costs
   b. prior service costs
   c. actuarial value of accumulated plan benefits
   d. vested benefits
   e. unfunded pension liabilities
2. Explain how the assumed rate of return on pension assets affects the actuarial value of accumulated plan benefits. How does a change in this assumption affect net income?
3. If Ford were required to capitalize pension fund assets and the related liabilities, what would be the effect on the company's financial structure?

EXHIBIT 1

Consolidated Statement of Income
For the Years Ended December 31, 1981, 1980 and 1979 (in millions)
Ford Motor Company and Consolidated Subsidiaries

	1981	1980	1979
Sales	$38,247.1	$37,085.5	$43,513.7
Costs and Expenses (Note 1)			
Costs, excluding items listed below (Notes 2 and 5)	34,626.2	34,700.6	38,448.3
Depreciation	1,168.7	1,057.2	895.9
Amortization of special tools	1,010.7	912.1	708.5
Selling and administrative	2,042.3	1,930.7	1,701.8
Employee retirement plans (Note 3)	655.0	763.2	811.2
Provision for supplemental compensation	0	0	31.0
Total costs and expenses (Note 4)	39,502.9	39,363.8	42,596.7
Operating Income (Loss)	(1,255.8)	(2,278.3)	917.0
Interest income			
Marketable securities and time deposits	361.4	360.9	535.8
Other	263.2	182.2	157.2
Interest expense	(674.7)	(432.5)	(246.8)
Net interest income (expense)	(50.1)	110.6	446.2
Equity in net income of unconsolidated subsidiaries and affiliates	167.8	187.0	146.2
Income (Loss) Before Income Taxes	(1,138.1)	(1,980.7)	1,509.4
Provision (credit) for income taxes (Note 5)	(68.3)	(435.4)	330.1
Income (Loss) Before Minority Interests	(1,069.8)	(1,545.3)	1,179.3
Minority interests in net income (loss) of consolidated subsidiaries	(9.7)	(2.0)	10.0
Net Income (Loss)	$(1,060.1)	$(1,543.3)	$ 1,169.3
Average number of shares of capital stock outstanding	120.3	120.3	119.9
Net Income (Loss) a Share (Note 6)	$(8.81)	$(12.83)	$9.75
Net Income a Share Assuming Full Dilution (Note 6)			$9.15
Cash Dividends a Share	$1.20	$2.60	$3.90

EXHIBIT 2

Consolidated Balance Sheet
December 31, 1981 and 1980 (in millions)
Ford Motor Company and Consolidated Subsidiaries

	1981	1980
Assets		
Current Assets		
Cash and cash items	$ 1,176.5	$ 2,164.1
Marketable securities (including, in 1981, $500 million of commercial paper of Ford Motor Credit Company), at cost and accrued interest (approximates market)	923.5	423.1
Receivables (Note 7)	2,595.8	2,998.1
Inventories (Notes 1 and 8)	4,642.9	5,129.6
Other current assets (Note 5)	838.2	844.1
Total current assets	10,176.9	11,559.0
Equities in Net Assets of Unconsolidated Subsidiaries and Affiliates (Note 9)	2,348.2	2,142.2
Property		
Land, plant and equipment, at cost (Note 10)	16,395.7	15,567.3
Less accumulated depreciation	8,959.4	7,992.2
Net land, plant and equipment	7,436.3	7,575.1
Unamortized special tools	2,410.1	2,450.8
Net property	9,846.4	10,025.9
Other Assets (Note 15)	649.9	620.5
Total Assets	$23,021.4	$24,347.6
Liabilities and Stockholders' Equity		
Current Liabilities		
Accounts payable		
Trade	$ 2,800.2	$ 3,370.6
Other	1,089.8	1,349.9
Total accounts payable	3,890.0	4,720.5
Income taxes	208.9	234.6
Short-term debt	2,049.0	2,321.8
Long-term debt payable within one year	128.7	83.8
Accrued liabilities (Note 11)	3,663.7	3,711.3
Total current liabilities	9,940.3	11,072.0
Long-Term Debt (Note 13)	2,709.7	2,058.8
Other Liabilities (Note 11)	1,856.2	1,444.4
Deferred Income Taxes (Note 5)	1,004.8	1,069.0
Minority Interests in Net Assets of Consolidated Subsidiaries	148.2	135.9
Guarantees and Commitments (Note 14)		
Stockholders' Equity		
Capital Stock, par value $2.00 a share (Notes 15 and 16)		
Common Stock, shares issued: 1981 – 107,859,065; 1980 – 107,365,711	215.7	214.8
Class B Stock, shares issued: 1981 – 12,717,003; 1980 – 13,209,749	25.5	26.4
Capital in excess of par value of stock	526.1	526.9
Earnings retained for use in the business (Note 9)	6,594.9	7,799.4
Total stockholders' equity	7,362.2	8,567.5
Total Liabilities and Stockholders' Equity	$23,021.4	$24,347.6

The accompanying notes are part of the financial statements.

Case 5—4

The Gillette Company

The Gillette Company is an international consumer products company engaged in developing, producing, and marketing a variety of products for personal use. Major product lines include blades and razors, toiletries and grooming aids, writing instruments, and cigarette lighters. The company also owns and operates Braun AG, a West German manufacturer of small household appliances and other consumer products.

Gillette's 1979 and 1980 balance sheets and income statements appear in Exhibits 1 and 2. Also, the notes to Gillette's 1980 consolidated financial statements included the following data:

Property, Plant, and Equipment

	1980	1979
Land	$ 18,554,000	$ 17,756,000
Buildings	184,040,000	170,457,000
Machinery and equipment	599,329,000	494,719,000
	$801,923,000	$682,932,000
Less: Accumulated depreciation	349,652,000	299,761,000
	$452,271,000	$383,171,000

Depreciation is computed primarily on a straight-line basis over the estimated useful lives of assets. Depreciation provisions are equivalent to weighted average rates of approximately 4% for buildings and 12% for machinery and equipment.

Income Taxes

Deferred taxes are provided for timing differences between financial and tax reporting, principally relating to depreciation.

Required

1. During 1980, Gillette sold and/or retired property, plant, and equipment carried at $8,197,000 in the financial statements. The original cost of these assets was $27,922,000. Compute the cost of property, plant and equipment acquired in 1980. Also compute the amount of depreciation recorded for the year.

This case was prepared from published financial statements of The Gillette Company.

2. Prepare a journal entry to record "Federal and foreign income taxes" for 1980.

3. Suppose that generally accepted accounting principles were changed to allow firms to "flow through" the tax effects of timing differences between taxable income and accounting income. Restate Gillette's 1980 income statement and balance sheet to reflect this change.

4. Assume that Gillette's average tax rate in recent years was 45%. Also assume that the use of accelerated depreciation for tax purposes was the only source of timing differences between accounting income and taxable income. Estimate the amount of property, plant, and equipment that Gillette would have reported in its 1980 balance sheet if the company had used accelerated depreciation methods for financial reporting purposes.

EXHIBIT 1

The Gillette Company and Subsidiary Companies
Consolidated Balance Sheet

(Thousands of dollars)

December 31, 1980 and 1979

Assets	1980	1979
Current Assets:		
Cash, time deposits and certificates of deposit	$ 82,895	$ 88,601
Marketable securities, at cost which approximates market value	5,845	4,484
Receivables, less allowances of $17,734 and $19,028	465,749	438,613
Inventories	513,034	435,374
Prepaid expenses	47,244	44,126
Total Current Assets	1,114,767	1,011,198
Property, Plant and Equipment, at cost less accumulated depreciation	452,271	383,171
Goodwill	92,448	87,063
Other Assets	49,018	46,316
	$1,708,504	$1,527,748

Liabilities and Stockholders' Equity

	1980	1979
Current Liabilities:		
Loans payable	$ 167,047	$ 137,035
Accounts payable and accrued liabilities	362,036	326,572
Dividends payable	14,348	12,974
Federal and foreign income taxes	57,500	50,000
Total Current Liabilities	600,931	526,581
Deferred Income Taxes	32,400	31,900
Other Liabilities, principally accrued pensions	75,464	68,930
Long-Term Debt	279,497	249,336
Minority Interest	3,571	3,093
Stockholders' Equity:		
Common stock, par value $1.00 per share	30,071	30,045
Additional paid-in capital	37,111	36,361
Earnings reinvested in the business	649,459	581,502
Total Stockholders' Equity	716,641	647,908
	$1,708,504	$1,527,748

EXHIBIT 2

The Gillette Company and Subsidiary Companies
Consolidated Statement of Income and Earnings Reinvested in the Business

(Thousands of dollars, except per share amounts)

Years Ended December 31, 1980, 1979 and 1978

	1980	1979	1978
Net sales	$2,315,294	$1,984,722	$1,710,471
Cost of sales	1,092,163	940,025	801,577
Operating expenses	945,524	806,472	698,457
	2,037,687	1,746,497	1,500,034
Profit from operations	277,607	238,225	210,437
Other income, including interest income of $10,246, $8,375 and $9,003	15,961	11,001	15,993
Other charges, including interest expense of $59,706, $37,485 and $35,462	79,991	59,908	54,066
Income before income taxes	213,577	189,318	172,364
Federal and foreign income taxes	89,600	78,700	77,800
Net income	123,977	110,618	94,564
Net income per share	$ 4.11	$ 3.67	$ 3.14
Earnings reinvested in the business at beginning of year	581,502	521,870	474,755
	705,479	632,488	569,319
Deduct: Dividends declared: $1.85½, $1.69 and $1.57½ per share	56,020	50,986	47,449
Earnings reinvested in the business at end of year	$ 649,459	$ 581,502	$ 521,870

Case 5-5

United Technologies Corporation

United Technologies (UT) is the seventh largest manufacturer and the second largest defense contractor in the United States. The company is a major competitor in three industries: aerospace, with Pratt and Whitney jet engines and Sikorsky Helicopter; building systems, with Otis Elevator and Carrier Air Conditioning; and electronics, with a number of firms engaged in avionics, semiconductor production, and automotive and medical instrumentation.

Despite gains in market share and increased government-related revenues, UT's sales were down slightly in 1982. The worldwide recession had a significant effect on most of the firm's commercial businesses. However, due to an accounting change for Investment Tax Credits and a tax-free extraordinary gain resulting from a debt for equity swap, net income increased by 16.5 percent over 1982.

The consolidated statement of income and consolidated balance sheet are included in Exhibits 1 and 2, respectively. Excerpts from Note 11 to the 1982 financial statements are included in Exhibit 3.

A. Deferred Taxes

United Technologies' 1982 income statement reports a tax expense totaling $318,244,000. Of this amount, $271,589,000 is currently payable and the remainder is deferred due to timing differences in the way transactions are treated for financial versus tax reporting.

Required

1. Compute the amount of taxes paid in 1982.
2. Note 11 provides a detailed breakdown of the 1982 deferred portion of federal income taxes totaling $59,025,000 (see Exhibit 3). For each item listed, briefly discuss the underlying cause(s) of the timing differences that result in deferred taxes. Would the accounting policies used for tax purposes be appropriate for financial reporting?

B. Investment Tax Credits

Note 2 to UT's 1982 financial statements includes the following description of the change in the method of accounting for the investment tax credit:

This case was prepared from the published financial statements of United Technologies Corporation.

Effective January 1, 1982, the Corporation changed its method of accounting for investment tax credits from the deferral method to the flow-through method in order to achieve greater comparability with the accounting practices of most other industrial concerns and, in the opinion of the Corporation, to more accurately reflect the economic impact of investment decisions on reported earnings. Under the flow-through method, the provision for federal income taxes is reduced by investment tax credits in the year the related assets are placed in service, rather than deferring such investment tax credits and amortizing them over the estimated useful lives of the related assets.

The effect of the change in 1982 was to increase net income by $81,425,000 or $1.53 per share on a primary basis and $1.22 per share on a fully diluted basis, of which $66,621,000 ($1.25 primary earnings per share and $1.00 fully diluted earnings per share) represents the cumulative effect of investment tax credits through 1981 and $14,804,000 ($.28 primary earnings per share and $.22 fully diluted earnings per share) represents the net effect of 1982 investment tax credits. Pro forma earnings and related per share amounts as if the flow-through method had been adopted retroactively are included in the Consolidated Statement of Income.

Required

1. The December 31, 1981, balance in "Deferred Income Taxes" includes $63,079,000 of deferrals related to the investment tax credit. Prepare the necessary journal entry to record income tax expense for 1982.

2. What would have been reported as income tax expense had the company continued to use deferral of the investment tax credit?

3. Comment on the company's stated reasons for changing this accounting policy.

C. Debt for Equity Swap

In June of 1982, UT exchanged 1,919,311 shares of common stock, valued at $65,611,000, and cash of $63,039,000 for $165,036,000 principal amounts of various debentures. The exchange resulted in an extraordinary gain, which was not subject to income taxes, of $40,226,000 after deducting expenses incurred in completing the swap (i.e., investment bankers' commissions and fees).

Required

1. Prepare the journal entry to record the swap.

2. In 1982, debt for equity swaps were completed for over 70 firms. Assume that it is the objective of management to maximize the discounted net present value of future cash flows for UT. Briefly outline the economic factors that are relevant in management's decision to swap debt for equity. Do you agree with their decision?

EXHIBIT 1

Consolidated Statement of Income

United Technologies Corporation

In Thousands of Dollars (except per share amounts)	Years Ended December 31, 1982	1981	1980
Revenues:			
Sales	$13,577,129	$13,667,758	$12,323,994
Other income, less other deductions	139,000	96,839	75,397
	$13,716,129	$13,764,597	$12,399,391
Costs and Expenses:			
Cost of goods and services sold	$ 9,956,151	$10,081,262	$ 9,038,161
Research and development	834,476	735,825	660,296
Selling, service and administrative expenses	1,916,892	1,827,256	1,684,046
Interest expense	250,886	244,839	229,848
	$12,958,405	$12,889,182	$11,612,351
Income before income taxes	$ 757,724	$ 875,415	$ 787,040
Income taxes	318,244	402,691	373,844
Income before minority interests	$ 439,480	$ 472,724	$ 413,196
Less — Minority interests in subsidiaries' earnings	12,606	15,038	19,813
Income before extraordinary item and cumulative effect of change in accounting principle	$ 426,874	$ 457,686	$ 393,383
Extraordinary gain	40,226	—	—
Cumulative effect of change in accounting principle	66,621	—	—
Net Income	$ 533,721	$ 457,686	$ 393,383
Preferred Stock Dividend Requirement	$ 69,570	$ 76,835	$ 81,239
Earnings Applicable to Common Stock	$ 464,151	$ 380,851	$ 312,144
Per Share of Common Stock:			
Primary:			
Income before extraordinary item and cumulative effect of change in accounting principle	$6.73	$7.71	$7.28
Extraordinary gain	.76	—	—
Cumulative effect of change in accounting principle	1.25	—	—
Net Income	$8.74	$7.71	$7.28
Fully Diluted:			
Income before extraordinary item and cumulative effect of change in accounting principle	$6.41	$7.05	$6.51
Extraordinary gain	.60	—	—
Cumulative effect of change in accounting principle	1.00	—	—
Net Income	$8.01	$7.05	$6.51
Pro forma assuming retroactive application of change in accounting principle:			
Income before extraordinary item	$ 426,874	$ 473,580	$ 408,305
Per Share of Common Stock			
Primary earnings	$6.73	$8.03	$7.63
Fully diluted earnings	$6.41	$7.29	$6.76
Net Income	$ 467,100	$ 473,580	$ 408,305
Per Share of Common Stock			
Primary earnings	$7.49	$8.03	$7.63
Fully diluted earnings	$7.01	$7.29	$6.76

See accompanying Notes to Financial Statements

EXHIBIT 2

Consolidated Balance Sheet   United Technologies Corporation

	December 31,	
In Thousands of Dollars	1982	1981
Assets		
Current Assets:		
Cash and short-term cash investments	$ 121,471	$ 167,955
Accounts receivable	1,552,304	1,506,740
Inventories and contracts in progress	4,968,588	4,600,221
Less — Progress payments and billings on contracts in progress	(2,102,596)	(1,868,063)
Prepaid expenses	64,005	81,673
Total Current Assets	$4,603,772	$4,488,526
Accounts and notes receivable due after one year	$ 152,388	$ 118,771
Unconsolidated subsidiaries and other investments	$ 298,436	$ 166,021
Fixed Assets, at cost:		
Land	$ 137,917	$ 140,707
Buildings and improvements	1,360,570	1,258,142
Machinery, tools and equipment	2,800,279	2,417,664
Under construction	242,474	275,626
	$4,541,240	$4,092,139
Less — Accumulated depreciation and amortization	(2,155,103)	(1,888,817)
	$2,386,137	$2,203,322
Deferred Charges:		
Costs in excess of net assets of acquired companies (net of amortization)	$ 532,428	$ 562,988
Other	20,215	15,475
	$ 552,643	$ 578,463
Total Assets	$7,993,376	$7,555,103
Liabilities and Shareowners' Equity		
Current Liabilities:		
Short-term borrowings	$ 449,391	$ 392,762
Accounts payable	871,092	869,942
Accrued salaries, wages and employee benefits	586,271	509,553
Other accrued liabilities	781,539	718,264
Long-term debt — currently due	55,153	74,378
Income taxes:		
Currently payable	101,032	140,750
Deferred	86,114	64,982
Advances on sales contracts	119,076	143,913
Total Current Liabilities	$3,049,668	$2,914,544
Deferred income taxes, and investment tax credits in 1981	$ 246,261	$ 283,817
Long-term debt	$ 927,180	$ 832,398
Other long-term liabilities	$ 219,888	$ 232,168
Commitments and contingent liabilities (Note 15)		
Minority interests in subsidiary companies	$ 68,589	$ 79,665
Shareowners' Equity:		
Capital Stock:		
Preferred Stock, $1 par value (Authorized — 100,000,000 shares)		
Outstanding — 24,330,271 and 26,368,013 shares, respectively	$ 697,774	$ 751,227
(Aggregate liquidating preference — $706,006,000)		
Common Stock, $5 par value (Authorized — 200,000,000 shares)		
Outstanding — 54,299,592 and 51,881,454 shares, respectively	1,143,981	1,058,729
Deferred foreign currency translation adjustments	(157,666)	(60,047)
Retained earnings	1,797,701	1,462,602
Total Shareowners' Equity	$3,481,790	$3,212,511
Total Liabilities and Shareowners' Equity	$7,993,376	$7,555,103

See accompanying Notes to Financial Statements

EXHIBIT 3

Note 11

Taxes on Income: The provision for income taxes for each of the three years ended December 31, 1982 comprised the following:

In Thousands of Dollars	1982	1981	1980
Currently payable:			
United States			
Federal	$ 78,344	$149,891	$ 13,479
State	50,740	30,457	14,881
Foreign	142,505	146,743	124,300
	$271,589	$327,091	$152,660
Deferred:			
United States			
Federal	$ 59,025	$ 38,697	$179,274
State	(6,941)	16,274	14,639
Foreign	(5,429)	3,867	11,331
	$ 46,655	$ 58,838	$205,244
Investment tax credit			
deferred, net	$ —	$ 16,762	$ 15,940
	$318,244	$402,691	$373,844

As discussed in Note 2, the Corporation adopted the flow-through method of accounting for investment tax credits effective January 1, 1982. The current tax provision for 1982 has been reduced by $27,044,000 for the effect of investment tax credits generated in 1982.

Deferred income taxes represent the tax effects of transactions which are reported in different periods for financial and tax reporting purposes.

Changes in deferred federal income taxes shown above, which represent the tax effects of transactions which are reported in different periods for financial and tax reporting purposes, include the income tax effects of:

In Thousands of Dollars	1982	1981	1980
Use of completed-contract method for reporting taxable income on long-term manufacturing contracts	$ 18,903	$(17,792)	$167,677
Tax depreciation or accelerated cost recovery in excess of financial statement depreciation	23,580	18,286	6,477
Capitalization of interest cost, less related depreciation	14,873	17,286	12,346
Adjustments of assets and liabilities for tax purposes, which tend to recur annually:			
Adjustment of inventories to tax basis	(6,365)	221	5,736
Expenditures (provisions) for warranty and correction of product deficiencies, tax deductible when paid	2,747	6,818	6,550
Employee severance, pension and vacation expense deductible on different bases for book and tax purposes	1,167	(2,948)	(2,585)
Customer allowances, tax deductible when paid or applied	974	25,663	(24,154)
Other items	3,146	(8,837)	7,227
	$ 59,025	$ 38,697	$179,274

Case 5–6

Aetna Life and Casualty Company

Aetna Life and Casualty is the nation's largest stockholder-owned insurance and financial services organization and, based on assets in excess of $44 billion, ranks among the 15 largest U.S. corporations. Aetna markets virtually all forms of business and personal insurance and pension products worldwide. Aetna has also diversified into areas such as real estate development and high technology.

As one of the nation's largest investors, Aetna's new investments of $5.6 billion in 1982 included direct loans to industry, mortgage loans and owned real estate, state and municipal bonds, and preferred and common stock.

Accounting for Future Tax Benefits

Aetna invests heavily in tax-exempt securities. Since the income from these securities is not taxable, while Aetna's costs of doing business are deductible, large tax losses resulted in 1982. These tax losses can be carried forward up to 15 years to offset future taxable income.

In 1967 the Accounting Principles Board, the accounting profession's self-regulatory body that preceded the Financial Accounting Standards Board, issued Opinion No. 11, which states that tax benefits cannot be recognized in the financial statements except in unusual circumstances where realization is assured "beyond any reasonable doubt." The opinion requires that all three of the following conditions be met to recognize in the current period the potential benefits of tax-loss carryforwards.

First, the tax loss must have resulted from "an identifiable, isolated, and non-recurring cause." Second, the company must have been continuously profitable over a long period or have suffered only occasional losses that were more than offset by taxable income in subsequent periods. Third, the taxable income must be large enough and occur soon enough (15 years under the current rules) to garner the benefits of the tax-loss carryforwards.

Aetna's *1982 Annual Report* contains the following discussion of management's reasoning behind its accounting for these potential future tax benefits.

> Generally accepted accounting principles provide for recognition of the tax benefit of operating loss carryforwards if, and only if, realization of those tax benefits is assured beyond any reasonable doubt at the time the loss carryforwards arise. AETNA's management believes that realization from future taxable income of the tax benefit of AETNA's tax losses is assured

---

This case was prepared from published financial statements of Aetna Life and Casualty Company.

beyond any reasonable doubt. Two specific factors reinforce management's assurance. First, AETNA has elected consolidation of its life companies (which generate substantial taxable income) with non-life companies for income tax purposes. This provides a partial offset against non-life losses. Second, investable funds generated by casualty-property operations and by casualty-property investment portfolios are being directed toward taxable investments as they have been since late 1981. Additionally, AETNA's non-insurance operations are expected to generate increasing amounts of taxable income in future years.

To provide further reinforcement of AETNA's assurance beyond any reasonable doubt that its tax benefits will be realized well within the 15 year carryforward period and to maximize shareholder returns in an environment where the tax benefit of tax loss carryforwards is not being currently recognized, AETNA is undertaking a program of economically sound steps to accelerate recovery of these benefits. These steps will include selective additional sales of tax-exempt securities for reinvestment in taxable bonds. The timing, manner and extent of these sales will be governed by market conditions and the development of other sources of taxable income within AETNA. As a part of this program, AETNA may also redeploy other assets for which the current market value is higher than the carrying value. In addition, the Company is considering various reinsurance programs that would allow it to accelerate the realization of taxable income through the release of reserves for claims far in the future.

As a result of these actions, the impact on operating results of not currently recognizing the tax benefit of tax loss carryforwards will be significantly reduced and the realization of the tax benefit asset will be accelerated. (For further discussion, see Notes 1 and 9 to the Financial Statements.)

Note 9 on federal income taxes contains the following additional information on the magnitude of the tax-loss carryforwards and their expiration dates.

At December 31, 1982, AETNA Life & Casualty has tax return operating loss carryforwards of $1,312.9 million. If not utilized to offset future taxable income $3 million will expire in 1993, $93.5 million will expire in 1995, $625.2 million will expire in 1996, and $591.2 million will expire in 1997. For financial statement purposes, tax benefits related to operating loss carryforwards in excess of amounts deducted from existing deferred taxes were recognized in 1981 of $26.6 million and in 1982 through nine months in the amount of $202.9 million. Management is assured beyond any reasonable doubt, that the tax benefits of these tax loss carryforwards will be realized. A tax benefit of $16 million for the fourth quarter of 1982 has not been reflected in the financial statements.

Exhibits 1, 2, and 3 present Aetna's consolidated balance sheets, statements of income and retained earnings, and statements of changes in financial position.

Required

1. In early 1983, the Securities and Exchange Commission (SEC) ordered AETNA to stop recognizing the possible future benefits of loss carryforwards in current earnings. Aetna agreed to halt the practice as of the fourth quarter

of 1982, but it did not restate earnings for the first three quarters of 1982. What would have been Aetna's operating earnings if (a) the company had not recognized any tax benefits in 1982? and (b) if tax benefits had been recognized for the entire year?

2. Do you agree with the SEC that the practice should be stopped? Or do you agree with Aetna and its accountants—Peat, Marwick, Mitchell & Co.—that the practice is proper? State your reasons.

3. Assuming that the tax benefits are assured of being realized "beyond any reasonable doubt," do you believe the benefits should be recognized in current earnings? How should the value of the benefits be determined? Is this the method Aetna appears to be using?

4. Many companies have tax losses that result in loss carryforwards. However, a computerized search of approximately 4,000 1981 corporate annual reports revealed that *only* Aetna was recognizing future tax benefits in current earnings. Speculate as to Aetna's purposes for booking the tax benefits.

EXHIBIT 1

CONSOLIDATED BALANCE SHEETS

(Millions)	1982	1981	1980
Assets Investments:			
Fixed maturities:			
Bonds	$13,277.2	$13,718.3	$13,920.2
Redeemable preferred stocks	835.7	844.1	855.9
Equity securities:			
Common stocks	857.5	675.0	757.3
Non-redeemable preferred stocks	192.3	215.1	250.1
Mortgage loans	10,069.1	9,562.3	8,502.1
Real estate	291.4	296.4	294.3
Policy loans	548.2	535.3	472.3
Other	123.0	84.4	78.0
Investments in international and diversified companies	1,141.3	680.3	360.4
Loans to diversified companies	329.1	285.1	389.7
Total investments	27,664.8	26,896.3	25,880.3
Cash and invested cash	962.9	304.1	596.6
Accrued investment income	458.2	450.1	425.9
Premiums due and other receivables	1,637.6	1,481.2	1,401.8
Deferred policy acquisition costs	726.0	704.1	681.9
Federal income taxes:			
Current	50.8	—	—
Tax benefits recoverable	229.5	26.6	—
Property and equipment	381.3	236.5	163.0
Other assets	663.4	445.4	413.2
Separate Accounts assets	11,436.3	8,088.9	5,257.7
Total assets	$44,210.8	$38,633.2	$34,820.4
Liabilities Liabilities:			
Future policy benefits	$10,238.7	$10,173.5	$ 9,917.1
Unpaid claims and claim expenses	7,790.5	7,280.6	6,406.3
Policyholders' funds left with the companies	8,862.6	8,478.6	8,757.8
Total insurance reserve liabilities	26,891.8	25,932.7	25,081.2
Dividends payable to shareholders	62.7	46.6	42.6
Short-term debt	2.8	35.2	3.8
Long-term debt	413.6	258.7	258.6
Other liabilities	650.2	629.8	642.9
Federal income taxes:			
Current	—	96.3	3.6
Deferred	74.9	9.9	163.2
Minority interests and Participating Department	131.9	124.1	114.1
Separate Accounts liabilities	11,401.4	8,056.6	5,229.3
Total liabilities	39,629.3	35,189.9	31,539.3
Shareholders' Equity Shareholders' Equity:			
Capital stock:			
Convertible preferred	—	.1	.1
Floating rate preferred	200.0	—	—
Common	781.9	120.2	118.9
Net unrealized capital losses on investments	(68.1)	(120.1)	(14.7)
Retained earnings	3,672.2	3,478.7	3,202.9
	4,586.0	3,478.9	3,307.2
Less treasury stock, at cost	4.5	35.6	26.1
Total shareholders' equity	4,581.5	3,443.3	3,281.1
Total liabilities and shareholders' equity	$44,210.8	$38,633.2	$34,820.4
Shareholders' equity per common share	$ 44.03	$ 42.89	$ 40.77

EXHIBIT 2

CONSOLIDATED STATEMENTS OF INCOME AND RETAINED EARNINGS

(Millions)	1982	1981	1980
Revenue Premiums.	$10,654.0	$11,065.0	$11,036.4
Net investment and other income	3,510.4	3,006.6	2,426.5
Total revenue	14,164.4	14,071.6	13,462.9
Benefits and Current and future benefits	11,850.8	11,912.6	11,293.8
Expenses Operating expenses	1,886.7	1,737.9	1,646.3
Interest expense	75.4	46.2	61.8
Federal income taxes (credits):			
Current.	(10.0)	76.9	5.0
Deferred	(135.7)	(163.2)	(13.3)
Minority interests and Participating Department	6.7	13.7	11.4
Total benefits and expenses	13,673.9	13,624.1	13,005.0
Insurance Operating Earnings	490.5	447.5	457.9
Earnings of International and Diversified Business			
Division	31.4	43.0	51.8
Operating Operating Earnings.	521.9	490.5	509.7
Earnings Realized capital gains (losses), net of taxes	(94.8)	(28.3)	51.9
Net Income Net Income	427.1	462.2	561.6
Dividends declared:			
Convertible preferred	—	—	(.1)
Floating rate preferred	(10.0)	—	—
Common	(223.6)	(186.4)	(170.6)
Retained earnings, beginning of year	3,478.7	3,202.9	2,812.0
Retained earnings, end of year	$ 3,672.2	$ 3,478.7	$ 3,202.9
Results Per Operating Earnings.	$ 5.80	$ 6.10	$ 6.32
Common Share Realized capital gains (losses), net of taxes	(1.08)	(.35)	.64
Net Income	$ 4.72	$ 5.75	$ 6.96

See Notes to Financial Statements.

EXHIBIT 3

CONSOLIDATED STATEMENTS OF CHANGES IN FINANCIAL POSITION

(Millions)	1982	1981	1980
Sources of Net income	$ 427.1	$ 462.2	$ 561.6
Funds Change in items not requiring (providing) funds:			
Insurance reserve liabilities.	959.1	851.5	3,046.6
Other, net.	(235.9)	(279.6)	(283.4)
Funds provided from operations.	1,150.3	1,034.1	3,324.8
Cost of investments sold, matured or repaid	2,439.7	2,544.5	1,976.4
Increase in long-term debt.	159.2	.9	6.0
Change in short-term debt.	(32.4)	31.4	(213.6)
Issuance of preferred stock	200.0	—	—
Issuance of common stock for Geosource			
and Federated acquisitions	657.4	—	—
Stock issued under benefit plans.	32.0	22.3	20.2
Total sources of funds	4,606.2	3,633.2	5,113.8
Uses of Cost of investments purchased	2,890.5	3,580.9	4,836.7
Funds Net increase in policy loans	12.9	63.0	74.4
Acquisition of Geosource.	446.1	—	—
Acquisition of Federated (less cash and			
invested cash of $31,284,000)	180.0	—	—
Additions to property and equipment.	151.4	94.0	47.0
Repayment of long-term debt	4.3	.8	34.8
Dividends paid to shareholders	217.5	182.4	164.4
Cost of treasury stock purchased.	21.3	32.1	27.9
Other, net.	23.4	(27.5)	67.9
Total uses of funds.	3,947.4	3,925.7	5,253.1
Net Increase Net increase (decrease) in funds.	658.8	(292.5)	(139.3)
(Decrease) Cash and invested cash, beginning of year	304.1	596.6	735.9
In Funds Cash and invested cash, end of year	$ 962.9	$ 304.1	$ 596.6

See Notes to Financial Statements.

6

OWNERS' EQUITY AND INTERCOMPANY INVESTMENTS

Case 6–1

Alaska Airlines, Inc.

Alaska Airlines is an Alaska corporation organized in 1937 to provide air transportation services within Alaska and between Alaska and the Lower 48 states. Since 1974, the company has carried more passengers between Alaska and the lower 48 states than any other airline.

In 1982, a year when most airlines were recording operating losses, Alaska Airlines reported a record profit as net income increased 38 percent over the previous year. Presented in Exhibits 1, 2, 3, and 4 are the company's balance sheets for 1981 and 1982, the statements of income and the statements of shareholders' equity for 1980, 1981, and 1982, and a seven-year summary of selected financial data. In addition, notes concerning the company's capital stock and stock options are provided (see Exhibit 5).

This case was prepared from published financial statements of Alaska Airlines, Inc.

Required

1. Given the information provided in the statement of shareholders' equity, prepare journal entries to record the transactions that affected shareholders' equity in 1980, 1981, and 1982.

2. Determine the market value of a common share at the time that the 575,000 "equity units" consisting of one common and one preferred share were issued.

3. Compute the average exercise price of the stock options exercised in each year.

4. Assume that, on January 1, 1983, Alaska Airlines sold all the common shares held in treasury stock for $12.50 per share. Prepare a journal entry to record this transaction. How would this transaction affect earnings per share in 1982? in 1983?

EXHIBIT 1

Balance Sheet
Alaska Airlines, Inc.

	December 31,	
	1981	1982
ASSETS	(amounts in thousands)	
CURRENT ASSETS		
Cash	$ 1,325	$ 1,612
Short-term investments, at cost which approximates market	8,852	42,095
Receivables — net of allowance for doubtful accounts of $296,000 in 1981 and $806,000 in 1982	17,771	21,538
Expendable parts and supplies at average cost net of allowance for obsolescence of $227,000 in 1981 and $242,000 in 1982	1,971	2,788
Prepaid expenses	1,328	2,448
TOTAL CURRENT ASSETS	31,247	70,481
PROPERTY AND EQUIPMENT — at cost		
Flight equipment	108,985	124,982
Other property and equipment	28,678	34,103
	137,663	159,085
Less accumulated depreciation and amortization	29,580	39,480
	108,083	119,605
DEFERRED CHARGES AND OTHER ASSETS	1,679	5,008
TOTAL ASSETS	$141,009	$195,094

LIABILITIES AND SHAREHOLDERS' EQUITY	(amounts in thousands)	
CURRENT LIABILITIES		
Accounts payable	$ 11,581	$ 13,563
Accrued salaries, wages, vacations and payroll taxes	6,450	8,378
Accrued income taxes	37	—
Other accrued liabilities	4,433	7,395
Air traffic liability	13,121	16,203
Current installments on long-term debt	5,706	7,394
TOTAL CURRENT LIABILITIES	41,328	52,933
LONG-TERM DEBT	47,700	55,769
OTHER LIABILITIES		
Deferred income taxes	5,469	13,701
Other deferred credits and liabilities	2,333	2,504
	7,802	16,205
SHAREHOLDERS' EQUITY		
Preferred stock, par value $1 per share		
Authorized: 5,000,000 shares		
Outstanding: $2.77 cumulative convertible		
1981 — 572,100 shares; 1982 — 0 shares	572	—
Capital in excess of par value	10,089	—
Common stock, par value $1 per share		
Authorized: 15,000,000 shares		
Issued: 1981 — 6,930,421 shares; 1982 — 10,659,438 shares	6,930	10,659
Capital in excess of par value	13,902	38,963
Treasury stock, at cost (103,305 shares)	(515)	(515)
Retained earnings	13,201	21,080
	44,179	70,187
COMMITMENTS — Note 8		
TOTAL LIABILITIES AND SHAREHOLDERS' EQUITY	$141,009	$195,094

EXHIBIT 2

Statement of Income
Alaska Airlines, Inc.

	Year Ended December 31,		
	1980	1981	1982
	(amounts in thousands)		
Operating revenues			
Passenger	$107,894	$151,199	$195,620
Freight and mail	13,665	18,207	25,357
Charter	1,396	2,032	1,740
Federal subsidy	2,124	3,507	3,705
Other — net	5,771	7,015	8,103
Total operating revenues	130,850	181,960	234,525
Operating expenses			
Flying operations	53,918	75,589	92,244
Maintenance	9,698	11,432	13,471
Passenger service	11,311	14,208	18,238
Aircraft and traffic servicing	25,446	31,662	38,697
Selling and advertising	14,262	19,971	27,530
General and administrative	5,760	7,572	9,880
Depreciation and amortization	5,350	7,419	9,323
Total operating expenses	125,745	167,853	209,383
Operating income	5,105	14,107	25,142
Other income (expense)			
Interest expense	(5,123)	(6,227)	(6,341)
Interest income	280	1,093	2,918
Interest capitalized	625	29	—
Gain (loss) from disposition of property and equipment	3,591	1,948	(95)
Other — net	(314)	(70)	(80)
	(941)	(3,227)	(3,598)
Income before income tax expense (credit)	4,164	10,880	21,544
Income tax expense (credit)	(964)	3,206	10,975
Net income	$ 5,128	$ 7,674	$ 10,569
Earnings per common share and common equivalent share	$ 1.04	$ 1.06	$ 1.26
Earnings per common share — assuming full dilution	$ 1.04	$ .97	$ 1.15

See accompanying notes to financial statements.

EXHIBIT 3

Statement of Shareholders' Equity
Alaska Airlines, Inc.

	Preferred Stock		Common Stock			
	$1 Par Value	Capital in Excess of Par Value	$1 Par Value	Capital in Excess of Par Value	Treasury Stock at Cost	Retained Earnings
	(amounts in thousands)					
Balances at December 31, 1979	$ —	$ —	$ 4,548	$ 3,581	$ (515)	$ 5,050
Net income for 1980						5,128
Five percent common stock dividend issued			218	846		(1,084)
Stock options exercised			3	10		
Balances at December 31, 1980	—	—	4,769	4,437	(515)	9,094
Net income for 1981						7,674
Issuance of 575,000 equity units consisting of one share of preferred stock and one share of common stock	575	10,140	575	2,012		
Conversion of preferred stock into common stock	(3)	(51)	10	44		
Issuance of 1,210,000 shares of common stock			1,210	5,479		
Cash dividends $2.39 per preferred share						(1,371)
Five percent common stock dividend issued			321	1,847		(2,196)
Stock options exercised			45	83		
Balances at December 31, 1981	572	10,089	6,930	13,902	(515)	13,201
Net income for 1982						10,569
Conversion of preferred stock into common stock	(572)	(10,089)	2,226	8,852		(599)
Cash dividends $2.08 per preferred share						(1,008)
Cash dividends $.12 per common share						(1,083)
Issuance of 1,500,000 shares of common stock			1,500	16,202		
Stock options exercised			3	7		
Balances at December 31, 1982	$ —	$ —	$10,659	$38,963	$ (515)	$21,080

See accompanying notes to financial statements.

EXHIBIT 4

Seven Year Summary of Selected Financial Data — Note A
Alaska Airlines, Inc.

	1976	1977	1978	1979	1980	1981	1982
	(dollar amounts in thousands, except for per share)						
Summary of Operations:							
Airline operating revenues	$69,475	$76,518	$84,246	$ 98,200	$130,850	$181,960	$234,525
Airline operating expenses	62,027	68,454	75,575	95,921	125,745	167,853	209,383
Airline operating income	7,448	8,064	8,671	2,279	5,105	14,107	25,142
Interest expense	(2,721)	(2,439)	(2,926)	(3,373)	(5,123)	(6,227)	(6,341)
Interest capitalized	—	13	7	427	625	29	—
Gain (loss) on disposition of property and equipment	2,031	(56)	2,417	2,938	3,591	1,948	(95)
Other income — net	362	135	689	514	(34)	1,023	2,838
Income before income tax expense (credit)	7,120	5,717	8,858	2,785	4,164	10,880	21,544
Income tax expense (credit)	3,379	2,206	2,699	(239)	(964)	3,206	10,975
Income from airline operations	$ 3,741	$ 3,511	$ 6,159	$ 3,024	$ 5,128	$ 7,674	$ 10,569
Average common shares and common equivalent shares outstanding (000)—Note B	4,932	4,967	4,998	4,918	4,920	5,939	7,566
Income from airline operations per Common share—Note B:							
Primary	$ .76	$ .71	$ 1.23	$ .62	$ 1.04	$ 1.06	$ 1.26
Fully diluted	$ .69	$ .67	$ 1.15	$ .59	$ 1.04	$ .97	$ 1.15
Dividends per share:							
Common — Note C:							
Cash			$ .10	$ .20			$ .12
Stock	5%	5%	5%	5%	5%	5%	
Preferred —							
Cash						$ 2.39	$ 2.08
Financial Data (as of December 31):							
Working capital	$ (441)	$ (5,415)	$ 2,327	$(10,369)	$ (7,569)	$ (10,081)	$ 17,548
Property and equipment, net of depreciation and amortization	$34,154	$41,818	$53,314	$ 55,820	$ 70,853	$108,083	$119,605
Assets of airline operations	$48,920	$53,991	$79,515	$ 70,772	$ 94,294	$141,009	$195,094
Long-term obligations	$26,472	$23,650	$36,035	$ 28,990	$ 42,125	$ 47,700	$ 55,769
Shareholders' equity	$15,726	$19,894	$25,892	$ 12,664	$ 17,785	$ 44,179	$ 70,187

Note A — The financial data presented is based on the Company's continuing air transportation operations, except that shareholders' equity for the years 1976-1978 includes the Company's investment in nonairline assets that were spun-off to shareholders in 1979. An additional year of financial data will be added to this table each year so that by 1985 a ten-year summary will be presented.

Note B — Per share data and average shares outstanding have been restated for all stock dividends.

Note C — Dividend of $.12 per common share declared in 1982, paid in 1983.

EXHIBIT 5

Note 5. Capital Stock	In February 1981, the Company sold 575,000 units of capital stock. Each unit consisted of one share of preferred stock and one share of common stock which were separately transferable immediately upon issuance. The units sold for $25.00 each. The Company received net proceeds of $13,302,000 of which $2,587,000 was allocated to the common stock based on its market value. The remaining $10,715,000 was allocated to the preferred stock. In connection with this stock issue, 105,000 shares of common stock are reserved for issuance at $6.79 per share under a Stock Purchase Warrant expiring February 26, 1986.

Each outstanding share of preferred stock had a scheduled annual cumulative dividend of $2.77, a liquidation preference of $25.00 and was convertible into 3.6816 shares of common stock at a conversion price of $6.79 per common share. In April 1982, the Company issued 600,000 shares of common stock in exchange for 130,435 shares of preferred stock. The exchange rate of 4.6 shares of common stock for each share of preferred stock caused $599,000 to be transferred from Retained Earnings to Common Stock — Capital in excess of par value. In November 1982, the Company called the remaining 441,665 outstanding shares of preferred stock for redemption on December 9, 1982. In November and December 1982, each share of preferred stock was converted into 3.6816 shares of common stock for a total issuance of 1,626,034 shares of common stock.

In September 1981, the Company sold 1,210,000 shares of common stock at a price to the public of $6.125 per share. The Company used the $6,689,000 net proceeds to reduce bank indebtedness.

In October 1982, the Company declared a $.12 per share cash dividend on the Company's common stock. The dividend was paid on January 5, 1983, to shareholders of record at the close of business on December 1, 1982. The total dividend payment was $1,083,000.

In December 1982, the Company sold 1,500,000 shares of common stock at a price to the public of $12.50 per share. The Company intends to use the $17,702,000 net proceeds primarily for the purchase of new equipment.

Note 6. Stock Options	The Company has two stock option plans which provide for the purchase of the Company's common stock by officers and key employees.

The 1966 Qualified Stock Option Plan provided that five-year options could be granted to purchase shares of common stock of the Company at the market price of the stock on the date that the options were granted. This Plan does not allow the granting of options after March 1980. Options to purchase a total of 38,488 and 31,537 shares were outstanding at December 31, 1981 and December 31, 1982, respectively.

The 1975 Stock Option Plan provides for up to ten-year options to purchase shares of common stock at market price on the date the options are granted. The Plan includes stock appreciation rights which permit an optionee to surrender for cancellation up to 50% of his stock options in return for credit by the Company in the amount by which the fair market value of the surrendered optioned shares exceeds the option price measured on the date of surrender of the option. For each optioned share surrendered in exercise of the stock appreciation rights, the optionee must concomitantly exercise one share, and the Company shall apply the stock appreciation credit to that exercise. The Company has made amendments to the Plan which would qualify future options granted under this Plan as incentive stock options under the Economic Recovery Tax Act of 1981. As of December 31, 1981 there were no options outstanding under this Plan. Options to purchase 79,500 shares were outstanding at December 31, 1982.

Transactions relating to the stock option plans during 1980, 1981 and 1982 are as follows:

	1980		1981		1982	
	Shares	Price	Shares	Price	Shares	Price
Outstanding at beginning of year	138,726	$3.174-$4.643	111,033	$2.057-$3.810	38,488	$3.158-$3.629
Granted	30,000	$4.000	—		79,500	$4.750-$5.125
Exercised	(2,547)	$2.160	(45,497)	$2.057-$3.810	(2,983)	$3.158-$3.629
Cancelled	(58,399)	$2.160-$4.000	—		(3,968)	$3.158-$3.629
Surrendered	(2,025)	$2.160	(28,866)	$2.057-$2.999	—	
Stock dividends adjustment	5,278		1,818		—	
Outstanding at end of year	111,033	$2.057-$3.810	38,488	$3.158-$3.629	111,037	$3.158-$5.125
Available for granting in future periods	111,687		117,271		37,771	
Currently exercisable	82,606		32,202		31,537	

The number of shares and the prices per share under the stock option plans are subject to adjustments because of stock dividends, recapitalization, merger, consolidation, stock split or other events affecting shares of stock. Accordingly, the number of shares and prices per share have been adjusted where applicable for certain transactions occurring in 1980 and 1981. No adjustments were necessary for 1982.

In addition, the Company in June 1982 granted to an executive officer a ten-year option to purchase up to 100,000 common shares of treasury stock at a price of $5.125 per common share, the market price of the Company's common stock at date of grant.

Case 6–2

Transamerica Corporation

Transamerica Corporation is a highly diversified company with subsidiaries in insurance and financial services, travel services, and manufacturing. In recent years, the company has been paying increased dividends to a decreasing number of outstanding shares. Selected notes from Transamerica's 1982 annual report are provided in Exhibit 1 and the consolidated balance sheets are presented in Exhibit 2.

A. Dividends

In Transamerica's 1982 annual report, the President's letter to shareholders and employees included the following statement:

> The board of directors raised Transamerica's dividend again in 1982, maintaining our policy of steady dividend increases at a rate that keeps ahead of inflation. The annual dividend rate on our common stock was increased from $1.40 to $1.50 per share, marking the twenty-first year of dividend increases to shareholders who have maintained their investments in Transamerica common stock. Over the last five years, our dividend's compound annual growth rate has been better than 13 percent.

Required

1. Prepare journal entries to record dividends declared and paid in 1980, 1981 and 1982.
2. Compute Transamerica's dividend payout (dividends divided by net income) in 1980, 1981 and 1982.
3. Predict Transamerica's 1983 dividends assuming a 5 percent inflation rate.
4. Note C discusses restrictions on the amount of dividends that can be paid to Transamerica by its subsidiaries and the payment of dividends by Transamerica to shareholders. Why do these dividend restrictions exist? Do these agreements result in any benefit to the company?

B. Treasury Stock

In November 1980, Transamerica announced its intentions to purchase two million of its own shares in the open market. In October 1981, the company announced plans to reacquire as many as five million additional shares.

This case was prepared from published financial statements of Transamerica Corporation.

Required

1. Prepare journal entries to record shares of common stock repurchased in 1980, 1981 and 1982. What was the average price paid for shares repurchased in each year?

2. Speculate as to why Transamerica's management established a policy of re-acquiring the company's shares. How might this policy be related to the company's dividend policy?

EXHIBIT 1

Note B. Shareholders' Equity

	Common Stock	Additional Paid-in Capital	Retained Earnings	Net Unrealized Gain (Loss) on Marketable Equity Securities	Foreign Currency Translation Adjustments
Balance at January 1, 1980	$65,334,000	$322,642,000	$ 964,187,000	$(27,210,000)	
Net income			244,979,000		
Dividends declared on common stock			(78,409,000)		
Common stock reacquired	(614,000)	(10,125,000)			
Other changes	504,000	5,754,000		(1,560,000)	
Balance at December 31, 1980	65,224,000	318,271,000	1,130,757,000	(28,770,000)	
Net income			223,336,000		
Dividends declared on common stock			(86,626,000)		
Common stock reacquired	(1,731,000)	(36,168,000)			
Other changes	614,000	7,865,000		5,274,000	
Balance at December 31, 1981	64,107,000	289,968,000	1,267,467,000	(23,496,000)	
Net income			186,234,000		
Dividends declared on common stock			(91,605,000)		
Common stock reacquired	(2,687,000)	(49,755,000)			
Translation adjustments, including effect of accounting change					$(11,907,000)
Other changes	1,554,000	27,094,000		25,261,000	
Balance at December 31, 1982	$62,974,000	$267,307,000	$1,362,096,000	$ 1,765,000	$(11,907,000)

At December 31, 1982, 1,200,000 shares of preferred stock ($100 par value) and 5,000,000 shares of preference stock (without par value) were authorized, but unissued.

Note C. Retained Earnings Restrictions

Under certain circumstances, the provisions of loan agreements and statutory requirements place limitations on the amount of funds which can be remitted to Transamerica by its consolidated subsidiaries. Of the adjusted net assets of Transamerica's consolidated subsidiaries at December 31, 1982, approximately $1,300,000,000 is so restricted, and $800,000,000 is free for remittance to Transamerica without restriction.

The payment of dividends by Transamerica is also limited to some extent by the provisions of certain loan agreements to which it is a party. These limitations are not considered to have a practical restrictive effect on Transamerica's ability to pay dividends to its shareholders.

Note D. Stock Option Plans

At December 31, 1982, under Transamerica's stock option plans, 4,566,122 shares of common stock (4,185,471 shares at December 31, 1981) were reserved for sale to key employees of the Corporation and subsidiaries at prices generally not less than market value on the date granted. During 1982, options for 135,000 shares were granted, options for 106,450 shares were cancelled due to the exercise of related stock appreciation rights, and options for 294,497 shares were cancelled due to forfeiture. Additionally, options for 805,763 shares were substituted for options granted by Fred. S. James & Co., Inc. prior to its acquisition by the Corporation. Options were exercised for 305,017 shares in 1982, 594,321 shares in 1981 and 321,406 shares in 1980 at aggregate option prices of $4,256,000, $8,060,000 and $2,999,000. Of the options for 3,433,024 shares outstanding at December 31, 1982 (3,198,225 shares at December 31, 1981) at an aggregate option price of $57,055,000, options for 1,591,850 shares were exercisable.

EXHIBIT 2

Consolidated Balance Sheet

Assets	1982	1981
Investments, principally of insurance subsidiaries:		
Equity securities, at market value (cost $138,821,000 in 1982 and $152,404,000 in 1981)	$ 141,307,000	$ 129,128,000
Fixed maturities, at amortized cost	2,523,587,000	2,219,931,000
Mortgage loans and real estate	1,519,702,000	1,415,341,000
Loans to life insurance policyholders	391,342,000	371,664,000
Short-term investments	238,188,000	276,955,000
	4,814,126,000	4,413,019,000
Finance receivables, of which $270,352,000 in 1982 and $305,157,000 in 1981 matures within one year	1,448,478,000	1,268,210,000
Less unearned discount ($103,158,000 in 1982 and $71,638,000 in 1981) and allowance for losses	145,590,000	113,544,000
	1,302,888,000	1,154,666,000
Cash, including temporary investments of $250,044,000 in 1982 and $124,796,000 in 1981	341,407,000	164,688,000
Trade and other accounts receivable	904,609,000	609,707,000
Insurance premiums in course of collection	258,099,000	282,963,000
Inventories of manufacturing subsidiaries	129,109,000	110,809,000
Property and equipment, less allowance for depreciation of $514,325,000 in 1982 and $432,267,000 in 1981:		
Land, buildings and equipment	443,806,000	364,497,000
Equipment held for lease	590,530,000	599,820,000
Aircraft and other flight equipment	344,872,000	312,731,000
Deferred policy acquisition costs of insurance subsidiaries	493,156,000	460,127,000
Separate accounts administered by life insurance subsidiaries	208,257,000	257,791,000
Renewal rights and goodwill, less allowance for amortization of $11,525,000 in 1982 and $7,652,000 in 1981	387,570,000	122,614,000
Other assets	204,909,000	188,910,000
	$10,423,338,000	$9,042,342,000

See notes to financial statements

EXHIBIT 2 *(Continued)*

Liabilities and Shareholders' Equity	Transamerica Corporation and Subsidiaries December 31 1982	1981
Insurance reserves and claims:		
Life insurance policy reserves	$ 3,517,227,000	$3,185,885,000
Property and casualty insurance unearned premiums	307,534,000	325,613,000
Reported and estimated unreported claims	809,936,000	775,748,000
	4,634,697,000	4,287,246,000
Notes and loans payable, of which $528,932,000 in 1982 and $315,718,000 in 1981 matures within one year:		
Consumer lending	1,347,884,000	1,136,339,000
Equipment leasing	303,649,000	273,944,000
Other	1,062,074,000	658,920,000
	2,713,607,000	2,069,203,000
Accounts payable and other liabilities	910,634,000	589,443,000
Income taxes, of which $193,910,000 in 1982 and $115,685,000 in 1981 is deferred	273,908,000	240,613,000
Separate account liabilities	208,257,000	257,791,000
Shareholders' equity:		
Common Stock ($1 par value):		
Authorized—150,000,000 shares		
Outstanding—62,973,907 shares in 1982 and 64,106,606 shares in 1981, after deducting shares in treasury (3,689,035 in 1982 and 2,556,336 in 1981)	62,974,000	64,107,000
Additional paid-in capital	267,307,000	289,968,000
Retained earnings	1,362,096,000	1,267,467,000
Net unrealized gain (loss) on marketable equity securities	1,765,000	(23,496,000)
Foreign currency translation adjustments	(11,907,000)	
	1,682,235,000	1,598,046,000
	$10,423,338,000	$9,042,342,000

Case 6–3

Carter Hawley Hale Stores, Inc.

Carter Hawley Hale Stores is a diversified North American retailer operating department stores, high-fashion specialty stores, and specialized merchandising operations through 11 divisions. The company markets apparel and accessories, home furnishings, books, and gifts.

The company's income statements and balance sheets for fiscal years 1977 and 1978 appear in Exhibits 1 and 2. In addition, the following information may be useful.

Common Stock

Cash dividends on common stock were $1.00 per share in fiscal 1978 and $0.98 per share in 1977. The market price of common stock ranged from a low of $16\frac{1}{2}$ to a high of $21\frac{1}{4}$. At year end, the stock price closed at $17\frac{5}{8}$, which was equal to the average stock price for fiscal 1978.

Preferred Stock

Cash dividends on cumulative preferred stock were $2.00 per share in 1978 and 1977. On average, 1,955,000 shares were outstanding in 1978, and 1,973,000 were outstanding in 1977. Par value is $5.00, and each share can be converted into 1.7 shares of common stock.

Convertible Debentures

Included in long-term debt, the company has outstanding $28,000,000 in $4\frac{3}{4}$% convertible debentures due in 1987. Each of these bonds can be converted into 24 shares of common stock (i.e., the conversion price is $41.67 per share).

Employee Stock Options

The company's stock option plans provide that employees may be granted options to purchase the common stock of the company at not less than the market price on the date of the grant. Options become exercisable one year after the date of the grant. At February 3, 1979, options for 274,500 shares were outstanding, of which 158,000 were exercisable.

This case was prepared from published financial statements of Carter Hawley Hale Stores, Inc.

Exercise Price	Number Outstanding	Number Exercisable
$17.00	84,600	72,000
$19.00	91,900	68,000
$21.00	98,000	18,000

Required

1. Compute earnings per share for Carter Hawley Hale Stores for fiscal 1978. How should the convertible securities and stock options be treated in this computation? Do not be concerned about having the correct answer but be prepared to defend the number you come up with.

EXHIBIT 1

Statement of Earnings
Carter Hawley Hale Stores, Inc. and Consolidated Subsidiaries

(In thousands, except per share data)	1978	1977
		(Restated)
Sales	$2,116,586	$1,647,642
Equity in net earnings of House of Fraser Limited,		
including net gain on sale of this investment		3,263
	2,116,586	1,650,905
Costs and expenses		
Cost of goods sold	1,203,120	934,219
Selling, operating and administrative expenses	603,314	461,731
Taxes other than income taxes	53,742	45,548
Rentals of real property	42,666	33,662
Depreciation and amortization	45,492	38,174
Net interest expense	51,232	39,304
	1,999,566	1,552,638
Earnings before income taxes	117,020	98,267
Income taxes	53,200	44,100
Net earnings	$ 63,820	$ 54,167
Net earnings per share of common stock		
Primary	$2.52	$2.16
Fully diluted	$2.32	$2.01

EXHIBIT 2

Balance Sheet

Carter Hawley Hale Stores, Inc. and Consolidated Subsidiaries

(In thousands)	February 3, 1979	January 28, 1978
		(Restated)
Assets		
Current assets		
Cash	$ 25,819	$ 27,035
Short term investments		53,000
Accounts receivable, net	238,188	193,511
Merchandise inventories	378,034	289,723
Other current assets	25,516	12,771
	667,557	576,040
Property and equipment, net	641,399	541,355
Investment in Carter Hawley Hale Credit Corp.	63,054	38,860
Other assets	23,477	21,812
	$1,395,487	$1,178,067
Liabilities and Shareholders' Equity		
Current liabilities		
Current installments on long term debt and		
capital lease obligations	$ 14,133	$ 12,612
Accounts payable and accrued expenses	194,625	145,031
Dividends payable	7,017	5,905
Current income taxes	18,954	20,522
Deferred income taxes	75,450	61,880
	310,179	245,950
Long term debt	305,034	218,218
Capital lease obligations	204,744	200,733
Other liabilities	44,368	29,544
Shareholders' equity		
Preferred stock, $5 par value (aggregate		
liquidation preference $87,562)	9,729	9,821
Common stock, $5 par value	120,741	117,348
Other paid-in capital	162,025	154,317
Accumulated earnings	238,667	202,136
	531,162	483,622
	$1,395,487	$1,178,067

Case 6–4

Corning Glass Works

Corning Glass Works is an international company specializing in the manufacture and sale of glass, ceramic, and related products. The company's products for the home are well known and include Pyrex and Corning Ware. Steuben Glass, a separate division, manufactures and sells Steuben crystal which is famous for its design, craftsmanship, and cost. The company also manufactures glass bulbs for television picture tubes; glass for incandescent, fluorescent, and neon lighting; glass-ceramic smooth-top cooking surfaces; and optical glass including blanks sold under the Sunsensor, Photogray, and Photosun trademarks.

In addition, the company manufactures a wide range of products used in industrial, scientific, and military applications.

Recording Investments in Other Companies

The company's "Principles of Consolidation" are included among its Statement of Accounting Policies:

> The consolidated financial statements include the accounts of all significant subsidiary companies. The major foreign subsidiaries are consolidated as of dates up to four weeks earlier than the consolidated balance sheet dates.

In note 6, Investments, the company provides additional information about its equity-basis companies and for Owens-Corning Fiberglass Corporation (OCF):

> The following information is presented for all equity-basis companies and for Owens-Corning Fiberglass:

In Thousands	1980	1979	1978
Equity in undistributed earnings of equity-basis companies included in retained earnings	$205,895	$180,326	$146,529
Dividends received from equity-basis companies	18,293	11,486	8,399
Dividends received from OCF	8,873	9,020	7,564
Excess of quoted market value over cost of investments in OCF	212,803	211,689	197,309

Under a consent decree, Corning is required to divest 90% of its OCF holdings by October 1986. Substantial extraordinary gains (measured by the difference between Corning's cost and the fair value of OCF stock) will be generated when the OCF stock is divested. If Corning exchanges these shares for outstanding Corning common shares, the Internal Revenue Service has

---

This case was prepared from published financial statements of Corning Glass Works.

advised that Corning would not be subject to a capital gains tax on the exchange. However, no decision has been made as to the timing or method of disposition.

Corning's 1980 and 1979 consolidated balance sheets and its 1980, 1979, and 1978 statements of income and retained earnings are presented in Exhibits 1 and 2.

Required

A. Short-term investments

1. What is the ending balance in the "Short-term investments" account for 1980? What distinguishes "Short-term investments" from "Investments" listed in the noncurrent asset section of the balance sheet?
2. Assume that all short-term investments are made up of equity securities (common and preferred stock) of other corporations. How would the ending balance in "Short-term investments" have been affected if the market value of the portfolio of securities had been substantially greater than its historical cost and if the market value had been substantially less than cost?
3. How would your answers to question 2 change if the short-term investment portfolio consisted entirely of debt securities?

B. Equity-basis investments

1. The balance sheets include "Investments in associated companies, at equity." The income statement includes "Equity in earnings of associated companies." Explain the rationale behind the equity method for accounting for investments in other companies. Why aren't they consolidated into the financial statements?
2. Dividends received from equity-basis associated companies amounted to $18,293,000 in 1980. Record 1980 journal entries relating to Corning's equity investments.

C. Cost-basis investments

1. The balance sheets also include "Investments other, at cost." The income statements include dividend income. Explain the rationale behind the cost method for accounting for investments in other companies.
2. Owens-Corning Fiberglass paid dividends of $1.20 per share in 1979 and 1980. How many shares of OCF did Corning hold (on average) in 1980? Given total outstanding shares of OCF were 30,628,063 at the end of 1980, is the use of the cost method to record Corning's investment in OCF appropriate?
3. Record journal entries related to Corning's investments in OCF during 1980. Assume that the average price of OCF shares sold during 1980 was $28 and that the historical cost of the shares was $.57.

4. OCF reported net income of $54,321,000 for 1980. Estimate Corning's 1980 net income as if the equity method had been used to record the company's investment in OCF?

5. Although it is not permissible under current generally accepted accounting principles, what would have been Corning's reported 1980 net income and total assets if the company had used current market value (instead of the cost method) to account for its investment in OCF?

EXHIBIT 1

Consolidated Balance Sheets

December 28, 1980, and December 30, 1979	1980	1979
Assets		
Current Assets		
Cash	$ 33,565	$ 33,113
Short-term investments, at cost which approximates market value	89,719	177,814
Receivables, net of doubtful accounts and allowances— $15,434/1980; $10,683/1979	223,445	197,361
Inventories	230,332	204,151
Prepaid expenses including deferred taxes on income	70,089	60,496
Total current assets	647,150	672,935
Investments		
Associated companies, at equity	280,187	221,659
Other, at cost	12,957	7,225
	293,144	228,884
Plant and Equipment, at Cost		
Land	17,949	15,768
Buildings	213,969	187,292
Equipment	883,482	784,534
Accumulated depreciation	(579,491)	(521,702)
	535,909	465,892
Goodwill	7,351	8,006
Other Assets	16,070	9,446
	$1,499,624	$1,385,163
Liabilities and Stockholders' Equity		
Current Liabilities		
Loans payable	$ 45,695	$ 55,217
Accounts payable	86,390	79,163
Taxes on income payable	70,221	65,895
Wages and employee benefits accrued	72,802	66,930
Other accrued liabilities	69,719	67,164
Total current liabilities	344,827	334,369
Accrued Furnace Repairs	23,752	19,630
Other Liabilities & Deferred Credits	33,210	27,971
Loans Payable Beyond One Year	153,606	147,146
Deferred Investment Credits and Deferred Taxes on Income	24,823	23,020
Minority Interest in Subsidiary Companies	6,699	5,063
Common Stockholders' Equity		
Common stock, including excess over par value— Par value $5 per share; authorized—25,000,000 shares (net of cost of 306,394 and 127,544 shares of common stock in treasury— $16,504/1980; $7,110/1979)	93,059	95,956
Retained earnings	819,648	732,008
Total common stockholders' equity	912,707	827,964
	$1,499,624	$1,385,163

EXHIBIT 2

Consolidated Statements of Income and Retained Earnings

Years Ending December 28, 1980, December 30, 1979, and December 31, 1978	1980	1979	1978
Net Sales	$1,529,670	$1,421,598	$1,251,728
Cost of sales	1,082,253	983,907	849,710
Gross Margin	447,417	437,691	402,018
Selling, general and administrative expenses	283,575	247,537	217,874
Research and development expenses	78,767	75,804	63,570
	362,342	323,341	281,444
Income from Operations	85,075	114,350	120,574
Royalty, interest and dividend income	29,011	38,846	27,061
Interest expense	(18,732)	(22,016)	(18,312)
Other income, net	27,060	12,260	8,195
Income before taxes on income	122,414	143,440	137,518
Taxes on income	46,951	61,539	60,531
Income before minority interest and equity earnings	75,463	81,901	76,987
Minority interest in earnings of subsidiaries	(2,518)	(2,202)	(1,566)
Equity in earnings of associated companies	41,775	45,244	28,942
Net Income (per share, $6.26/1980; $7.05/1979; $5.89/1978)	114,720	124,943	104,363
Retained Earnings at Beginning of Year	732,008	641,436	567,763
Effect on Retained Earnings at beginning of year of the business combination with Gilford Instrument Laboratories, Inc.	11,923		
Dividends on Common Stock (per share/$2.17/1980; $1.94/1979; $1.73/1978)	(39,003)	(34,371)	(30,690)
Retained Earnings at End of Year	$ 819,648	$ 732,008	$ 641,436

In thousands, except per share amounts.

Case 6–5

General Motors Corporation

General Motors Corporation (GM) is a vertically integrated business involved in the manufacture, assembly, and sale of automobiles, trucks, and related parts and accessories. GM sales account for 20% of worldwide auto production and 43% of U.S. sales, making it the world's largest automotive products company. GM's products are marketed through retail dealers and distributors throughout the world. GMAC, a wholly owned subsidiary, provides financial services and insurance to dealers and customers.

Note 1 to GM's 1982 consolidated financial statements provided the following explanation of the company's consolidation policy:

Principles of Consolidation

The consolidated financial statements include the accounts of the Corporation and all domestic and foreign subsidiaries which are more than 50% owned and engaged principally in manufacturing or wholesale marketing of General Motors products. General Motors' share of earnings or losses of nonconsolidated subsidiaries and of associates in which at least 20% of the voting securities is owned is generally included in consolidated income under the equity method of accounting.

General Motors' 1981 and 1982 balance sheets and income statements are provided in Exhibits 1 and 2. Also provided is a condensed financial statement for GMAC (Exhibit 3).

Required

1. Prepare a journal entry to record General Motors' equity in the earnings of GMAC.
2. What entry did GM make to record dividends received from GMAC?
3. Assume that General Motors consolidated its investment in GMAC. Prepare the necessary consolidation and elimination entries. State your assumptions.
4. What would have been the effect on 1982 net income had GM consolidated GMAC?
5. What would have been the effect on the 1982 balance sheet had GM consolidated GMAC?
6. Speculate as to why General Motors accounts for investments in GMAC using the equity method rather than consolidation.

This case was prepared from published financial statements of the General Motors Corporation.

EXHIBIT 1

CONSOLIDATED BALANCE SHEET

December 31, 1982 and 1981
(Dollars in Millions Except Per Share Amounts)

ASSETS	1982	1981
Current Assets		
Cash	$ 279.6	$ 204.1
United States Government and other marketable securities and time deposits—at cost, which approximates market of $2,835.5 and $1,086.3	2,846.6	1,116.6
Total cash and marketable securities	3,126.2	1,320.7
Accounts and notes receivable (including GMAC and its subsidiaries—$312.0 and $636.2)—less allowances	2,864.5	3,643.3
Inventories (less allowances) (Note 1)	6,184.2	7,222.7
Prepaid expenses and deferred income taxes	1,868.2	1,527.1
Total Current Assets	14,043.1	13,713.8
Equity in Net Assets of Nonconsolidated Subsidiaries and Associates (principally GMAC and its subsidiaries—Note 8)	4,231.1	3,369.5
Other Investments and Miscellaneous Assets—at cost (less allowances)	1,550.0	1,783.5
Common Stock Held for the Incentive Program (Note 3)	35.2	71.5
Property		
Real estate, plants and equipment—at cost (Note 9)	37,687.2	34,811.5
Less accumulated depreciation (Note 9)	18,148.9	16,317.4
Net real estate, plants and equipment	19,538.3	18,494.1
Special tools—at cost (less amortization)	2,000.1	1,546.6
Total Property	21,538.4	20,040.7
Total Assets	$41,397.8	$38,979.0

LIABILITIES AND STOCKHOLDERS' EQUITY	1982	1981
Current Liabilities		
Accounts payable (principally trade)	$ 3,600.7	$ 3,699.7
Loans payable (principally overseas) (Note 11)	1,182.5	1,727.8
Accrued liabilities (Note 10)	7,601.8	7,127.5
Total Current Liabilities	12,385.0	12,555.0
Long-Term Debt (Note 11)	4,452.0	3,801.1
Capitalized Leases	293.1	242.9
Other Liabilities (including GMAC and its subsidiaries—$876.0 and $424.0)	4,259.8	3,092.7
Deferred Credits (including investment tax credits—$1,158.7 and $1,111.1)	1,720.8	1,566.2
Stockholders' Equity (Notes 3 and 12)		
Preferred stocks ($5.00 series, $183.6; $3.75 series, $100.0)	283.6	283.6
Common stock (issued, 312,363,657 and 304,804,228 shares)	520.6	508.0
Capital surplus (principally additional paid-in capital)	1,930.4	1,589.5
Net income retained for use in the business	15,552.5	15,340.0
Total Stockholders' Equity	18,287.1	17,721.1
Total Liabilities and Stockholders' Equity	$41,397.8	$38,979.0

EXHIBIT 2

STATEMENT OF CONSOLIDATED INCOME

For the Years Ended December 31, 1982, 1981 and 1980
(Dollars in Millions Except Per Share Amounts)

	1982	1981	1980
Net Sales (Note 2)	$60,025.6	$62,698.5	$57,728.5
Costs and Expenses			
Cost of sales and other operating charges, exclusive of items listed below	51,548.3	55,185.2	52,099.8
Selling, general and administrative expenses	2,964.9	2,715.0	2,636.7
Depreciation of real estate, plants and equipment	2,403.0	1,837.3	1,458.1
Amortization of special tools	2,147.5	2,568.9	2,719.6
Total Costs and Expenses	59,063.7	62,306.4	58,914.2
Operating Income (Loss)	961.9	392.1	(1,185.7)
Other income less income deductions—net (Note 4)	476.3	367.7	348.7
Interest expense (Note 1)	(1,415.4)	(897.9)	(531.9)
Income (Loss) before Income Taxes	22.8	(138.1)	(1,368.9)
United States, foreign and other income taxes (credit) (Note 6)	(252.2)	(123.1)	(385.3)
Income (Loss) after Income Taxes	275.0	(15.0)	(983.6)
Equity in earnings of nonconsolidated subsidiaries and associates (dividends received amounted to $412.7 in 1982, $189.7 in 1981 and $116.8 in 1980)	687.7	348.4	221.1
Net Income (Loss)	962.7	333.4	(762.5)
Dividends on preferred stocks	12.9	12.9	12.9
Earnings (Loss) on Common Stock	$ 949.8	$ 320.5	($ 775.4)
Average number of shares of common stock outstanding (in millions)	307.4	299.1	292.4
Earnings (Loss) Per Share of Common Stock (Note 7)	$3.09	$1.07	($2.65)

EXHIBIT 3

NOTE 8. General Motors Acceptance Corporation and Subsidiaries

Condensed Consolidated Balance Sheet (Dollars in Millions)	1982	1981
Cash and investments in securities	$ 1,674.2	$ 1,709.9
Finance receivables—net (including GM and affiliates—$876.0 and $424.0)	41,771.1	39,692.5
Other assets	969.4	446.2
Total Assets	$44,414.7	$41,848.6
Short-term debt	$22,114.1	$23,256.1
Accounts payable and other liabilities (including GM and affiliates—$312.0 and $636.2)	2,689.0	2,507.5
Long-term debt	15,695.5	12,849.9
Stockholder's equity	3,916.1	3,235.1
Total Liabilities and Stockholder's Equity	$44,414.7	$41,848.6

Condensed Consolidated Statement of Income (Dollars in Millions)	1982	1981	1980
Gross Revenue	$7,255.4	$6,153.9	$4,566.8
Interest and discount	4,482.1	4,174.7	2,889.6
Other expenses	2,085.3	1,614.0	1,446.2
Total Expenses	6,567.4	5,788.7	4,335.8
Net Income	$ 688.0	$ 365.2	$ 231.0

7

FUNDS FLOW AND FINANCIAL STATEMENT ANALYSIS

Case 7–1

Danly Machine Corporation

Danly Machine Corporation manufactures precision-built machine tools and accessories including hydraulic stamping presses, woodworking machines, metal cutting machines, die sets, and die-makers' supplies. Danly markets its products throughout the United States and Canada as well as in Europe, South America, Australia, and Japan. The company was founded in 1922. Danly's 1978 and 1977 consolidated balance sheets and consolidated statements of income and retained earnings are presented in Exhibits 1 and 2.

A. Statement of Changes in Financial Position

The following information was obtained from the notes to Danly's consolidated financial statements:

This case was prepared from published financial statements of Danly Machine Corporation.

1. During 1978, Danly recorded depreciation of property, plant, and equipment totaling $2,317,000.
2. During fiscal 1978, Danly sold property, plant, and equipment for $52,000. These assets had a book value of $9,000.
3. Proceeds from long-term borrowings totaled $14,500,000 during 1978, including $10,000,000 from an insurance company for an 8⅞% note.

Required

1. Prepare the journal entries to record
   a. depreciation of property, plant, and equipment during 1978
   b. the sale of property, plant, and equipment described in point 2
   c. property, plant, and equipment purchased during 1978
2. Prepare a journal entry to record
   a. the issuance of long-term debt as described in point 3
   b. the retirement of long-term debt and/or reclassification of long-term debt as current maturities
3. Prepare a statement of changes in financial position for Danly Machine Corporation using a working capital definition of funds.

B. Cash Flow Statements

Some accountants have argued that the statement of changes in financial position does not adequately portray a firm's solvency when based on working capital flows. Cash flow statements have been suggested as a supplement or replacement for the statement of changes.

Required

1. Convert "working capital provided by operations" as computed in part A into "cash flow provided by operations." State your assumptions.
2. Under what circumstances might these two measures of funds flow tell different stories about a firm's solvency?

EXHIBIT 1
Danly Machine Corporation
Consolidated Balance Sheets
(in thousands)

	June 30	
	1978	1977
Assets		
Current Assets:		
Cash	$ 4,689	$ 4,626
Accounts receivable	14,895	16,353
Inventories:		
Finished goods	4,494	3,660
Work in process	18,055	8,900
Raw materials and factory supplies	12,631	10,568
Total inventories	35,180	23,128
Prepaid expenses	367	538
Total current assets	55,131	44,645
Other Receivables and Investments	869	444
Property, Plant and Equipment	47,239	41,379
Less accumulated depreciation	32,429	30,810
Net property, plant and equipment	14,810	10,569
	$70,810	$55,658
Liabilities and Shareholders' Equity		
Current Liabilities:		
Notes payable—banks	$10,171	$ 2,059
Current maturities of long-term debt	607	805
Accounts payable	6,523	4,531
Accrued expenses:		
Salaries, wages and vacation pay	2,056	2,317
Payroll, property and other taxes	1,455	1,275
Income taxes	1,020	1,757
Pension contribution	2,000	1,986
Other	677	439
Advance payments from customers	983	265
Total current liabilities	25,492	15,434
Long-Term Debt, Exclusive of Current Maturities		
(Notes 2 and 5)	13,852	11,916
Shareholders' Equity:		
Common capital stock, $5.00 par value per share.		
Authorized 1,000,000 shares; issued 849,670 shares	4,248	4,248
Additional paid-in capital	2,672	2,672
Retained earnings (Note 2)	24,546	21,388
Total shareholders' equity	31,466	28,308
	$70,810	$55,658

EXHIBIT 2
Danly Machine Corporation
Consolidated Statements of Net Income and Retained Earnings
(in thousands, except per share data)

	Year Ended June 30	
	1978	1977
Net Sales	$86,672	$75,119
Cost of Goods Sold	65,033	54,820
Gross Profit on Sales	21,639	20,299
Selling, Die Set Stockroom, Assembly and Shipping and Administrative and General Expenses	14,772	13,131
Operating Profit	6,867	7,168
Other Income	1,468	1,052
	8,335	8,220
Other Deductions:		
Interest	1,491	1,069
Other	172	258
	1,663	1,327
Income Before Income Taxes	6,672	6,893
Income Taxes (Note 4)	2,664	3,251
Net Income (per share: 1978—$4.72; 1977—$4.29)	4,008	3,642
Retained Earnings at Beginning of Year	21,388	18,341
	25,396	21,983
Less Cash Dividends Paid (per share: 1978—$1.00; 1977—$.70)	850	595
Retained Earnings at End of Year	$24,546	$21,388

Case 7–2

American Stores

American Stores Company (ASC) is engaged primarily in the retail food and grocery business. It is the sixth largest supermarket chain and the eleventh largest retailing business in the United States. The company operates 760 supermarkets, 446 of which are located in seven East Coast states. The remaining stores are located in Arizona and California. The company also buys and develops commercial properties through its real estate subsidiary, which accounts for less than five percent of sales.

ASC's consolidated income statements and balance sheets for the years ended March 31, 1979, and April 1, 1978, are presented in Exhibits 1 and 2, along with selected notes to the financial statements (Exhibit 3). In addition, the following information may be useful:

a. ASC leases most of its supermarket, drug, and general merchandise stores under long-term leases covering 15 to 20 years. During fiscal 1979, the company entered into several new lease agreements which were classified as capital leases. The present value of future minimum lease payments on these leases was $21,253,000.

b. Purchases of property, plant and equipment totaled $74,519,000 in 1979.

c. Amortization of leased property under capital leases was included among depreciation and amortization expense in the statement of earnings.

d. Long-term borrowing totaled $923,000 in 1979.

e. During 1979, officers and key management employees exercised stock options on 60,962 shares of common stock (see Note 7). Proceeds from the sale of stock under the stock option plan totaled $1,120,000.

Required

1. Prepare a statement of changes in financial position using a working capital definition of funds.

This case was prepared from published financial statements of American Stores Company.

EXHIBIT 1

American Stores Company and Subsidiaries
Consolidated Statements of Earnings
Fiscal years ended March 31, 1979 and April 1, 1978

Current Earnings	1979	1978*
Sales	$4,183,222,000	3,737,634,000
Cost of merchandise sold, including warehousing and transportation expenses	3,286,278,000	2,951,464,000
Gross profit	896,944,000	786,170,000
Wages, rents, advertising, administrative and other operating expenses	778,384,000	686,436,000
Depreciation and amortization (notes 3 and 5)	46,255,000	41,423,000
	824,639,000	727,859,000
Operating profit	72,305,000	58,311,000
Other income:		
Gain on sale and retirement of assets, etc.	5,653,000	1,690,000
Interest income	10,295,000	5,941,000
	15,948,000	7,631,000
Other deductions:		
Interest on long-term indebtedness	19,461,000	19,045,000
Other interest	656,000	616,000
	20,117,000	19,661,000
Earnings before income taxes	68,136,000	46,281,000
Federal and state income taxes (note 6)	30,045,000	20,290,000
Net earnings	$ 38,091,000	25,991,000
Net earnings per share of common stock	$7.15	4.92

EXHIBIT 2

American Stores Company and Subsidiaries
Consolidated Balance Sheets
March 31, 1979 and April 1, 1978

Assets	1979	1978*
Current assets:		
Cash	$ 1,243,000	13,619,000
Time deposits and certificates of deposit	65,990,000	73,381,000
Short-term marketable securities, at approximate market	2,093,000	19,883,000
Receivables:		
Trade	13,829,000	13,271,000
Other	5,436,000	4,311,000
	19,265,000	17,582,000
Less allowance for doubtful receivables	125,000	110,000
	19,140,000	17,472,000
Inventories (note 2):		
Merchandise	316,242,000	264,259,000
Supplies	9,173,000	8,204,000
	325,415,000	272,463,000
Prepaid expenses	23,062,000	16,937,000
Properties to be developed and sold within one year	6,263,000	6,164,000
Total current assets	443,206,000	419,919,000
Property, plant and equipment, at cost (note 4)		
Land	22,369,000	16,736,000
Buildings	73,802,000	76,371,000
Machinery, equipment and fixtures	295,784,000	250,853,000
Leasehold costs and improvements	51,845,000	40,298,000
	443,800,000	384,258,000
Less accumulated depreciation and amortization (note 3)	191,122,000	165,104,000
Net property, plant and equipment	252,678,000	219,154,000
Leased property under capital leases, less accumulated amortization of $63,016,000 in 1979 and $60,344,000 in 1978 (note 5)	97,421,000	84,326,000
Other assets	14,620,000	8,400,000
	$807,925,000	731,799,000

EXHIBIT 2 *(Continued)*

Liabilities and Shareholders' Equity	1979	1978*
Current liabilities:		
Current instalments of long-term debt (note 4)	$ 3,735,000	5,454,000
Current obligations under capital leases (note 5)	6,857,000	5,921,000
Accounts payable:		
Trade	166,856,000	147,068,000
Taxes withheld from employees	5,836,000	7,915,000
Other	11,864,000	9,158,000
	184,556,000	164,141,000
Accrued expenses:		
Payrolls	38,915,000	33,379,000
Taxes, other than income taxes	9,285,000	11,016,000
Interest	2,809,000	2,574,000
Other	30,407,000	22,018,000
	81,416,000	68,987,000
Dividend payable	2,997,000	2,782,000
Federal and state income taxes (note 6)	13,496,000	6,653,000
Construction and other loans on properties to be sold	927,000	1,866,000
Total current liabilities	293,984,000	255,804,000
Long-term debt, excluding current instalments (note 4)	95,364,000	101,133,000
Obligations under capital leases, less current portion (note 5)	109,102,000	94,951,000
Deferred income taxes (note 6)	17,036,000	14,857,000
Other liabilities	2,564,000	2,443,000
Shareholders' equity:		
Preferred stock of $1 par value. Authorized 1,000,000 shares; issued none	—	—
Common stock of $1 par value. Authorized 10,000,000 shares; issued 5,402,774 shares in 1979 and 5,341,812 shares in 1978 (note 7)	5,403,000	5,342,000
Capital in excess of par value of common stock (note 7)	134,413,000	133,354,000
Earnings retained for use in the business (note 4)	151,078,000	124,934,000
	290,894,000	263,630,000
Less 41,064 shares common treasury stock, at cost	1,019,000	1,019,000
Total shareholders' equity	289,875,000	262,611,000
Lease commitments and litigation (notes 5 and 9)		
	$807,925,000	731,799,000

EXHIBIT 3

American Stores Company and Subsidiaries
Notes to Financial Statements
March 31, 1979 and April 1, 1978

(1) Summary of Significant Accounting Policies

Definition of Fiscal Year

The company's fiscal year ends on the Saturday nearest to March 31. Fiscal year 1979 ended March 31, 1979; fiscal year 1978 ended April 1, 1978. Both of these years comprised 52 weeks.

Basis of Consolidation

The consolidated financial statements include the accounts of the company and all subsidiaries. All significant inter-company accounts and transactions have been eliminated in consolidation.

Inventories

Inventories are stated at the lower of cost or market. The last-in, first-out (LIFO) method is used to determine the cost of certain categories of grocery inventories. Cost of the balance of grocery inventories and all other inventories is computed by either the first-in, first-out (FIFO) or average cost methods.

Property, Plant and Equipment

Depreciation and amortization charged to earnings for financial statement purposes are generally computed using the straight-line method applied to individual property items. For income tax purposes, depreciation is computed by accelerated methods applied to composite groupings of assets.

Maintenance, repairs, renewals and minor betterments are charged to earnings. Where betterments are significant in amount and tend to increase operating efficiency or capacity, they are capitalized and depreciated.

At the time of sale or retirement of plant and equipment, the cost and related accumulated depreciation or amortization are removed from the accounts and the resulting gains or losses are carried to earnings.

Costs of Opening and Closing Stores

The costs of opening new stores are charged against earnings in the year in which they are incurred. When operations are discontinued and a store is closed, the remaining investment in fixtures and improvements, net of expected salvage, is charged against earnings and provision made for the remaining liability under the lease, net of expected sublease recovery.

Income Taxes

The company provides deferred income taxes or credits where there are timing differences in recording income and expenses for financial reporting and tax purposes. These timing differences relate primarily to accelerated depreciation, capitalized leases and reserves not currently tax deductible.

The company reduces its current income tax provision for investment tax credits in the year in which the credits arise.

Pension Costs

Pension costs are actuarially computed and include amortization of prior service cost over periods ranging to 30 years. The company's policy is to fund pension costs accrued.

Net Earnings Per Share

Net earnings per share of common stock are based on the average number of common shares outstanding during the year. Common share equivalents in the form of stock options are excluded from the calculation since they have no material dilutive effect on per share figures.

(2) Inventories

The dry grocery inventories located in both stores and warehouses of the company's food store subsidiaries are valued at last-in, first-out (LIFO) cost. Such inventories amounted to $140,469,000 at March 31, 1979 and $125,844,000 at April 1, 1978. If the first-in, first-out (FIFO) and average cost methods had been used, inventories would have been $50,094,000 higher at March 31, 1979 and $38,237,000 higher at April 1, 1978.

The amounts of the opening and closing inventories used in computing cost of merchandise sold are stated hereunder:

April 2, 1977	$244,475,000
April 1, 1978	264,259,000
March 31, 1979	316,242,000

(3) Depreciation and Amortization

Depreciation and amortization are recorded at rates estimated to provide for the retirement of buildings

EXHIBIT 3 *(Continued)*

and machinery, equipment and fixtures at the end of their useful lives. The annual depreciation rates generally used are as follows:

Buildings	2% to 20%
	(principally 4%)
Machinery, equipment and fixtures:	
Retail store fixtures	7½% to 33⅓%
Other machinery, equipment and fixtures	5% to 33⅓%
Trucks and automobiles	10% to 25%

Leasehold costs and improvements are amortized generally over the term of the related leases.

(4) Indebtedness

A summary of long-term debt at March 31, 1979 and April 1, 1978 is shown below:

	1979	1978
9⅝% sinking fund debentures due July 1, 2001	$ 50,000,000	50,000,000
9⅞% sinking fund debentures due August 1, 1990	16,711,000	20,320,000
Notes payable due June 30, 1980	8,500,000	10,500,000
Mortgage loans payable	17,804,000	19,424,000
Industrial development revenue bonds due April 1, 1995	3,700,000	3,700,000
Purchase agreement	2,384,000	2,643,000
	99,099,000	106,587,000
Current instalments	3,735,000	5,454,000
Long-term	$ 95,364,000	101,133,000

Sinking fund payments, sufficient to retire $2,500,000 principal amount of the 9⅝% sinking fund debentures, are due annually beginning July 1, 1982. Annual payments of $1,560,000 are required to the sinking fund for the 9⅞% debentures. The company has repurchased $2,049,000 principal amount of 9⅞% debentures which reduce March 31, 1979 figures in the above summary. Such reacquired debentures will be used to satisfy all of the August 1, 1979 sinking fund payment and a part of the subsequent year requirement.

The notes payable due June 30, 1980 bear interest at prime rate plus ½% (12¼% at March 31, 1979) with a maximum average rate of 7½% to maturity. The notes are payable in quarterly instalments of $500,000 until March 31, 1980 with the remainder of $6,500,000 payable at maturity.

The various mortgage loans are payable in monthly instalments of approximately $256,000 through October 1, 1979 and lesser amounts thereafter through December 1, 2004 (applied first to interest and then to principal) and are secured by property, plant and equipment with a carrying value of $22,952,000. The loans bear interest at various rates, ranging from 6% to 10% (average 9⅜%).

Industrial development revenue bonds (average interest rate 7.4%) were issued to finance part of the cost of a food processing plant of a subsidiary leased from the municipality in which it is located. The annual payments made by the subsidiary are in amounts sufficient to pay principal and interest expense on the bonds. Repayments of this debt are scheduled to commence on April 1, 1980 ($500,000) and range in amount from $200,000 in 1984 to $1,500,000 in 1995. The cost of the plant and related facilities have been included in property, plant and equipment as if they were owned by the company.

The purchase agreement relates to a distribution center property and requires equal semi-annual payments through 1986 applied first to interest (at 4¾%) and the remainder to principal.

The aggregate amounts of long-term debt maturing in each of the five fiscal years subsequent to March 31, 1979 are: 1980—$3,735,000; 1981—$9,914,000; 1982—$2,639,000; 1983—$5,180,000 and 1984—$5,145,000.

Lines of credit are made available to the company by commercial banks. At March 31, 1979, the unused and available lines of credit totaled $63,300,000, under which the company has agreed to maintain compensating balances totaling approximately $6,330,000, which is less than normal bank balances required to cover day-to-day transactions. In the event the lines are drawn upon, additional cash balances may be required by the banks. There were no short-term borrowings during fiscal years 1979 and 1978 except the construction and other loans on properties to be sold.

The various loan agreements impose certain restrictions with respect to maintenance of working capital, amount of liabilities, payment of dividends and purchase of capital shares. Under the most restrictive

EXHIBIT 3 *(Continued)*

American Stores Company and Subsidiaries

Notes to Financial Statements (continued)

covenant, earnings retained for use in the business in the approximate amount of $34,257,000 at March 31, 1979, were free of restriction.

(5) Leases

At March 31, 1979, the company and subsidiaries were lessees under leases covering retail locations and certain distribution center properties. The major part of retail store operations are conducted from leased premises and the initial terms of such leases generally range from 15 to 20 years. Certain store leases provide for additional rentals based on sales volume in excess of a specified level. In addition, most of the leases contain renewal options which give the company the right to extend the leases for varying additional periods, often at reduced rentals.

In fiscal year 1979, the company changed its accounting for leases as required by the provisions of Statement of Financial Accounting Standards No. 13 ("SFAS 13"), and restated its financial statements for prior years. Under the new method, leases defined as "capital leases" by SFAS 13 are recorded as an asset, subject to amortization over the lease term, and the related lease obligation shown as a liability. The accounting change decreased 1979 net earnings by $976,000 (18¢ a share) and previously reported 1978 net earnings by $605,000 (11¢ a share). Earnings retained for use in the business for years prior to 1978 were reduced $7,413,000 by the retroactive application of SFAS 13.

Aggregate future minimum lease payments as of March 31, 1979 for both capital leases and other leases (referred to as "operating leases"), net of sublease rentals which are minor in amount, are as follows for the fiscal years indicated:

Fiscal year	Operating leases	Capital leases
1980	$ 23,712,000	18,423,000
1981	22,273,000	17,999,000
1982	22,399,000	18,671,000
1983	19,138,000	16,536,000
1984	16,190,000	14,182,000
Thereafter	164,423,000	146,151,000
Total minimum lease payments	$268,135,000	231,962,000
Less estimated executory costs (such as taxes, insurance and maintenance) included in capital leases		13,764,000
Net minimum lease payments		218,198,000
Less amount representing interest		102,239,000
Present value of net minimum lease payments, including $6,857,000 due within one year		$115,959,000

The amounts of amortization of leased property and interest on lease obligations charged to earnings are as follows for the fiscal years indicated.

Fiscal year	Depreciation and amortization	Interest on long-term indebtedness
1978	$ 7,595,000	9,000,000
1979	8,158,000	9,871,000

Rental expense (under operating leases) for fiscal years 1979 and 1978 was as follows:

	1979	1978
Minimum rentals, net of minor sublease rentals	$25,827,000	23,782,000
Rentals based on sales	3,172,000	2,027,000
	$28,999,000	25,809,000

Rentals based on sales applicable to capital leases amounted to $4,768,000 in 1979 and $2,989,000 in 1978.

EXHIBIT 3 *(Continued)*

(6) Income Taxes

Federal and state income taxes charged to earnings are summarized below:

	1979	1978
Current:		
Federal (before investment credits)	$26,873,000	19,670,000
Investment credits	(4,800,000)	(3,823,000)
State	5,793,000	3,402,000
Deferred:		
Federal	1,866,000	906,000
State	313,000	135,000
	$30,045,000	20,290,000

The effective income tax rate was less than the statutory Federal income tax rate as shown below:

	1979	1978
Computed "expected" tax rate	47.5%	48.0%
State income taxes, net of Federal income tax benefit	4.7	4.0
Investment credits	(7.1)	(8.3)
Other, net	(1.0)	0.1
Effective income tax rate	44.1%	43.8%

The Federal income tax returns of the company for fiscal years 1969 and 1970 have been examined by the Internal Revenue Service, and all issues have been settled except one relating to imposition of a minor deficiency which the company is contesting. The examination of returns for fiscal years 1971 and 1972 has been completed and certain disallowances by the Service are being protested. Returns for fiscal years 1973 through 1975 are currently under examination. Management believes that any adjustments arising from final tax settlements will not have a material effect on the consolidated earnings or consolidated financial position of the company.

(7) Common Stock and Capital in Excess of Par Value of Common Stock

Changes in common stock and capital in excess of par value of common stock are as follows:

	Common stock		Capital in excess of par value of common stock
	Shares	Amount	
Balance at April 2, 1977	5,305,004	$5,305,000	132,792,000
Sale of stock under stock option plan	36,808	37,000	562,000
Balance at April 1, 1978	5,341,812	5,342,000	133,354,000
Sale of stock under stock option plan	60,962	61,000	1,059,000
Balance at March 31, 1979	5,402,774	$5,403,000	134,413,000

Under the company's stock option plans approved by the shareholders in 1964 and 1974, there were outstanding at March 31, 1979 options granted to officers and key management employees to purchase 113,329 shares of common stock at prices ranging from $21.54 to $30.13, such prices being equal to market value on the respective dates of granting. The 1974 option plan provides for grant of either qualified or nonqualified options. Qualified options are exercisable on a cumulative basis over periods of five years or less and expire on or before April 27, 1981. Nonqualified options are exercisable on a cumulative basis over periods of ten years or less and expire on or before January 25, 1988.

Case 7–3

Brass-Craft
Manufacturing Company

Brass-Craft manufactures and markets a broad line of brass, copper, steel, and plastic plumbing supply products. The company is the originator of flexible plumbing, and its products are designed primarily for use by the journeyman plumber trade. Principal product items include chrome-plated brass shut-off valves to control the flow from water sources; fittings and specially designed flexible tubing to connect faucets, fixtures, and appliances to water and gas service piping; plastic tubular drainage waste and trap systems; and stainless steel sinks.

Brass-Craft is based in Detroit and has six manufacturing plants in the United States and Canada. The company's consolidated income statements, statements of shareholders' equity, balance sheets, and statements of changes in financial position appear in Exhibits 1–3.

Required

1. Compute the amount of cash that Brass-Craft collected from customers in 1978.
2. Prepare journal entries to record
   a. depreciation of properties in 1978
   b. properties purchased or acquired
   c. properties disposed of during the year
3. What amount of long-term debt (including current maturities) did Brass-Craft repay in 1978?
4. Prepare a journal entry to record income tax expense for 1978. What amount of income taxes did Brass-Craft actually pay during the year?
5. Why is the amount of deferred taxes reported in the 1978 income statement different from the amount reported in the statement of changes in financial position? Where does this difference show up in the balance sheet?
6. Prepare a journal entry to record dividends declared and paid during 1978.
7. What journal entry did Brass-Craft's accountants make to record the 5-for-4 stock split executed by the company during the year?
8. Prepare a statement of changes in financial position using a "cash plus cash equivalents" definition of funds for 1978.

This case was prepared from published financial statements of Brass-Craft Manufacturing Company.

EXHIBIT 1

Consolidated Statements of Operations

Brass-Craft Manufacturing Company and Subsidiaries
Years ended December 31, 1978 and 1977

	1978	1977
Net sales	$56,627,587	$50,320,117
Other income	379,650	351,359
	57,007,237	50,671,476
Costs and expenses:		
Cost of products sold	39,692,120	35,150,807
Selling and administrative	7,504,582	6,568,702
Interest	202,319	91,370
	47,399,021	41,810,879
Earnings Before Income Taxes	9,608,216	8,860,597
Federal and foreign income taxes — Note A:		
Current	4,175,000	3,770,000
Deferred	155,000	190,000
State income taxes	200,000	205,000
	4,530,000	4,165,000
Net Earnings	$ 5,078,216	$ 4,695,597
Net earnings per share — Note C	$1.92	$1.77

Consolidated Statements of Shareholders' Equity

	Total	Common Stock	Additional Paid-In Capital	Retained Earnings
Balances at January 1, 1977	$26,636,827	$2,118,784	$518,482	$23,999,561
Net earnings for 1977	4,695,597			4,695,597
Cash dividends — $.25 per share, as adjusted for stock split	(656,823)			(656,823)
Balances at December 31, 1977	30,675,601	2,118,784	518,482	28,038,335
Net earnings for 1978	5,078,216			5,078,216
5-for-4 stock split (529,586 shares), including cash paid in lieu of fractional shares	(1,789)	529,586	(518,482)	(12,893)
Cash dividends — $.38 per share, as adjusted for stock split	(1,006,389)			(1,006,389)
Balances at December 31, 1978	$34,745,639	$2,648,370	$ -0-	$32,097,269

EXHIBIT 2

Consolidated Balance Sheets

Brass-Craft Manufacturing Company and Subsidiaries
December 31, 1978 and 1977

	1978	1977
ASSETS		
Current Assets		
Cash	$ 416,867	$ 330,191
Short-term investments — Note A	3,412,994	5,400,590
Trade accounts receivable, less allowance of $225,000	7,457,110	5,626,710
Inventories — Note A:		
Finished and in-process products	14,163,032	11,786,915
Raw materials	5,162,981	4,111,268
	19,326,013	15,898,183
Other current assets	303,063	243,003
Total Current Assets	30,916,047	27,498,677
Properties — Notes A and B		
Land	338,700	340,706
Buildings	4,231,020	4,304,455
Machinery and equipment	9,973,865	8,793,262
	14,543,585	13,438,423
Less allowances for depreciation	5,097,597	4,650,702
	9,445,988	8,787,721
	$40,362,035	$36,286,398

EXHIBIT 2 *(Continued)*

	1978	1977
LIABILITIES AND SHAREHOLDERS' EQUITY		
Current Liabilities		
Accounts payable	$ 1,600,571	$ 1,239,539
Compensation and other employee benefits	1,069,344	1,105,171
Taxes, other than income taxes	131,553	176,325
Income taxes	642,583	985,825
Current maturities of long-term debt	61,526	57,604
Total Current Liabilities	3,505,577	3,564,464
Long-Term Debt — Note B	992,819	1,054,333
Deferred Income Taxes	1,118,000	992,000
Shareholders' Equity — Note C		
Preferred stock, par value $1 per share:		
Authorized and unissued — 500,000 shares		
Common stock, par value $1 per share:		
Authorized — 4,000,000 shares		
Outstanding — 2,648,370 shares		
(2,118,784 in 1977)	2,648,370	2,118,784
Additional paid-in capital	-0-	518,482
Retained earnings	32,097,269	28,038,335
	34,745,639	30,675,601
	$40,362,035	$36,286,398

EXHIBIT 3

Consolidated Statements of Changes in Financial Position

Brass-Craft Manufacturing Company and Subsidiaries
Years ended December 31, 1978 and 1977

	1978	1977
Sources of Funds		
Net earnings	$ 5,078,216	$ 4,695,597
Add charges not requiring a current outlay of funds:		
Noncurrent deferred income taxes	126,000	168,000
Depreciation	1,218,963	1,073,079
Total from Operations	6,423,179	5,936,676
Net carrying amount of property disposals	80,921	5,931
	6,504,100	5,942,607
Applications of Funds		
Property additions	1,958,151	1,489,739
Reduction of long-term debt	61,514	57,604
Cash dividends	1,006,389	656,823
Cash paid in lieu of fractional shares on stock split	1,789	-0-
	3,027,843	2,204,166
Increase in Working Capital	3,476,257	3,738,441
Working capital at beginning of year	23,934,213	20,195,772
Working Capital at End of Year	$27,410,470	$23,934,213
Changes in Components of Working Capital		
Increase (decrease) in current assets:		
Cash and short-term investments	$ (1,900,920)	$ 197,530
Trade accounts receivable	1,830,400	660,329
Inventories	3,427,830	2,170,788
Other current assets	60,060	30,258
	3,417,370	3,058,905
Increase (decrease) in current liabilities:		
Accounts payable	361,032	(44,776)
Compensation and other employee benefits	(35,827)	127,701
Income and other taxes	(388,014)	(766,827)
Current maturities of long-term debt	3,922	4,366
	(58,887)	(679,536)
Increase in Working Capital	$ 3,476,257	$ 3,738,441

Case 7–4

Almadén Vineyards

Almadén Vineyards, originally established in 1852 by Charles LeFranc, produces and markets a variety of California wines including table wines, dessert wines, sparkling wines, and brandy. Since 1967, the company has been a majority-owned subsidiary of National Distillers and Chemical Corporation.

Almadén's sales rank the company among the largest wine producers in the world. The company operates more than 6,700 acres of vineyards which produce approximately 15% of the varietal grapes used in making wine. The remaining 85% of the needed grapes are purchased from independent growers.

Almadén's 1975 and 1976 balance sheets, statements of income and retained earnings, and statements of changes in working capital are presented in Exhibits 1, 2, and 3. Also, the following information concerning Almaden's inventories was taken from Almadén's summary of accounting policies and notes to the financial statements.

Inventories

Inventories are valued at the lower of cost or market. Cost is determined primarily using the first-in, first-out method. Wine and brandy in storage for aging over a number of years is included in current assets in accordance with general practices in the wine and distilling industries.

At December 31, inventories consisted of the following:

	1976	1975
Finished goods	$ 7,057,000	$ 5,538,000
Bulk wines	39,288,000	36,122,000
Bulk brandy	2,894,000	3,232,000
Bottling supplies	1,426,000	1,945,000
	$50,665,000	$46,846,000

During 1975 the company sold certain bulk brandy inventory that was in excess of anticipated current requirements and realized a gross profit of $393,000 which has been included in the statement of income as a reduction of cost of goods sold. In 1976 gross profit on sales of bulk brandy aggregated $61,000.

Required

1. Compute Almadén's current ratios as of December 31, 1975 and 1976.

This case was prepared from published financial statements of Almadén Vineyards.

2. The notes to Almadén's financial statements explain that Almadén is required to repay the long-term note payable to National Distillers and Chemical Corporation in equal annual installments of $1,800,000 (plus interest). Almadén apparently made its 1977 payment during fiscal 1976. How did this early payment affect Almadén's current ratio?

3. Comment on Almadén's classification of inventories as a current asset. How does this policy affect your assessment of the company's liquidity?

4. Estimate the average length of time that Almadén holds inventories before they are sold to customers. What assumptions are implicit in your estimate?

5. Compute the amount of cash collected from customers in 1976. Estimate the average collection period (i.e., the length of time from the date that the wine is delivered to the customer until the date that cash is collected).

6. Prepare a cash-flow statement for 1976.

EXHIBIT 1

Balance Sheet		*Almadén Vineyards, Inc.*

	At December 31	
Assets	1976	1975
Current Assets		
Cash	$ 940,000	$ 704,000
Accounts receivable	9,732,000	8,190,000
Inventories (Note 2)	50,665,000	46,846,000
Prepaid taxes and expenses	953,000	1,084,000
Total current assets	62,290,000	56,824,000
Property, Plant and Equipment—net (Notes 3 and 5)	33,927,000	33,526,000
Goodwill and Trademarks—at cost	500,000	500,000
	$96,717,000	$90,850,000

Liabilities and Stockholders' Equity

Current Liabilities		
Accounts payable	$ 7,852,000	$ 3,625,000
Accrued expenses	911,000	930,000
Taxes on income (Note 4)	1,259,000	1,117,000
Payable to National Distillers and Chemical Corporation (Notes 1 and 5)		
Accounts payable	632,000	305,000
Current portion of term note		1,800,000
Current portion of other long-term debt (Note 5)	172,000	257,000
Total current liabilities	10,826,000	8,034,000
Term Note Payable to National Distillers and Chemical Corporation, less current portion (Notes 1 and 5)	12,600,000	14,400,000
Other Long-Term Debt, less current portion (Notes 1 and 5)	1,821,000	1,994,000
Deferred Taxes on Income (Note 4)	6,427,000	5,659,000
	31,674,000	30,087,000
Stockholders' Equity		
Common stock—$.10 par value		
Authorized—12,000,000 shares		
Issued and outstanding—10,003,766 shares	1,000,000	1,000,000
Paid-in capital	43,202,000	43,202,000
Retained earnings	20,841,000	16,561,000
	65,043,000	60,763,000
Commitments (Note 6)		
	$96,717,000	$90,850,000

EXHIBIT 2

Statement of Income and Retained Earnings		Almadén Vineyards, Inc.
	Year Ended December 31	
	1976	1975
Net sales	$77,200,000	$69,466,000
Cost of goods sold (Note 2)	56,833,000	51,062,000
Gross profit	20,367,000	18,404,000
Expenses		
Selling	2,909,000	2,542,000
Advertising and promotion	3,373,000	2,995,000
General and administrative (Note 1)	1,468,000	1,300,000
Interest (Note 5)	1,264,000	1,669,000
	9,014,000	8,506,000
Income before income taxes	11,353,000	9,898,000
Provision for income taxes (Note 4)	5,873,000	4,981,000
Net income for the year	5,480,000	4,917,000
Retained earnings at beginning of year	16,561,000	12,844,000
	22,041,000	17,761,000
Dividends paid 1976—$.12 per share; 1975—$.12 per share	1,200,000	1,200,000
Retained earnings at end of year	$20,841,000	$16,561,000
Earnings per share	$ .55	$ .49
Shares outstanding during the year	10,003,766	10,003,766

EXHIBIT 3

Statement of Changes in Working Capital		Almadén Vineyards, Inc.
	Year ended December 31	
	1976	1975
Working capital was provided by		
Net income	$ 5,480,000	$ 4,917,000
Charges to net income not requiring use of working capital		
Depreciation and amortization	1,728,000	1,676,000
Deferred taxes on income	768,000	531,000
Total from operations	7,976,000	7,124,000
Disposals of property, plant and equipment	91,000	25,000
	8,067,000	7,149,000
Working capital was used for		
Expenditures for property, plant and equipment	2,220,000	2,103,000
Reduction of long-term debt	1,973,000	2,021,000
Dividends	1,200,000	1,200,000
	5,393,000	5,324,000
Increase in working capital	$ 2,674,000	$ 1,825,000
Working capital changes—increase (decrease)		
Cash	$ 236,000	$ (27,000)
Accounts receivable	1,542,000	(948,000)
Inventories	3,819,000	(4,293,000)
Prepaid taxes and expenses	(131,000)	269,000
Accounts payable	(4,227,000)	2,082,000
Accrued expenses	19,000	75,000
Taxes on income	(142,000)	(282,000)
Payables to National Distillers and Chemical Corporation	1,473,000	4,854,000
Current portion of other long-term debt	85,000	95,000
	$ 2,674,000	$ 1,825,000

Case 7–5

J. A. Wilson and Company

Ann Clark hurried back to her office and canceled her plans to spend the weekend in the mountains. The president of International Oil Company had asked her to evaluate a potential acquisition candidate and prepare to present her results to the board of directors. Since the board was meeting on Monday, Ann knew that she would spend most of the weekend at her desk.

In 1973, as a result of the worldwide oil crisis, International Oil Company adopted a policy of diversification into businesses other than oil. As part of this long-range diversification program, International was considering the acquisition of J. A. Wilson and Company, a large, well-known, retailing firm. "Wilson's" began as a chain of small variety stores selling mostly low-priced merchandise, but in recent years the company has shifted to larger, full-line, department stores that were in competition with retailers such as Sears, Roebuck and J. C. Penney. The president of International believed that J. A. Wilson and Company would be a profitable investment in a field unrelated to the energy business. He asked Ann to analyze Wilson's financial statements in detail and be prepared to answer several specific questions:

What caused the drop in earnings for 1974 (i.e., the fiscal year ended January 31, 1974)? Is this downturn of a long-term or short-term nature?

What action, if any, is needed by management to correct the situation?

Are there other problems of a managerial or financial nature that should be brought to the attention of the board?

Given the president's desire to expand into the retailing business, does J. A. Wilson and Company appear to be an attractive acquisition candidate?

Provided on the following pages are excerpts from J. A. Wilson and Company's annual report, including the letter to stockholders (Exhibit 1), financial highlights (Exhibit 2), income statements (Exhibit 3), balance sheets (Exhibit 4), statements of changes in financial position for the most recent five years (Exhibit 5), and the notes to the financial statements (Exhibit 6).

Required

1. Assuming that you are Ann Clark, prepare your report for the board of directors of International Oil Company.

This case was prepared by Professor Roland E. Dukes of the University of Washington.

EXHIBIT 1
J. A. Wilson and Company
Letter to Stockholders

To Our Stockholders

During the last six years your Company opened 410 large stores of over 50,000 square feet, enlarged 36 successful stores, and closed 307 smaller units. Retailing is synonymous with change. Selling methods, size and types of stores, and lines or departments of merchandise change as the demands of the American consumer dictate. The Management of your Company recognized this inevitable shift from smaller, limited stores to larger "full-line" stores and committed itself to the complete restructuring of the Company.

As this program proceeded, a frequent statement was, "We do not understand or recognize your image." Ten years ago, the Company had been "understood and recognized" as a large chain of variety stores. Our image was clear. We sold limited-price items in smallwares, wearing apparel, and soft goods for the home. Times changed and retailing changed . . . to the one-stop, complete store of over 50,000 square feet. That is the direction your Company followed.

To convert a chain of approximately 1,000 successful limited variety stores to a Company with approximately half its units composed of "full-line" stores, while at the same time adding all the necessary backup services, merchandise distribution centers, data processing, and major appliance warehousing, home delivery, and service in a relatively short span of time was not easily accomplished. Our image may have become blurred. We do have both small and large stores. This has to be. Ten years ago, from Maine to California, we operated small stores with limited merchandise assortments. Today in hundreds of communities our store is recognized as a store with complete assortments of merchandise for the home and family. Our stores may not yet have the general acceptance of some of our major competitors, but we firmly believe that our quality is good, our pricing and values excellent, and our reputation and acceptance as a full-line store improves each year. We are still relatively new to the full line store field, but we intend to stay—and to improve each year.

In this Letter to Stockholders we will cover more fully the factors influencing operations in 1973 and our prospects for the future.

Effects of Price Controls

Phase IV price controls seriously impaired our profit potential in 1973. While every retailer was under Phase IV price controls, your Company was more seriously affected than others . . . WHY?

In January 1972, we started promotional pricing, on a regular basis, of selected easily recognizable items to reinforce our value image. This promotional emphasis plan was successful and developed the pattern that we expected. By aggressively stocking and promoting these low-markup items, large quantities were sold in 1972, and as a result, our total selling margins declined. As we started 1973, our sales increases continued, but the mix of promotionally priced merchandise with items carrying higher selling margins came back into balance, and selling margins began to return to the more normal levels of 1970 and 1971. The Phase IV price control regulations

EXHIBIT 1 *(Continued)*

imposed in August 1973 specified that selling margins by merchandise category could not, for the full year 1973, exceed the selling margin for the same merchandise category during the year 1972. In August, when these regulations became effective, we were already above our 1972 selling margins by category in most departments—not because of increased selling margins but because the merchandise mix had changed as planned. With this turn of events, we felt compelled to lower our selling margins during the second half of 1973 to comply with government regulations; this involuntary action caused a substantial profit decrease.

Revolving Credit Plan

In 1946, the Company introduced a credit service to aid its customers to purchase wanted merchandise and pay on an installment plan. The stores were small and stocked with merchandise limited in lines and price. The credit coupon book was selected as the most practical method as these coupons could be used as cash and the customer did not have to wait for individual sales slips on each item purchased. It gave us a method of granting credit without incurring the expense of a sophisticated credit system to keep customer credit limits under control. For smaller stores, this type was not only popular with customers but it was tailor-made for the simplified operation of this small unit. However, as the Company developed new full-line stores, customers indicated a preference for the revolving credit charge plan. In addition, government regulations have made it increasingly difficult and expensive to administer the coupon-type credit plan. Primarily, in recognition of the customer preference for revolving credit charge accounts, the plan was promoted in 1973, and this emphasis will be continued in the future. This change from the credit coupon book plan produces less service charge revenue and is more expensive to operate. During 1973, although credit sales were $45,000,000 higher, service charge revenues were down by over $7,000,000. On the other hand, our experience in the past year indicates that customers prefer the revolving credit charge and will purchase more merchandise with this plan.

Inventories

At midyear, Management decided that the levels of inventory were higher than desirable. A planned program was instituted to reduce inventories, and this program was implemented on a progressive basis throughout the remainder of the year. At year-end, inventories were in satisfactory condition. The additional $51,000,000 of merchandise represented an increase that was equal to the sales increase of 12.5% and included the inventory investment necessary to stock the 5,606,000 square feet of new stores opened in 1973. The planned inventory reduction had an adverse effect on the sales trend in the fourth quarter.

Much publicity has been given to the growth of "point-of-sales" equipment in retail stores, designed to record sales and capture data for inventory management and allied functions. Beginning in 1972 and continuing through 1973, we installed point-of-sale systems in 6 stores. The decision has been made to further test point-of-sale equipment in 28 stores in 1974, using the systems of two manufacturers. The purpose of adding 28 additional units is

EXHIBIT 1 *(Continued)*

to study the problems of training, service backup, and utilization of data in a larger group than the original test stores. The experience gained in this program, with particular attention to the potential for better merchandise information, added efficiency and cost saving, will give us meaningful direction for succeeding years.

Continued Growth and Improvement

In 1973 the Company opened 77 new stores and enlarged 4 existing units, for an additional 5,606,000 square feet of new store space. In addition, construction of the new 475,000-square-foot distribution center in Hartford, Connecticut, was completed in late fall 1973.

In 1974, we will open approximately 45 new stores and enlarge 1 unit for a gain of approximately 3,000,000 square feet. The reduction, both in number of stores and square footage, from 1973 levels is due to developers encountering difficulty in securing necessary materials to complete centers on schedule, inability to start some projects because of the high cost of interim financing, and the increased time required to be spent before beginning a project in satisfying environmental control requirements. It is our estimate at this time that the 1975 program will be of the same magnitude as 1974, or smaller, and management feels that this is a more workable program in view of present conditions. This will, of course, reduce preopening costs and the additional funds required for investment in capital expenditures and inventories and to carry customer receivables, from the peaks of the last few years.

The program of closing older stores, typically of a smaller size, was accelerated in 1973 with 96 closings. All expenses pertaining to this program were charged to the year of closing. Since the closing of unprofitable stores not only reduces investment in inventory but eliminates the burden of operating costs, this program will be continued in 1974.

Financing

Every corporation is financed with a mixture of stockholders' equity and debt (both long and short term). Our rapid expansion during the last six years, coupled with the necessary service facilities to support the new stores, required substantial investments in inventories and customer credit receivables.

At the beginning of 1973, the Company had outstanding three long-term debt issues totaling $126,672,000, with interest rates of 4% and 4¾%. In July 1973, the Company concluded a loan arrangement, with eight of the largest banks in the United States, for $100,000,000 for five years, with interest at the minimum commercial lending rate of the Morgan Guaranty Trust Company of New York that ranged between 8% and 10% during the balance of 1973.

The balance of Company financing, as in previous years, was done in the short-term commercial paper market—with bank lines of credit always in effect for more than the total short term borrowings. These short-term borrowings were always less than customer account receivables, which at year-end totaled $602,000,000 and are made up of 2,900,000 individual accounts, located in all sections of the country.

Interest rates in the United States, which reached record levels in the second half of 1973, directly affected the cost of a substantial portion of

EXHIBIT 1 *(Continued)*

our borrowings. For the year, total interest costs were $30,000,000 greater than for the year 1972.

Dividends and Common Stock

Dividends of $1.50 per share on the common stock and $3.75 per share on the preferred stock were paid in 1973. Based on fiscal 1973 earnings, your Directors felt that prudent financial management dictated a reduction in the dividend payout. At the February 26, 1974 meeting of the Board, a quarterly dividend of $.15 per share was declared on the common stock, payable April 1, 1974. The new dividend will reduce the cash payout, with a consequent conservation of the Company's cash resources.

The Management of the Company takes this opportunity to express appreciation to its stockholders for the cooperation, support and loyalty they have shown over the years. We are proud of the fact that the number of common stockholders last year increased by 10,000, from 20,000 to over 30,000.

The growth in numbers and the support of our stockholders reflect, in good measure, the effects of the Employees' Stock Purchase Plan instituted 24 years ago to put Company ownership within the reach of thousands of employees. Over the years employees have paid for and been issued over 3,000,000 shares of stock. Additionally, The Foundation, established by Mr. James A. Wilson, the Company's founder, owns or has a beneficial interest in approximately 2,500,000 shares, while various other trusts established by him hold in addition an aggregate of over 1,300,000 shares. We are proud of this Company ownership in the hands of people associated with the Company.

Outlook

We are now in the year 1974. Price control limitations on retailers have been removed. Short-term interest rates are currently trending downward. We will continue opening full line stores and will continue to expand our revolving credit charge account plan. This year, the economy will be uncertain, but Management will continue to take aggressive steps to strengthen its entire operation, whether in limited or full-line stores. We will continue to change the Company to meet the demands of customers. In the final analysis, our customers will determine the success of the Company. We feel that customers are aware of the positive changes that are occurring and that, as a result, the acceptance of our full-line stores will continue to increase.

> Charles A. Wilson
> President and
> Chairman of the Board

EXHIBIT 2
J. A. Wilson and Company
Financial Highlights, 1970–1974

	Years Ended January 31,				
	1974	*1973*	*1972*	*1971*	*1970*
Sales (000s)	$1,849,802	$1,644,747	$1,374,812	$1,254,131	$1,210,918
Net earnings (000s)	8,429	37,787	35,212	39,577	41,809
Earnings per common share	$0.59	$2.70	$2.51	$2.87	$2.99
Pretax earnings per sales dollar	0.2¢	3.7¢	4.4¢	5.7¢	6.6¢
Dividends paid to shareholders (000s)	21,121	21,142	21,139	20,821	19,737
Dividends per common share	$1.50	$1.50	$1.50	$1.50	$1.40
Capital expenditures (000s)	23,537	26,983	26,476	15,995	13,668
Depreciation and amortization of properties (000s)	13,579	12,004	10,577	9,619	8,972
Number of stores	1,189	1,208	1,168	1,116	1,095
Number of new stores opened	77	92	83	65	52
Number of stores enlarged	4	5	5	8	3

EXHIBIT 3

J. A. Wilson and Company

Consolidated statement of Earnings (in 000s), 1970-1974

	Years Ended January 31,				
	1974	1973	1972	1971	1970
Sales	$1,849,802	$1,644,747	$1,374,812	$1,254,131	$1,210,918
Income from concessions	3,971	3,753	3,439	4,985	3,748
	1,853,773	1,648,500	1,378,251	1,259,116	1,214,666
Cost of merchandise sold; buying and occupancy costs	1,282,945	1,125,261	931,237	843,192	817,671
Selling, general, and administrative expenses	518,279	442,211	371,503	327,244	303,478
Interest expense	51,047	21,127	16,452	18,874	14,919
	1,852,271	1,588,599	1,319,192	1,189,310	1,136,068
Interest and other income	1,502	59,901	59,059	69,806	78,598
	3,062	1,188	1,533	1,476	1,615
Earnings before income taxes	4,564	61,089	60,592	71,282	80,213
Provisions for income taxes	786	28,417	29,331	35,880	41,736
Earnings before unconsolidated subsidiaries	3,778	32,672	31,261	35,402	38,477
Equity in net earnings of unconsolidated subsidiaries	4,651	5,115	3,951	4,175	3,332
Net earnings	$ 8,429	$ 37,787	$ 35,212	$ 39,577	$ 41,809
Net earnings per common share	$0.59	$2.70	$2.51	$2.87	$2.99

183

EXHIBIT 4

J. A. Wilson and Company

Consolidated Statements of Financial Position (in 000s), 1970-1974

		At January 31,			
	1974	1973	1972	1971	1970
Assets					
Current assets					
Cash and securities	$ 45,951	$ 30,943	$ 49,851	$ 34,009	$ 32,977
Net accounts receivable	598,799	542,751	477,324	419,731	368,267
Merchandise inventories	450,637	399,533	298,676	260,492	222,128
Prepaid expenses	7,299	6,649	5,378	4,950	5,037
Total current assets	1,102,686	979,876	831,229	719,182	628,409
Investment in unconsolidated subsidiaries	44,251	34,981	29,538	21,204	17,992
Properties, fixtures, and improvements	100,984	91,420	77,173	61,832	55,311
Other assets	5,062	4,421	6,730	5,410	5,083
Total assets	$1,252,983	$1,110,698	$944,670	$807,628	$706,795

Liabilities					
Current liabilities					
Short-term commercial notes and bank loans	$ 453,097	$ 390,034	$237,741	$246,420	$182,132
Accounts payable and accrued expenses	103,910	104,416	115,513	104,524	94,584
Federal income taxes payable	—	8,480	9,477	13,567	9,560
Deferred credits (primarily income taxes)	133,057	130,137	112,846	94,489	80,443
Total current liabilities	690,064	633,067	475,577	459,000	366,719
Long-term debt	220,336	126,672	128,432	32,301	35,402
Deferred federal income taxes	14,649	11,926	9,664	8,518	8,287
Other liabilities	4,195	4,694	5,252	5,773	5,699
Capital					
Cumulative preferred stock	7,465	8,600	9,053	9,600	11,450
Common stock	67,813	64,586	72,184	62,001	67,559
Earnings retained for use in the business	248,461	261,153	244,508	230,435	211,679
Total liabilities and capital	$1,252,983	$1,110,698	$944,670	$807,628	$706,795

EXHIBIT 5
J. A. Wilson and Company
Consolidated Statement of Changes in Financial Position (in 000s), 1970-1974

	Years Ended January 31,				
	1974	1973	1972	1971	1970
Sources of funds					
Net earnings	$ 8,429	$37,787	$ 35,212	$39,577	$41,809
Adjustments to earnings not affecting working capital					
Equity in undistributed earnings of unconsolidated subsidiaries	(3,570)	(3,403)	(2,383)	(2,777)	(2,083)
Depreciation and amortization of properties	13,579	12,004	10,577	9,619	8,972
Increase in deferred federal income taxes	2,723	2,262	1,146	231	345
Increase (decrease) in other liabilities	(499)	(558)	(521)	74	180
Total from operations	20,662	48,092	44,031	46,724	49,223
Increase in long-term debt	100,000	–	100,000	–	–
Increase (decrease) in common stock, net	3,227	(7,598)	10,183	(5,558)	(9,751)
Total funds provided	123,889	40,494	154,214	41,166	39,472
Application of funds					
Investments in properties, fixtures, and improvements	23,143	26,251	25,918	16,140	14,352
Investments in unconsolidated subsidiaries	5,700	2,040	5,951	435	–
Increase (decrease) in other assets, net	641	(2,309)	1,320	327	281
Long-term debt retired or converted into common stock	6,336	1,760	3,869	3,101	7,774
Purchase and cancellation of preferred stock	1,135	453	547	1,850	1,800
Dividends paid to shareholders	21,121	21,142	21,139	20,821	19,737
Total funds applied	58,076	49,337	58,744	42,674	43,944
Working capital increase (decrease)	$ 65,813	($8,843)	$ 95,470	($1,508)	($4,472)

EXHIBIT 6
J. A. Wilson and Company
Notes to the Consolidated Financial Statements

Summary of Significant Accounting Policies

The financial statements include the accounts of the Company and its two wholly owned subsidiaries, Wilson Financial Corporation and Jewel Studios, Inc.

The Company carries its 51% investment in McDermott Ltd., a Canadian company, at equity and has included in earnings its equity in the net earnings of the subsidiary. McDermott has consistently followed the policy of distributing approximately 40–50% of current earnings and permanently reinvesting the remainder. No U.S. deferred income taxes or Canadian withholding taxes have been provided on such undistributed earnings, as such taxes would be substantially offset by available foreign tax credits.

Gross profits on sales on the installment basis are reflected in the financial statements when the sales are made, whereas for federal income tax purposes, such profits are reported as income when collections are received. The resulting difference between taxes accrued and taxes actually payable is included as "Deferred credits (primarily income taxes)" among current liabilities.

At January 31, 1974, accumulated depreciation of approximately $30,094,500 has been deducted for tax purposes in excess of the amount (using the straight-line method) reflected in the financial statements. The resulting tax difference is included in "Deferred federal income taxes."

Investment credits (using the flowthrough method) totaling approximately $1,509,000 have been added to refundable federal income taxes for the year ended January 31, 1974 and $1,750,000 has been deducted from the provision for federal income taxes for the year ended January 31, 1973.

Merchandise inventories are carried at the lower of cost, determined principally by the retail inventory method, or market.

The Company has an Employees' Retirement Plan available to all its employees. The amounts charged to operations for the years ended January 31, 1974 and 1973 for this plan were $1,247,202 and $1,261,018, respectively. The Company funds pension costs accrued.

Expenses associated with the opening of new stores are written off in the year of store opening.

Net earnings per share of common stock (equivalent to fully diluted), after deduction of dividends on preferred stock, have been determined based on the average number of shares outstanding during each year.

Income Taxes

The Company's federal income tax returns for the years ended January 31, 1964 through 1971 have been examined by the Internal Revenue Service. Certain adjustments proposed by the Internal Revenue Service related to the tax treatment of gross profit under one of the Company's installment plans were successfully defended in the Tax Court for the years ended January 31, 1964 and 1965; however, during the year the United States Court of Appeals ruled in favor of the Internal Revenue Service. The Company has petitioned the United States Supreme Court for review. In the opinion of management, adequate provision has been made for all possible interest payments and all tax assessments have been provided for.

EXHIBIT 6 *(Continued)*

Accounts Receivable and Interest

Unearned credit insurance premiums amounted to $4,922,700 and $8,768,405 at January 31, 1974 and 1973, respectively.

Finance charges on customers' installment accounts, included as a reduction of selling, general, and administrative expenses, amounted to approximately $69,756,000 and $76,826,000 for the years ended January 31, 1974 and 1973, respectively. Pro forma interest expense and operating expenses related to the credit operations exceeded finance charges to customers.

Customers' installment accounts range in maturities up to 36 months, with finance charges, where appropriate, ranging up to an annual percentage rate of approximately 18%.

Interest earned for the years ended January 31, 1974 and 1973 includes $777,339 and $267,281, respectively, on investments in debentures of unconsolidated subsidiaries. For the years ended January 31, 1974 and 1973, interest expense on long-term debt amounted to $11,300,900 and $6,070,375, respectively.

Short-Term Borrowing

Maturities on short-term commercial notes range from 1 to 270 days from the date of issuance.

The average interest rate on short-term commercial notes outstanding at January 31, 1974 and 1973, was approximately 9.6% and 5.7%, respectively. The average interest rate on bank loans at January 31, 1973 was approximately 6.0% and in connection with such bank loans, the Company agreed to maintain compensating balances which amounted to $705,000 at such date.

The following relates to aggregate short-term borrowings for the years ended:

	January 31,	
	1974	1973
Maximum amount outstanding at any month end	$518,871,000	$407,661,000
Average daily amount outstanding	465,204,000	314,101,000
Weighted average daily interest rate	8.55%	4.76%

The Company's line of credit arrangements for short-term borrowings with banks amounted to $493,182,500 and $509,532,500 at January 31, 1974 and 1973, respectively, upon such terms as the Company and the banks may mutually agree. The arrangements do not have termination dates but are reviewed annually for renewal. At January 31, 1974 and 1973, the unused portion of such credit lines were $493,182,500 and $499,532,500, respectively, providing coverage for commercial paper outstanding. The Company maintained cash balances at such banks amounting to $597,000 and $369,000 at January 31, 1974 and 1973, respectively. Subsequent to January 31, 1974, the Company has felt it prudent to reduce its borrowing in the commercial paper field and place a greater reliance on its banks for short-term loans.

EXHIBIT 6 *(Continued)*

Compensating balances are not restricted as to withdrawal, serve as a compensation to the banks for their account handling function and other services, and additionally serve as part of the Company's minimum operating cash balances.

Long-Term Debt

At January 31,	1974	1973
4¾% convertible subordinated debentures dated April 15, 1971 and due April 15, 1996	$ 95,507,000	$100,000,000
4¾% sinking fund debentures dated January 1, 1962 and due January 1, 1987 (annual sinking fund payment of $1,500,000)	23,995,000	25,576,000
4% convertible subordinated debentures dated June 1, 1965 and due June 1, 1990	834,000	1,096,000
Notes payable to banks (see below)	100,000,000	—
	$220,336,000	$126,672,000

In July 1973, the Company borrowed $100,000,000 from several banks. These notes are due in eight equal quarterly installments commencing October 1, 1976, bearing interest payable quarterly at the minimum commercial lending rate of the Morgan Guaranty Trust Company of New York from October 1, 1973 to June 30, 1975, and at one-fourth of 1% above that rate thereafter. The understanding is that the Company will maintain compensating balances equal to 15% of the outstanding notes payable, which amounted to $15,000,000 at January 31, 1974.

Long-term debt at January 31, 1974 matures as follows: years ending January 31, 1975—none; 1976—$1,500,000; 1977—$26,500,000; 1978—$51,500,000; 1979—$26,500,000; and thereafter—the balance of $114,336,000.

As of January 31, 1974 and 1973, 29,785 and 39,142 shares, respectively, of common stock of the Company were reserved for conversion of the 4% convertible subordinated debentures at the conversion price of $28 a share. In addition, at January 31, 1974 and 1973, 1,308,315 and 1,369,863 shares, respectively, were reserved for conversion of the 4¾% convertible subordinated debentures, at the conversion price of $73 a share.

Included in miscellaneous income is the gain totaling $1,959,769 and $315,733 for the years ended January 31, 1974 and 1973, respectively, on retirement of long-term debt.

Under the terms of the various indentures, at January 31, 1974 the Company may incur additional unsubordinated long-term debt of approximately $139,000,000; under the most restrictive of such indentures, approximately $19,000,000 of earnings retained for use in the business was available for the declaration of cash dividends, the purchase of capital stock and investments in certain subsidiaries. The Company can, at its election, increase the amount unrestricted by including its financial subsidiary for purposes of debt covenant calculation. If the Company had made such election at January 31, 1974,

EXHIBIT 6 *(Continued)*

approximately $165,000,000 would have been available for the declaration of dividends, the purchase of capital stock and investments in certain subsidiaries.

Leases

Total rental expenses for all leases amounted to

	Years Ended January 31,	
	1974	1973
Financing leases		
Minimum rentals	$101,236,977	$87,659,988
Contingent rentals	2,300,195	2,176,237
Other leases		
Minimum rentals	3,577,735	2,227,950
Less: Rentals from subleases	1,747,848	1,821,251
	$105,367,059	$90,242,924

The contingent rentals are based upon various percentages of sales in excess of specified minimums.

The future minimum rental commitments as of January 31, 1974 for all noncancellable leases (as defined by ASR No. 147) are as follows (in thousands):

Years Ended January 31,	Financing Leases		Other Leases	Less: Rental From Subleases	Total
	Real Estate	Equipment	Real Estate	Of Real Estate	
1975	$ 95,512	$8,522	$ 3,162	$1,539	$105,657
1976	94,013	8,522	3,090	1,240	104,385
1977	91,292	8,522	3,021	1,077	101,758
1978	88,087	7,272	2,993	916	97,436
1979	85,546	7,272	2,993	844	94,967
1980-1984	385,846	1,859	12,522	2,777	397,450
1985-1989	319,693	1,859	12,522	1,379	332,695
1990-1994	167,626	681	12,522	731	180,098
1995 and beyond	8,391	—	8,139	113	16,417

Capital

The 3¾% cumulative preferred stock is redeemable at the Company's option in whole or in part at $100 per share.

At January 31, 1974 and 1973, 238,165 and 289,615 shares, respectively, of the Company's unissued common stock were reserved under the 1960 Employees' Stock Purchase Plan. An additional 1,000,000 shares of unissued

EXHIBIT 6 *(Continued)*

common stock have been reserved under the 1970 Employees' Stock Purchase Plan. Contracts for the sale of such shares, on a deferred payment basis, are made at approximate market prices at date of contracts. Shares are issued after completion of payments.

Accountants' Report

Board of Directors and Stockholders
J. A. Wilson and Company
919 West State Street
Chicago, Illinois

We have examined the consolidated financial statements of J. A. Wilson and Company and consolidated subsidiaries for the years ended January 31, 1974 and 1973. Our examinations were made in accordance with generally accepted auditing standards, and accordingly included such tests of the accounting records and such other auditing procedures as we considered necessary in the circumstances. The amounts included in the financial statements for the years ended January 31, 1974 and 1973 for McDermott Ltd. are based solely on the report of other independent accountants who have examined the financial statements of such company.

In our opinion, based on our examination and the report of other independent accountants for the year ended January 31, 1974 of McDermott Ltd. referred to above, the accompanying consolidated statements of financial position, operations, and changes in financial position present fairly the consolidated financial position of J. A. Wilson and Company and consolidated subsidiaries at January 31, 1974 and 1973, and the consolidated results of their operations, and changes in financial position for the years then ended, in conformity with generally accepted accounting principles applied on a consistent basis.

Chicago, Illinois
March 18, 1974

Coopers and Anderson

8

ACCOUNTING FOR
CHANGING PRICES

Case 8–1 _____

General Electric Company

The General Electric Company is a diversified manufacturer of consumer products, industrial products and components, power systems, technical systems and materials, and transportation systems. Through subsidiary companies, GE is also engaged in the exploration, development, and extraction of coal, uranium, and other natural resources throughout the world.

GE made inflation accounting the theme of its *1979 Annual Report* to stockholders, highlighting the disclosure requirements adopted by the Financial Accounting Standards Board in September of that year (see Exhibit 1). On the cover, the company stated "Inflation increasingly widens the gap between reported and real profits—drastically weakening U.S. business investments in keeping competitive." In a letter to shareholders included in that report, Chief Executive Officer Reginald H. Jones commented on the effects of inflation:

This case was prepared from published financial statements of the General Electric Company.

Of the challenges facing the U.S. economy, none is more serious than the present double-digit inflation. As indicated by this report's cover, severe inflation distorts the financial reporting of business, giving the illusion of soaring profits when, in fact, real profits—profits stripped of their inflationary increments—have failed to keep pace with the rising costs of replacing buildings, machinery and equipment, maintaining inventories, and supporting research and development. This reduction in real corporate retained earnings has weakened capital investment, with resulting lowered levels of productivity and international competitiveness.

It is a situation that calls for sharp changes in national direction. Believing that the first step toward this goal is greater public understanding of inflation's impact on the vital process of capital formation, your management welcomes the initiative taken in 1979 by the Financial Accounting Standards Board (FASB). Under FASB leadership, some 1,200 U.S. companies will include, in their 1979 annual reports, inflation adjusted supplementary data that will show how inflation escalates reported sales and earnings, causes shortfalls in depreciation provisions, and boosts effective tax rates to counterproductive levels.

You will note from our supplementary data that, after pre-tax earnings are adjusted for the impact of inflation and then reduced by taxes and dividends, your Company retained for reinvestment and growth only 16% of pre-tax earnings over the 1975–1979 period. The comparable amount for all U.S. nonfinancial corporations was even lower, at 10%. This somewhat more favorable situation for your Company provides little satisfaction, however, when we see how our inflation-adjusted data scale down our sales and earnings and show that our reported depreciation expenses understate our real capital recovery needs by some $356 million in 1979 alone.

Industrywide data generated by this FASB initiative will underscore the case for restructuring U.S. corporate income tax provisions and policies so as to mitigate the impact of inflation on the capital formation process. The results of the more realistic capital recovery allowances and other remedial measures that businessmen are advocating to our legislators will benefit not only industry but the nation as a whole.

GE's supplemental disclosure on the effects of inflation are presented in Exhibit 2. In addition, Exhibit 3 presents a summary of financial data prepared under "traditional" historical cost assumptions for the five-year period, 1975 to 1979.

Required

1. Explain the difference between constant dollar accounting and current cost accounting. What is the purpose of each of these alternatives to historical cost accounting?

2. The supplemental disclosure required by FASB Statement No. 33 does not include a complete set of financial statements for either the constant dollar or the current cost alternatives. Examine the information provided by GE and comment. What information is omitted from the disclosure?

3. Compare the three alternative income statements presented in Table 1 of Exhibit 2. What can be determined from such a comparison?

4. Refer to Table 2 of Exhibit 2. What is meant by "current cost information in dollars of 1979 purchasing power"?

5. Table 2 (see Exhibit 2) contains the following item: "(Loss)/gain in general purchasing power of net monetary items." Why isn't this gain/loss included in the earnings statements?

6. In your opinion, does the supplemental disclosure required by Statement No. 33 adequately reflect the effects of inflation on the operations of GE? Why or why not?

7. Why is GE so strongly in favor of supplemental disclosure of the effects of inflation? What types of companies would you expect to support this disclosure? Which firms would be opposed?

EXHIBIT 1
General Electric Company
From GE's *1979 Annual Report*

The cover:
Inflation feeds itself by weakening U.S. industry's ability to invest in the productivity improvements that help keep inflation in check. The cover shows how inflation distorts financial results and produces a widening gap between the reported after-tax profits and real after-tax profits of U.S. nonfinancial corporations. Three factors account for this gap: underdepreciation, reflecting the difference between what facilities cost originally and what they would cost if replaced at current prices; "phantom" profits on inventories valued via FIFO (first-in, first-out) accounting; and the decrease in the purchasing power of the dollar caused by general inflation. Compounding of these problems by the present U.S. tax system results in decreasing the resources available for industry to invest in improving productivity and in supporting technological innovations such as those that underlie the GE operations illustrated on the cover. The impact of inflation is discussed further by the Chairman on page 5, and in the supplementary information on pages 28-30.

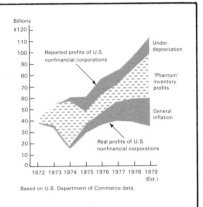

EXHIBIT 2
General Electric Company
Supplemental Disclosure on the Effects of Inflation

Financial issues:
the impact of inflation

Inflation is commonly defined as a loss in value of money due to an increase in the volume of money and credit relative to available goods and services, resulting in a rise in the level of prices. Inflation in the U.S. is generally recognized to be caused by a combination of factors, including government deficits, sharp increases in energy costs, and low productivity gains including the effect of proliferating government regulations.

Although loss of purchasing power of the dollar impacts all areas of the economy, it is particularly onerous in its effect on savings — of both individuals in forms such as savings accounts, securities and pensions, and of corporations in the form of retained earnings.

For the individual, with inflation of 6% a year, the dollar saved by a person at age 50 will have lost three-fifths of its value by the time the person is age 65. With a 10% inflation rate, almost four-fifths of the dollar's value is lost in 15 years. This problem affects almost everyone, including those presently working and especially those who are on fixed incomes.

The situation is rendered even more difficult by the progressive income tax system. A Congressional staff study reports that a family of four with an income of $8,132 in 1964 would need a 1979 income of $18,918 to have kept pace with the increase in the Consumer Price Index over the years. However, the 1979 income of $18,918 puts the family into a higher tax bracket which, when coupled with increased Social Security taxes, reduces real after-tax income $1,068 below the equivalent 1964 level.

Your Company and all U.S. businesses face a similar problem. Business savings are in the form of retained earnings — the earnings a company keeps after paying employees, suppliers and vendors, and after payment of taxes to government and dividends to share owners. If a company is to continue in business, much less grow, it must be able to save or retain sufficient earnings, after providing a return to its share owners, to fund the cost of replacing — at today's inflated prices — the productive assets used up. Retention of capital in these inflationary times under existing tax laws is a challenge facing all businesses.

U.S. tax regulations permit recognition of the impact of inflation on a company's inventory costs by use of the LIFO (last-in, first-out) inventory method. In general, under the LIFO method, a company charges off to operations the current cost of inventories consumed during the year. With inflation averaging over 11% last year, the negative impact on operations of using current costs with respect to a supply of goods is substantial. Financial results are portrayed more accurately when the LIFO method is used in periods of high inflation, and GE has used LIFO for most of its U.S. manufacturing inventories for a quarter-century. The Statement of Earnings on page 32 is on that basis. As

supplementary information to that Statement of Earnings: use of the LIFO method increased 1979 and 1978 operating costs by $430.8 million and $224.1 million (to $20,330.7 million and $17,695.9 million), respectively, with a corresponding reduction of reported pre-tax profits.

Unfortunately, U.S. tax regulations fail to provide an equivalent to LIFO for the impact of inflation on a company's costs of property, plant and equipment. Instead, deductions for wear and tear on these assets are based on original purchase costs rather than today's replacement costs. In general, the resulting shortfall must be funded from after-tax earnings.

The supplementary information shown in Table 1 restates operating results to eliminate the major effects of inflation discussed above. Table 1 compares GE operating results as reported on page 32 with results adjusted in two ways. First, results are restated to show the effects of general inflation — the loss of the dollar's purchasing power — on inventories and fixed assets. The second restatement shows results restated for changes in specific prices — the current costs of replacing those assets. Your management feels that the last column in Table 1 is the more meaningful and has therefore shown, in Table 2 on page 30, five years of results on that basis, also adjusted to equivalent 1979 dollars to make the years comparable. While the techniques used are not precise, they do produce reasonable approximations.

In these earnings statements, specific adjustments are made to (1) *cost of goods sold* for the current cost of replacing inventories and (2) *depreciation* for the current costs of plant and equipment. The restatements for inventories are relatively small because GE's extensive use of LIFO accounting already largely reflects current costs in the traditional statements. However, a substantial restatement is made for the impact of inflation on fixed assets, which have relatively long lives. The $624 million of depreciation as traditionally reported, when restated for general inflation, increases to a total of $880 million. But the restatement necessary to reflect replacement of these assets at current costs grows to $980 million. The net effect of these restatements lowers reported income of $6.20 a share to $4.68 on a general inflation-adjusted basis and $4.34 on a specific current cost basis.

It is significant to note that for the five years 1975-1979, even after adjustment for inflation, your Company has shown real growth in earnings and a steady increase in share owners' equity over the entire period. After adjusting earnings for current costs and restating all years to equivalent 1979 dollars, your Company's average annual growth rate in real earnings was 21% since 1975 and 8% since 1976. This means that the growth in GE's earnings has been real, not just the product of inflation.

An important insight from these data is depicted in the pie charts at right. These show that, over the five years 1975-1979, because of inflation 10% more of GE's earnings were taxed away than appeared to have been the case using traditional financial statements. While the traditional earnings statements indicated an effective tax rate of 41% over this period, the "real" tax rate averaged 51% of profits before taxes. Consequently, earnings

EXHIBIT 2 *(Continued)*

Table 1: supplementary information – effect of changing prices (a)

(In millions, except per-share amounts)   The notes on page 30 are an integral part of this statement.

For the year ended December 31, 1979	As reported in the traditional statements	Adjusted for general inflation	Adjusted for changes in specific prices (current costs) (b)
Sales of products and services to customers	$22,461	$22,461	$22,461
Cost of goods sold	15,991	16,093	16,074
Selling, general and administrative expense	3,716	3,716	3,716
Depreciation, depletion and amortization	624	880	980
Interest and other financial charges	258	258	258
Other income	(519)	(519)	(519)
Earnings before income taxes and minority interest	2,391	2,033	1,952
Provision for income taxes	953	953	953
Minority interest in earnings of consolidated affiliates	29	16	13
Net earnings applicable to common stock	$ 1,409	$ 1,064	$ 986
Earnings per common share	$ 6.20	$ 4.68	$ 4.34
Share owners' equity at year end (net assets) (c)	$ 7,362	$10,436	$11,153

Use of each dollar of earnings
Based on total earnings before taxes 1975-1979

As Reported

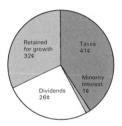

Adjusted for changes in specific prices (current costs)

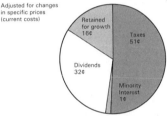

retained for growth were cut in half to 16% of income before tax, not 32% as reflected in the traditional financial statements. Over the period, share owners received a measure of protection against inflation's impact as about two-thirds of after-tax earnings were distributed — equivalent to an average annual growth rate of about 8% in *real* dividends.

An area receiving special attention by management is experimentation with the use of inflation-adjusted measurements at the individual business and project level for capital budgeting. Since 1973, your Company has been experimenting with various techniques to measure the impact of inflation, to incorporate the perspectives provided by such measurements into decision-making, and to stimulate awareness by all levels of management of the need to develop constructive business strategies to deal with inflation. The objective is to ensure that investments needed for new business growth, productivity improvements and capacity expansions earn appropriate

real rates of return commensurate with the risks involved. Such supplemental measurements can assist in the entire resource allocation process, starting with initial project approval, implementation and subsequent review.

Improving productivity to offset inflationary forces is a primary goal established by top management that is being stressed throughout General Electric. As discussed on the back cover of this Annual Report, the Company has committed significant levels of resources to research and development activities to accelerate innovation and increase productivity. In addition, General Electric's production base continues to be expanded and modernized through increasing investments in plant and equipment. For example, $1,262 million and $1,055 million were spent on strengthening General Electric's production base in 1979 and 1978, respectively. Imaginative and diligent coupling of production techniques and equipment is critical to the maintenance and improvement of your Company's profitability.

EXHIBIT 2 *(Continued)*

Table 2: supplementary information – effect of changing prices (a)

(In millions, except per-share amounts)

Current cost information in dollars of 1979 purchasing power (b)

(All amounts expressed in average 1979 dollars)	1979	1978	1977	1976	1975
Sales of products and services to customers	$22,461	$21,867	$20,984	$20,015	$19,022
Cost of goods sold	16,074	15,548	14,793	14,145	13,914
Selling, general and administrative expense	3,716	3,566	3,606	3,360	3,018
Depreciation, depletion and amortization	980	1,000	986	979	1,006
Interest and other financial charges	258	249	238	222	251
Other income	(519)	(466)	(467)	(350)	(235)
Earnings before income taxes and minority interest	1,952	1,970	1,828	1,659	1,068
Provision for income taxes	953	995	926	853	620
Minority interest in earnings of consolidated affiliates	13	13	20	26	26
Net earnings applicable to common stock	$ 986	$ 962	$ 882	$ 780	$ 422
Earnings per common share	$ 4.34	$ 4.22	$ 3.88	$ 3.45	$ 1.88
Share owners' equity at year end (net assets) (c)	$11,153	$11,020	$10,656	$10,526	$10,056
Other inflation information					
Average Consumer Price Index (1967 = 100)	217.4	195.4	181.5	170.5	161.2
(Loss)/gain in general purchasing power of net monetary items	$(209)	$(128)	$ (61)	$ (20)	$ 19
Dividends declared per common share	2.75	2.78	2.52	2.17	2.16
Market price per common share at year end	47⅞	50½	58¼	69⅜	60¼

Notes to supplementary information — Tables 1 and 2

(a) This information has been prepared in accordance with requirements of the Financial Accounting Standards Board (FASB). Proper use of this information requires an understanding of certain basic concepts and definitions.

The heading "As reported in the traditional statements" refers to information drawn directly from the financial statements presented on pages 32 to 44. This information is prepared using the set of generally accepted accounting principles which renders an accounting based on the number of actual dollars involved in transactions, with no recognition given to the fact that the value of the dollar changes over time.

The heading "Adjusted for general inflation" refers to information prepared using a different approach to transactions involving inventory and property, plant and equipment assets. Under this procedure, the number of dollars involved in transactions at different dates are all restated to equivalent amounts in terms of the general purchasing power of the dollar as it is measured by the Consumer Price Index for all Urban Consumers (CPI-U). For example, $1,000 invested in a building asset in 1967 would be restated to its 1979 dollar purchasing power equivalent of $2,174 to value the asset and calculate depreciation charges. Similarly, 1978 purchases of non-LIFO inventory sold in 1979 would be accounted for at their equivalent in terms of 1979 dollars, rather than in terms of the actual number of dollars spent.

The heading "Adjusted for changes in specific prices (current costs)" refers to information prepared using yet another approach to transactions involving inventory and property, plant and equipment assets. In this case, rather than restating to dollars of the same general purchasing power, estimates of current costs of the assets are used.

In presenting results of either of the supplementary accounting methods for more than one year, "real" trends are more evident when results for all years are expressed in terms of the general purchasing power of the dollar for a designated period. Results of such restatements are generally called "constant dollar" presentations. In the five-year presentations shown above, dollar results for earlier periods have been restated to their equivalent number of constant dollars of 1979 general purchasing power (CPI-U basis).

Since none of these restatements is allowable for tax purposes under existing regulations, income tax amounts are the same as in the traditional statements (but expressed in constant dollars in the five-year summary).

There are a number of other terms and concepts which may be of interest in assessing the significance of the supplementary information shown in Tables 1 and 2. However, it is management's opinion that the basic concepts discussed above are the most significant for the reader to have in mind while reviewing this information.

(b) Principal types of information used to adjust for changes in specific prices (current costs) are (1) for inventory costs, GE-generated indices of price changes for specific goods and services, and (2) for property, plant and equipment, externally generated indices of price changes for major classes of assets.

(c) At December 31, 1979, the current cost of inventory was $5,251 million, and of property, plant and equipment was $7,004 million. Estimated current costs applicable to the sum of such amounts held during all or part of 1979 increased by approximately $1,111 million, which was $329 million less than the $1,440-million increase which could be expected because of general inflation.

EXHIBIT 3
General Electric Company
Five-Year Summary of Operations, 1975–1979

(Dollar amounts in millions; per-share amounts in dollars)	1979	1978	1977	1976	1975
Summary of operations					
Sales of products and services to customers	$22,460.6	$19,653.8	$17,518.6	$15,697.3	$14,105.1
Cost of goods sold	15,990.7	13,915.1	12,287.7	11,048.3	10,209.8
Selling, general and administrative expense	3,715.9	3,204.4	3,010.8	2,634.9	2,238.2
Depreciation, depletion and amortization	624.1	576.4	522.1	486.2	470.5
Operating costs	20,330.7	17,695.9	15,820.6	14,169.4	12,918.5
Operating margin	2,129.9	1,957.9	1,698.0	1,527.9	1,186.6
Other income	519.4	419.0	390.3	274.3	174.2
Interest and other financial charges	(258.6)	(224.4)	(199.5)	(174.7)	(186.8)
Earnings before income taxes and minority interest	2,390.7	2,152.5	1,888.8	1,627.5	1,174.0
Provision for income taxes	(953.4)	(893.9)	(773.1)	(668.6)	(459.8)
Minority interest	(28.5)	(28.9)	(27.5)	(28.3)	(25.7)
Net earnings	$ 1,408.8	$ 1,229.7	$ 1,088.2	$ 930.6	$ 688.5
Earnings per common share (b)	$ 6.20	$ 5.39	$ 4.79	$ 4.12	$ 3.07
Dividends declared per common share (c)	$ 2.75	$ 2.50	$ 2.10	$ 1.70	$ 1.60
Earnings as a percentage of sales	6.3%	6.3%	6.2%	5.9%	4.9%
Earned on average share owners' equity	20.2%	19.6%	19.4%	18.9%	15.7%
Dividends–General Electric	$ 623.6	$ 569.8	$ 476.9	$ 332.5	$ 293.1
Dividends–Utah International Inc. (d)	—	—	—	$ 28.3	$ 33.1
Shares outstanding–average (in thousands) (e)	227,173	227,985	227,154	225,791	224,262
Share owner accounts–average	540,000	552,000	553,000	566,000	582,000
Market price range per share (c) (f)	55⅛-45	57⅝-43⅝	57¼-47⅜	59¼-46	52⅞-32⅜
Price/earnings ratio range (c)	9-7	11-8	12-10	14-11	17-10
Current assets	$ 9,384.5	$ 8,755.0	$ 7,865.2	$ 6,685.0	$ 5,750.4
Current liabilities	6,871.8	6,175.2	5,417.0	4,604.9	4,163.0
Working capital	$ 2,512.7	$ 2,579.8	$ 2,448.2	$ 2,080.1	$ 1,587.4
Short-term borrowings	$ 871.0	$ 960.3	$ 772.1	$ 611.1	$ 667.2
Long-term borrowings	946.8	993.8	1,284.3	1,322.3	1,239.5
Minority interest in equity of consolidated affiliates	151.7	150.8	131.4	119.0	104.6
Share owners' equity	7,362.3	6,586.7	5,942.9	5,252.9	4,617.0
Total capital invested	$ 9,331.8	$ 8,691.6	$ 8,130.7	$ 7,305.3	$ 6,628.3
Earned on average total capital invested	17.6%	16.3%	15.8%	15.1%	12.5%
Share owners' equity per common share–year end (b)	$ 32.31	$ 28.88	$ 26.05	$ 23.18	$ 20.49
Property, plant and equipment additions	$ 1,262.3	$ 1,055.1	$ 822.5	$ 740.4	$ 588.2
Employees–average worldwide	405,000	401,000	384,000	380,000	380,000

(a) Unless specifically noted, all years are adjusted to include Utah International Inc., which became a wholly owned affiliate of General Electric on December 20, 1976, through the exchange of 41,002,034 shares of General Electric common stock for all of the outstanding shares of Utah.
(b) Computed using outstanding shares as described in note (e).
(c) For General Electric common stock as reported in the years shown.
(d) Reflects transactions prior to merger date.

(e) Includes General Electric outstanding average shares or year-end shares as appropriate plus, in 1976 and prior years, outstanding shares previously reported by Utah multiplied by 1.3. Adjustments have been made for a two-for-one GE stock split in 1971 and the two-for-one Utah stock split effected in the form of stock dividends in 1973.
(f) Represents high and low market prices as reported on New York Stock Exchange through January 23, 1976, and as reported on the Consolidated Tape thereafter.

Case 8–2

Sperry Corporation

Sperry (formerly Sperry Univac) is a multinational corporation with diversified operations in information processing systems and services, defense and aerospace systems, specialized farm machinery, and fluid power equipment.

As are other major U.S. corporations, Sperry was required by FASB Statement No. 33 to disclose supplementary information on the effects of inflation. The statement focused on three items most affected by changing prices. First, Statement No. 33 required adjustments to inventories and properties, and related cost of sales and depreciation, for changes in the general purchasing power of the dollar, as measured by the Consumer Price Index for all Urban Consumers (CPI-U). These "constant dollar" adjustments are displayed in the middle column of Sperry's inflation-adjusted income statement (Exhibit 1). Second, Statement No. 33 required adjustments to cost of sales and depreciation for changes in the prices of goods and services specifically used by the company. This "current cost" information is disclosed in the third column of Exhibit 1. Third, Statement No. 33 required firms to disclose information on the effect of general inflation on monetary assets and liabilities. In 1982, Sperry reported a $1.5 million loss from the decline in the purchasing power of net monetary assets.

Also provided are Exhibit 2, other excerpts from Sperry's 1982 supplementary information on inflation accounting, including a five-year comparison of selected financial data expressed in dollars of 1982 purchasing power and management's discussion of the impact of inflation on financial data; Exhibit 3, consolidated balance sheets for 1981 and 1982; and Exhibit 4, consolidated statements of income and retained earnings for 1980, 1981, and 1982.

Required

1. Contrast constant dollar and current cost accounting. Why does Sperry's net income vary so dramatically among historical cost, constant dollar, and current cost accounting?

2. Refer to Exhibit 2. Do you agree with management's position "that the current cost basis results in a more appropriate matching of its revenue and inflation-adjusted expenses than the constant dollar basis"? Give specific reasons.

3. The company notes that Statement No. 33 "is experimental in nature and should be viewed in that context and not as complete or precise measurements of the effects of inflation." What appears to be incomplete or imprecise about the disclosures?

4. What is the cause of Sperry's monetary losses in 1981 and 1982? Why aren't

---

This case was prepared from published financial statements of the Sperry Corporation.

these losses included in the income statements? Do you believe these losses are typical of most large corporations?

5. Refer to Exhibits 2 and 3. Revenues of $5,571.4 million for fiscal 1982 are reported in both statements. However, for 1981, the five-year comparison reports revenues of $5,938.9 million versus $5,427.2 million disclosed in the historical cost income statement. Reconcile this difference and explain the purpose of the five-year comparison.

6. Management notes that the effective tax rate is higher for both constant dollar and current cost accounting than that reported under historical cost (see Exhibit 2). Using the 1982 income statements provided in Exhibit 1, compute income before taxes and the effective tax rate under each basis. Comment on the resulting numbers.

7. What is your overall reaction to the supplemental disclosures on the effects of inflation?

EXHIBIT 1
Sperry Corporation
1982 Income Statements Adjusted for Changing Prices
(And Other 1982 Data in Millions of Dollars)

Pursuant to Statement No. 33, a pro forma consolidated statement of income for the year ended March 31, 1982 (based on historical costs before giving effect to the change in accounting for foreign currency translation described in Note 2) adjusted for the effects of changing prices follows:

	Pro Forma Basis	Adjusted for General Inflation (Constant Dollar)	Adjusted for Changes in Specific Prices (Current Cost)
Revenue	$5,571.4	$5,571.4	$5,571.4
Cost of sales of products, rentals and services (a)	3,343.2	3,433.9	3,350.1
Selling, general and administrative expenses (a)	1,095.8	1,095.8	1,095.8
Depreciation (b)	212.9	271.8	259.0
Other expenses, net...................	694.4	694.4	694.4
Provision for taxes on income	73.3	73.3	73.3
	5,419.6	5,569.2	5,472.6
Net income	$ 151.8	$ 2.2	$ 98.8
Net income per share (fully diluted and primary).........................	$ 3.59	$ .05	$ 2.34
Net assets at March 31, 1982............	$2,450.0	$2,820.0	$2,847.9
(Loss) from decline in purchasing power of net monetary assets		$ (1.5)	$ (1.5)
Increase in general price level of inventories, rental machines and other property, plant and equipment held during the year			$ 193.9
Effect of increase in specific prices (c)			79.3
Excess of increase in general price level over increase in specific prices.............................			$ 114.6

(a) *Excludes depreciation.*

(b) *Depreciation expense for both the constant dollar and current cost disclosures was determined using the depreciation methods and estimates of useful lives used in the preparation of the primary financial statements.*

(c) *At March 31, 1982 the current cost of inventories, less progress payments, was $1,517.7 million and the current cost of rental machines and other property, plant and equipment, net of accumulated depreciation, was $1,227.9 million.*

EXHIBIT 2
Sperry Corporation
Five-Year Comparison of Selected Financial Data
In Dollars of 1982 Purchasing Power (in Millions of Dollars)
and Management Discussion, 1978–1982

The following five-year comparison shows selected historical financial data adjusted to average fiscal year 1982 dollars as measured by the CPI-U:

	Years ended March 31				
	1982	1981	1980	1979	1978
Revenue	$5,571.4	$5,938.9	$5,905.1	$5,793.8	$5,490.1
Information Adjusted for General Inflation:					
Net income	2.2	158.9	168.3		
Net income per share:					
Fully diluted	$.05	$3.83	$4.26		
Primary	$.05	$3.90	$4.62		
Net assets at year end ..	2,820.0	2,854.4	2,720.9		
Information Adjusted for Changes in Specific Prices:					
Net income	98.8	257.5	280.7		
Net income per share:					
Fully diluted	$2.34	$6.18	$7.01		
Primary	$2.34	$6.31	$7.70		
Net assets at year end ..	2,847.9	2,874.6	2,762.3		
(Loss) gain from change in purchasing power of net monetary items ...	(1.5)	(2.7)	4.4		
Excess of increase in general price level over increase in specific prices	114.6	169.5	257.5		
Cash dividends declared per share	$1.92	$1.93	$1.93	$1.83	$1.68
Market price per share at year end	$27.19	$60.57	$53.50	$66.17	$50.79
Average consumer price index	277.4	253.5	224.8	200.1	184.4

Impact of Inflation on Financial Data—The Company believes that the current cost basis results in a more appropriate matching of its revenue and inflation-adjusted expenses than the constant dollar basis. The specific costs and expenses of the Company generally have not increased at the pace of general inflation primarily due to offsetting productivity gains and advances in technology. The CPI-U (which is prescribed by the FASB) is not an appropriate index because it (a) encompasses a wide range of items such as food, housing and fuel costs, and (b) would not be applicable to the Company's operations outside the U.S. We therefore do not believe that the constant dollar basis properly measures the effects of inflation on the Company. Accordingly, the current cost basis may provide a more reasonable measure of the impact of changing prices on the Company's operations.

The impact of inflation on earnings, as presented by the constant dollar or current cost adjustments, is not deductible for income tax purposes. As a result, the effective income tax rate on both bases is higher than that reported in the financial statements. This supports the view that present U.S. tax policy should be revised to recognize the effects of inflation on taxable income.

EXHIBIT 3
Sperry Corporation
Consolidated Balance Sheets, 1981–1982 (in Millions of Dollars)

At March 31	1982	1981
ASSETS		
Current Assets		
Cash, including interest-bearing time and call deposits: 1982, $41.8; 1981, $31.7	$ 66.2	$ 62.7
Accounts and notes receivable (Note 8):		
United States Government contracts, direct and indirect	71.1	70.1
Sales-type leases, less allowance for unearned income: 1982, $192.1; 1981, $155.9	390.5	350.9
Commercial, less allowance for doubtful accounts: 1982, $28.1; 1981, $25.7	633.3	640.8
Due from wholly-owned finance company	19.7	116.0
Inventories (Note 9)	1,331.2	1,461.7
Prepaid expenses	116.6	106.4
Total Current Assets	2,628.6	2,808.6
Long-Term Receivables (Note 10)		
Sales-type leases, less allowance for unearned income: 1982, $261.1; 1981, $243.5	1,320.5	1,181.4
Other, less allowance for doubtful accounts: 1982, $2.1; 1981, $2.7	120.7	140.7
	1,441.2	1,322.1
Investments at Equity (Note 11)		
Wholly-owned finance and insurance companies	283.9	221.0
Other companies	73.1	60.6
	357.0	281.6
Other Assets	42.7	44.3
Property, Plant and Equipment, at cost		
Land	32.3	33.5
Buildings and leasehold improvements	425.2	376.0
Machinery and equipment	782.5	689.4
	1,240.0	1,098.9
Less allowance for depreciation and amortization	569.4	511.8
	670.6	587.1
Rental machines	737.8	787.6
Less allowance for depreciation and obsolescence	534.9	588.8
	202.9	198.8
Property, Plant and Equipment, Net	873.5	785.9
	$5,343.0	$5,242.5

See notes to financial statements.

EXHIBIT 3 *(Continued)*

	At March 31	1982	1981
LIABILITIES			
Current Liabilities			
Bank and other loans (Note 12)		$ 527.6	$ 394.4
Accounts payable		201.9	223.5
Other payables and accruals (Note 15)		714.9	717.0
Accrued federal and foreign income taxes		267.3	228.5
Current maturities on long-term liabilities		53.5	48.9
Dividend payable		20.6	18.2
Total Current Liabilities		1,785.8	1,630.5
Long-Term Liabilities (Note 13)		716.8	798.6
Deferred Income Taxes		456.0	490.3
STOCKHOLDERS' EQUITY			
Capital Stock			
Series preferred stock, no par value			
Authorized and unissued—5,000,000 shares			
Common stock, $.50 par value (Note 16)			
Authorized—60,000,000 shares			
Outstanding shares: 1982, 42,950,606; 1981, 41,279,217		21.5	20.6
Additional Paid-In Capital (Note 16)		544.4	488.8
Retained Earnings (Note 17)		1,954.1	1,813.7
Accumulated Translation Adjustment (Note 18)		(135.6)	—
Total Stockholders' Equity		2,384.4	2,323.1
		$5,343.0	$5,242.5

EXHIBIT 4

Sperry Corporation

Consolidated Statements of Income and Retained Earnings, 1980-1982

(in Millions of Dollars)

Years ended March 31	1982	1981	1980
Revenue			
Net sales of products	$4,195.0	$4,239.8	$3,717.2
Rentals and services	1,376.4	1,187.4	1,068.2
Total	5,571.4	5,427.2	4,785.4
Interest and Other Income (Note 3)	47.1	64.1	64.6
	5,618.5	5,491.3	4,850.0
Costs and Expenses			
Cost of sales of products	2,687.5	2,598.9	2,286.6
Cost of rentals and services	745.2	666.5	605.7
Selling, general and administrative expenses	1,146.6	1,118.5	995.1
Research and development	397.6	336.5	279.8
Interest (Note 4)	294.1	211.6	158.5
Foreign exchange (gains) losses	(7.3)	21.4	22.8
	5,263.7	4,953.4	4,348.5
Income before Taxes on Income	354.8	537.9	501.5
Provision for Taxes on Income (Note 5)	133.0	226.7	227.1
Net Income (Note 2)	221.8	311.2	274.4
Retained Earnings, Beginning of Year (Note 2)	1,813.7	1,574.2	1,357.3
Cash Dividends Declared	(81.4)	(71.7)	(57.5)
Retained Earnings, End of Year	$1,954.1	$1,813.7	$1,574.2
Net Income per Share (Notes 2 and 6)			
Fully Diluted	$5.25	$7.46	$6.83
Primary	$5.25	$7.63	$7.53
Cash Dividends Declared per Share	$1.92	$1.76	$1.56

See notes to financial statements.

Case 8–3

Exxon Corporation

Exxon is the world's largest company in the energy industry. Primary activities include exploration for and production of crude oil and natural gas, manufacturing of petroleum products, and transportation and sale of crude oil, natural gas, and petroleum products; exploration, mining, and sale of coal and uranium; and the fabrication of nuclear fuel. Exxon Chemical Company is a major manufacturer of petrochemicals. Reliance Electric Company, an affiliate, manufactures, markets, and services a broad line of industrial equipment. In addition, Exxon is involved in a variety of other activities unrelated to energy.

Provided on the following pages is Exxon's "Supplemental Information on Inflation Accounting" (see Exhibit 1), which was required by Financial Accounting Standards Board Statement No. 33. Table I presents fiscal 1981 income statements prepared on a historical cost basis (column 1), adjusted for general inflation, sometimes referred to as a constant dollar basis (column 2), and adjusted for specific price changes, sometimes called a current cost basis (column 3). Table II presents 1981 balance sheets for each alternative and Table III presents selected financial data for prior periods in dollars of average 1981 purchasing power.

Required

1. Explain the differences in income from continuing operations based on each of these three alternatives. What is the purpose of the adjustments to historical cost accounting? What do you infer about Exxon's performance in 1981?

2. Refer to Table I. Why aren't "Total revenue," "Other costs and deductions," and "Income, excise and other taxes" adjusted for the effects of changing prices?

3. Exxon reports that 98% (79%) of current cost (constant dollar) income from continuing operations is being distributed in cash dividends. What implications does this have for capital expenditures, research and development, and exploration activities?

4. Explain how Exxon benefits from the "gain from the decline in purchasing power of net amounts owed."

5. Explain how shareholders' equity measured on a current cost basis can be more than double that of the historical cost basis in the balance sheet while 1981 current cost income from continuing operations is less than half that of historical cost.

This case was prepared from published financial statements of Exxon Corporation.

EXHIBIT 1

Supplemental Information on Inflation Accounting

Background During 1981, inflation in the United States continued at a high rate which further eroded the purchasing power of the dollar. This trend causes a distortion in the conventional measures of financial performance.

Historical dollar accounting (as reflected in the financial statements) does not provide for the change in the purchasing power of the dollar due to inflation. Since the purchasing power of the dollar has declined significantly (the 1981 dollar, for example, is worth only $.45 compared with the 1971 dollar), this decline should be considered for a proper assessment of economic results.

Inflation affects monetary assets, such as cash and receivables, which lose a part of their purchasing power during periods of inflation since they will purchase fewer goods or services in the future. Conversely, holders of liabilities benefit during periods of inflation because less purchasing power will be required to satisfy these obligations in the future. Thus, a 1971 debt of one dollar can be satisfied with a payment of a 1981 dollar which has the equivalent purchasing power of $.45.

Inflation also affects plant and equipment, which is reflected in the financial statements at the purchasing power of the dollars of the years in which the investments were made rather than in today's purchasing power. This tends to understate depreciation charges in the current year, and thus overstate earnings.

The information on this and the following two pages is presented in an experimental fashion in an attempt to overcome these shortcomings of historical accounting.

General Methodology The supplemental data presented here include adjustments made to the historical dollar results in accordance with Financial Accounting Standards Board Statement No. 33 – Financial Reporting and Changing Prices, as modified by Statement No. 39. Two methods are used in these adjustments to show the effect of (1) general inflation and (2) changes in specific costs.

The first method adjusts the historical dollars in the financial statements to dollars of the same general purchasing power. For example, if the inflation rate is 5 percent from one year to the next year, then 5 percent more dollars are needed in the second year just to maintain the same general purchasing power. This adjustment to common units of measurement – constant dollars – is accomplished by using an index which measures general inflation. Statement No. 33 prescribes the use of the Consumer Price Index for All Urban Consumers (CPI). Thus, the constant dollar method starts with historical dollars as recorded using generally accepted accounting principles and adjusts these amounts to reflect changes in purchasing power using the CPI to show the effect of general inflation.

The second method adjusts for the current, or specific, costs of inventory and plant and equipment. Current replacement costs have been used for these items. That is, specific prices that would have to be paid currently have been used as replacement costs for the inventory of crude oil and products and for property, plant and equipment.

For the most part, the specific cost data used here represent replacement in-place and in-kind. No consideration has been given to possible replacement of assets of a different type, at a different location or with improved operating cost efficiencies. The specific costs used, while believed reasonable, are necessarily subjective. They do not necessarily represent amounts for which the assets could be sold or costs which will be incurred, or the manner and extent in which actual replacement of assets will occur.

More specifically, land, other than oil and gas acreage, has been valued based on appraisal or estimated current market prices. Oil and gas acreage costs have been updated using the constant dollar (CPI) index. Development costs of oil and gas properties were measured by use of appropriate indices or estimates of current drilling, material and equipment costs. Other plant and equipment, for the most part, was updated by use of internally developed construction cost indices. Items such as automotive equipment and office buildings were costed at current market prices.

Supplemental Data Adjustments for the effect of changing prices under both the aforementioned methods are reflected in the tables on the following pages and in subsequent comments.

Table I shows the results of operations in 1981 as reflected in the Consolidated Statement of Income (page 26), as adjusted for general inflation, and as adjusted for specific costs. Adjustments under both methods reflect an increase in the 1981 cost of goods sold as shown in the historical dollar accounts for the $261 million of profit realized on sales of quantities from LIFO inventories, this being the amount necessary to bring total cost of goods sold to current costs in average 1981 dollars. Depreciation is adjusted upward by $2,030 million for general inflation to restate this cost in terms of 1981 dollars, based on the restatement of property, plant and equipment as shown in Table II. In adjusting for specific costs, an additional depreciation charge of $622 million is necessary to reflect the increases of the specific costs of the facilities over the effect of general inflation. The two depreciation adjustments maintain the same methods, useful lives and salvage values as used in computing historical depreciation.

After these adjustments, the income from continuing operations is lowered in terms of constant purchasing power (general inflation) and further lowered on the basis of specific prices. Dividends paid in 1981 represent 47 percent, 79 percent and 98 percent, respectively, of historical, constant dollar and specific cost incomes.

Statement No. 33 requires that income taxes paid not be modified for the effects of either general inflation or specific cost adjustments. Therefore, the 48 percent effective tax rate for historical earnings becomes an effective 54 percent for the results adjusted for general inflation and 59 percent for the specific cost results. This indicates the hidden additional tax that results from inflation which restricts capital recovery.

EXHIBIT 1 *(Continued)*

Table I also shows changes in shareholders' equity, other than income from continuing operations, which occurred during the year as a result of inflation. The first of these is a gain, applicable to both methods, resulting from the effect of the decline in the purchasing power of the dollar on the net monetary amounts owed by the company. Most of the company's current assets, except inventories, and the current liabilities and long-term debt are considered to be monetary items. This gain represents the decline in the amount of purchasing power required at the end of 1981 to pay these net liabilities versus the amount that would have been required to pay them at the end of 1980.

The second change in shareholders' equity is applicable only to the specific cost method and represents the additional increase or decrease during the year in the specific prices for inventory and property, plant and equipment over or less than the increase attributed to the effects of general inflation as measured by the CPI. This additional cost of plant and equipment is charged to income from continuing operations by means of the increased depreciation charge previously mentioned.

These changes in shareholders' equity, when added to income from continuing operations, result in adjusted net income of $4,343 million using the general inflation method. Under the specific cost method, the $3,576 million net change in shareholders' equity from these items excludes foreign exchange effects on asset values for property, plant and equipment.

Table I – Income from continuing operations and changes in shareholders' equity adjusted for changing prices
For the year ended December 31, 1981

	As reported on page 26	General inflation	Specific costs
	(millions of dollars)	(millions of average 1981 dollars)	
Income from continuing operations			
Total revenue	$115,148	$115,148	$115,148
Costs and other deductions			
Crude oil and product purchases	64,324	64,585	64,585
Depreciation and depletion	2,948	4,978	5,600
Other costs and deductions	18,985	18,985	18,985
Income, excise and other taxes	23,324	23,324	23,324
Total costs and other deductions	109,581	111,872	112,494
Income from continuing operations	5,567	3,276	2,654
Gain from decline in the purchasing power of net amounts owed		1,067	1,067
Excess of increase (decrease) in specific prices over general inflation			
Inventories			(344)
Property, plant and equipment			199
Net income	**$ 5,567**		
Adjusted net income		**$ 4,343**	
Net change in shareholders' equity from above	$ 5,567	$ 4,343	**$ 3,576**

Table II presents a summarized balance sheet at year-end 1981 based on the historical dollar balance sheet shown on page 25 and as adjusted for inflation.

Adjustments to the balance sheet for general inflation include the restatement of inventories and property, plant and equipment on the basis of constant dollars using the CPI index. The adjustments shown in the table restate these prior year additions in terms of average 1981 dollars. For example, an inventory or plant addition made in 1971 is increased in amount (about doubled) to reflect the increased number of 1981 dollars required to equal the general purchasing power originally invested.

Under the specific cost method, additional adjustments are necessary for those items which have increased in cost faster than the CPI. Inventories and plant have been restated based upon the cost of replacing them at current costs. Since the purchase prices of crude oil and petroleum products have increased faster than general inflation, particularly in the late 1970s and since the inventories have been carried on the LIFO basis, the specific costs of the inventories is about $6 billion greater than after restatement for general inflation. The adjustment to property, plant and equipment, made in a similar fashion, results in an additional $11 billion adjustment.

Under both inflation-adjustment methods, the Table II categories of "All other assets" and "Total liabilities" have been restated from the year-end 1981 dollar amounts to average 1981 dollar amounts using the CPI.

The sum of all the foregoing balance sheet adjustments results in the restatement of shareholders' equity–the invest-

Table II – Summarized balance sheet adjusted for changing prices at December 31, 1981

	As reported on page 25	General inflation	Specific costs
	(millions of dollars)	(millions of average 1981 dollars)	
Assets			
Inventories	$ 7,584	$ 11,075	$ 17,095
Property, plant and equipment	36,094	50,561	61,257
All other assets	19,253	18,723	18,723
Total assets	62,931	80,359	97,075
Total liabilities	34,414	33,414	33,414
Shareholders' equity	**$ 28,517**	**$ 46,945**	**$ 63,661**

EXHIBIT 1 *(Continued)*

ment base. The adjustments for general inflation increase the historical shareholders' equity of about $29 billion to a basis of $47 billion. In other words, it would take $47 billion 1981 dollars to provide the same purchasing power as the $29 billion historical dollars represented in the financial statements. Additional adjustments for specific costs raise the shareholders' equity on this basis to $64 billion.

Table III summarizes the earnings results, shareholders' equity and returns over a five-year period. In this table, the historical cost data for the years 1977 through 1980 have been adjusted for the effects of general inflation and for specific costs in the same manner as has been discussed for the year 1981. Income from continuing operations is composed of the same factors as shown in Table I. As shown, the returns on average shareholders' equity are considerably lower than reflected in the financial statements when both the results and the investment base are adjusted for the effects of general inflation and for specific costs. These decreases in returns show the erosion taking place in the capital base of the company from the continuing high levels of inflation being faced by the general public, the oil and gas industry, and Exxon.

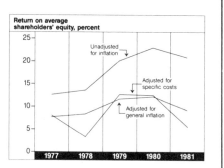

Return on average shareholders' equity, percent

Table III–Summary of income, shareholders' equity and return (millions of dollars except per share amounts)

	1977	1978	1979	1980	1981
			Years ended December 31		
Unadjusted for inflation					
Income from continuing operations (net income)	$ 2,443	$ 2,763	$ 4,295	$ 5,650	$ 5,567
Per share*	2.73	3.10	4.87	6.49	6.44
Shareholders' equity at year-end	19,121	20,229	22,552	25,413	28,517
Return of net income on average shareholders' equity, percent	**13.1**	**14.0**	**20.1**	**23.6**	**20.6**
Adjusted for general inflation (average 1981 dollars)					
Income from continuing operations	2,485	2,570	3,824	4,338	3,276
Per share*	2.77	2.88	4.34	4.99	3.79
Gain from decline in purchasing power of net amounts owed	552	774	1,251	1,280	1,067
Adjusted net income	3,037	3,344	5,075	5,618	4,343
Per share*	3.39	3.75	5.76	6.46	5.02
Shareholders' equity at year-end	39,904	40,846	43,446	45,610	46,945
Return of adjusted net income on average shareholders' equity, percent	**7.7**	**8.3**	**12.0**	**12.6**	**9.4**
Adjusted for specific costs (average 1981 dollars)					
Income from continuing operations	1,673	1,559	2,994	3,460	2,654
Per share*	1.87	1.75	3.40	3.98	3.07
Gain from decline in purchasing power of net amounts owed	552	774	1,251	1,280	1,067
Excess of increase (decrease) in specific prices over general inflation	2,265	(472)	3,382	3,327	(145)
Net change in shareholders' equity	4,490	1,861	7,627	8,067	3,576
Per share*	5.01	2.09	8.65	9.27	4.13
Shareholders' equity at year-end	55,936	55,396	60,481	65,359	63,661
Return of net change in shareholders' equity on average shareholders' equity, percent	**8.2**	**3.3**	**13.2**	**12.8**	**5.5**

Table IV–Supplementary data adjusted for general inflation (average 1981 dollars)

	1977	1978	1979	1980	1981
Total revenue (millions)	$87,738	$90,735	$106,463	$121,831	$115,148
Dividends per share*	2.25	2.30	2.44	2.98	3.00
Market price at year-end, per share*	35¼	33	32⅝	42½	30¼
Average consumer price index (1967 = 100)	181.5	195.4	217.4	246.8	272.4

*Reflects May 1981 two-for-one stock split. See Note 3, page 30.

Case 8–4

Weyerhaeuser Company

Weyerhaeuser, incorporated as Weyerhaeuser Timber Company in 1900 in the State of Washington, is principally a forest products company engaged in the growing and harvesting of timber as well as the manufacture, distribution, and sale of wood products. In addition, Weyerhaeuser Real Estate Company, a wholly owned subsidiary, is engaged in on-site construction and sale of residential real estate, mortgage banking, and other real estate activities. Real estate company revenues represented less than 10% of total company revenues in 1979.

At the end of 1979, the company owned approximately 5.9 million acres of forest land, of which approximately 2.8 million acres were in the Pacific Northwest and 3.1 million acres in the South. Company data indicated that the volume of merchantable timber on company-owned lands in the United States was approximately 11.5 billion cubic feet of solid wood. The company also owned selective harvesting rights on over 9 million acres in Canada and 1.5 million acres in the Far East.

Financial Reporting and Changing Prices

During 1979, the Financial Accounting Standards Board issued Statement No. 33, which required supplementary financial information on the effects of general inflation and the effects of firm-specific changes in costs. Unlike many other major corporations, Weyerhaeuser's reaction was unfavorable.

> The Company believes that the two supplementary earnings computations, one dealing with the effects of general inflation and the other dealing with the effects of specific changes in the prices of resources used by the Company, are apt to be misunderstood and inappropriate conclusions drawn therefrom. Particularly unfortunate, in the view of the Company, is the fact that the disciplines of Statement No. 33 do not deal with the probable effects upon revenues if the Company's costs were, in fact, those costs portrayed in the two supplementary earnings computations, and if the costs of the Company's competitors were similarly and as pervasively affected by changing prices. What has been lost sight of is the observable phenomenon that as, on an industry basis, operating costs rise, revenues must rise to provide an adequate return on invested capital. Although management is obligated to replace assets consumed in the earnings process, that obligation holds only as long as the cost of replacement is justified in terms of reasonably anticipated future, not present, revenues and future, not present, rates of return. U.S. companies bend to the pressures of competition and delay the imposition of increases in product prices which may in fact be justified on the basis of current costs. The consumer is the beneficiary of pricing based

---

This case was prepared from published financial statements of the Weyerhaeuser Company.

212 Accounting for Changing Prices

traditionally, to a large extent, on historical cost. Only when operating cost increases pervade an entire industry do operating cost increases, absent governmental intervention, become immediately translatable into revenue increases. If, as the supplementary earnings computations suggest, operating costs on a generalized, industry-pervasive basis increase, then it is likely that, in time, operating revenues, too, would increase. Otherwise, replacement capital could not be found, and it is with this matter that Statement No. 33 does not deal. To deal unilaterally with rising costs, however measured, without considering the effect of those rising costs upon revenues and upon earnings were those costs, in fact, to be incurred and be used to measure performance, renders computations so dealing with rising costs suspect and capable of misinterpretation.

Of further concern to the Company is the failure of Statement No. 33 to deal with the earnings aspects of holding assets during periods of changing prices, i.e., holding gains and losses. That such gains and losses do in fact occur is not disputed, but their measurement and classification for financial reporting purposes, in the Company's view, remain issues yet to be satisfactorily resolved.

Included is the following supplementary financial information: statements of consolidated earnings adjusted for changing prices and statements of net assets adjusted for changing prices (Exhibit 1), a five-year comparison of selected supplementary financial information adjusted for the effects of changing prices in 1979 average dollars (Exhibit 2).

Required

1. Why does Weyerhaeuser management believe that supplementary earnings computations "are apt to be misunderstood and inappropriate conclusions drawn therefrom?"

2. Evaluate the following: "The consumer is the beneficiary of pricing based traditionally, to a large extent, on historical cost. Only when operating cost increases pervade an entire industry do operating cost increases, absent governmental intervention, become immediately translatable into revenue increases."

3. Statement No. 33 permitted timber, timberlands, and directly related facilities to be excluded from specific price adjustments (pending further study by the FASB). Speculate on the magnitude of "Earnings before income taxes" and "Net assets" if timber, timberlands, and so on were adjusted for changes in specific prices. Comments?

4. Why does the company believe that holding gains and/or losses are not adequately addressed in Statement No. 33?

5. Historical cost "Net sales" were $4,422,653,000 and $3,799,441,000 for 1979 and 1978, respectively. Explain how the company arrived at $4,227,258,000 for net sales in 1978 in the five-year comparison.

6. What modification(s) to Statement No. 33 disclosures would you suggest for the FASB to adopt for forest product companies such as Weyerhaeuser?

EXHIBIT 1

Weyerhaeuser Company and Subsidiaries

Following is the supplementary financial information required by Statement No. 33:

Consolidated Earnings Adjusted for Changing Prices

		Adjusted For	
For the year ended December 30, 1979	As Reported	General Inflation	Specific Prices
Net sales	$4,422,653	$4,422,653	$4,422,653
Weyerhaeuser Real Estate Company earnings	57,117	57,117	57,117
Other income, net	37,005	37,005	37,005
	4,516,775	4,516,775	4,516,775
Operating costs and expenses:			
Other than depreciation, amortization and fee stumpage—Note A	3,340,630	3,350,171	3,349,721
Depreciation, amortization and fee stumpage	332,594	501,157	509,920
Interest expense	104,607	104,607	104,607
	3,777,831	3,955,935	3,964,248
Earnings before income taxes	738,944	560,840	552,527
Income taxes	226,700	226,700	226,700
Net earnings	$ 512,244	$ 334,140	$ 325,827
Per common share	$ 4.02	$ 2.59	$ 2.52
Gain from decline in the purchasing power of net amounts owed		$ 174,012	$ 174,012

Note A: The Company uses the last-in, first-out (LIFO) method of accounting for product inventories. Operating costs have been adjusted to give effect to changing prices upon liquidations of LIFO layers during the current year.

Net Assets Adjusted for Changing Prices

		Adjusted For	
December 30, 1979	As Reported	General Inflation	Specific Prices
Product inventories	$ 341,301	$ 457,974	$ 515,203
Materials and supplies	124,141	131,726	132,524
Property and equipment	2,485,243	3,373,996	3,457,257
Timber and timberlands	608,312	1,463,519	1,463,519
Leased property under capital leases	150,608	180,399	180,399
All other assets, net	396,023	396,023	396,023
	4,105,628	6,003,637	6,144,925
Deduct net monetary liabilities	1,369,761	1,369,761	1,369,761
Net assets	$2,735,867	$4,633,876	$4,775,164

Note: Dollar amounts in thousands except per share data.

EXHIBIT 2

Weyerhaeuser Company and Subsidiaries

Five Year Comparison of Selected Supplementary Financial Information
Adjusted for Effects of Changing Prices in 1979 Average Dollars

	1979	1978	1977	1976	1975
Net sales and other operating revenues	$4,422,653	$4,227,258	$3,932,099	$3,657,470	$3,265,326
Historical cost information adjusted for general inflation:					
Net earnings	$ 334,140	—	—	—	—
Per common share	$ 2.59	—	—	—	—
Net assets at end of year	$4,633,876	—	—	—	—
Current cost information:					
Net earnings	$ 325,827	—	—	—	—
Per common share	$ 2.52	—	—	—	—
Excess of increase in specific prices over increase in the general price level	$ 141,288	—	—	—	—
Net assets at end of year	$4,775,164	—	—	—	—
Gain from decline in purchasing power of net amounts owed	$ 174,012	—	—	—	—
Dividends per common share	$ 1.06	$ .94	$ .96	$ 1.02	$ 1.07
Market price per common share at end of year	$ 30.90	$ 26.39	$ 31.98	$ 58.00	$ 48.53
Average consumer price index	217.4*	195.4	181.5	170.5	161.2

*Estimated—based on latest data available.

Note: Dollar amounts in thousands except per share data.